Praise from Job Seekers for the *Knock 'em Dead* Books

"I got the position! I was interviewed by three people and the third person asked me all the questions in *Knock 'em Dead*. I had all the right answers!"
— **D.J., Scottsdale, Arizona**

"I just finished writing the letter I have dreamed of writing for three years: my letter of resignation from the Company from Hell. Thanks to you and the book, *Knock 'em Dead*, I have been offered and have accepted an excellent position with a major international service corporation."
— **C.C., Atlanta, Georgia**

"My previous employer asked me to resign. Your book got me through my depression, and in only four weeks, got me four job offers. This is the first time in my career I have this many options to choose from."
— **D.H., North Canton, Ohio**

"After college graduation, I searched and searched for a job, and ended up taking a few low-paying ones I was overqualified for. Finally, I read your book and have been offered *every* job I have applied for since."
— **L.E. (no address given)**

"I followed the advice in *Knock 'em Dead* religiously and got more money, less hours, a better hospital plan, and negotiated to keep my three weeks vacation. I start my new job immediately!"
— **A.B., St. Louis, Missouri**

"I found your book to be absolutely invaluable during my recent job search. Since then I have had a chance to speak with my interviewer, who informed me that it was my strong interview that landed me my job offer. He went on to outline what had turned him off about other candidates, and it was some of the very same mistakes I used to make before reading your book!"
— **D.D., Houlton, Maine**

"Every time I've used your book, I've gotten an offer! This book is incredible. Thanks for publishing such a great tool."
— **W.Z., Columbia, Maryland**

"Just a quick note to let you know how much your book has helped me. I was chosen for my job out of over one hundred applicants! I later loaned the book to a friend and circled the things that had helped me. She interviewed on a Thursday, and she was offered the position that Thursday night! Thanks for writing such a helpful book."

— S.G., Sacramento, California

"Your book is simply fantastic. This one book improved my yearly income by several thousand dollars, and my future income by untold amounts. Your work has made my family and myself very happy."

— M.Z., St. Clair Shores, Michigan

"Thank you for all the wonderfully helpful information you provided in your book. I lost my job almost one year ago. I spent almost eight months looking for a comparable position. Then I had the good sense to buy your book. Two months later, I accepted a new position. You helped me turn one of the worst experiences of my life into a blessing in disguise."

— L.G., Watervliet, New York

"I was out of work for four months—within five weeks of reading your book, I had four job offers."

— S.K., Dallas, Texas

"Yesterday I received two job offers in the space of fifteen minutes. I am now using the 'Negotiating the Offer' chapter to evaluate these positions."

— W.B., Thornhill, Ontario

"I read every page in the book and, after a two-month search, got ten interviews with top-performing companies and six offers (five of which I declined)."

— M.V., Millington, Tennessee

"I was sending out hordes of resumes and hardly getting a nibble—and I have top-notch skills and experience in my field. I wasn't prepared for this tough job market. When I read your book, however, I immediately began applying some of your techniques. My few nibbles increased to so many job interviews I could hardly keep up with them!"

— C.S., Chicago, Illinois

RESUMES THAT KnOCK 'em DEaD

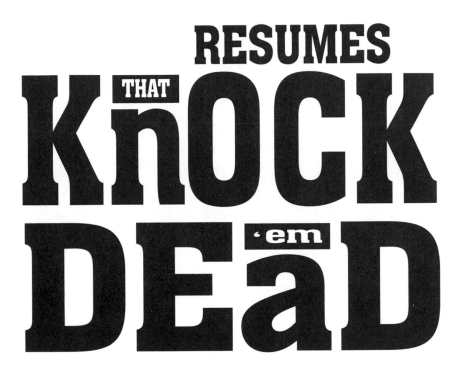

Martin Yate

Adams Media Corporation
Avon, Massachusetts

Acknowledgments

Knock 'em Dead is now in its 15th year of publication, and has become a staple for job hunters around the world. This is due to the ongoing support of my publisher Bob Adams, and the tireless encouragement of the Adams Media sales team headed by Wayne Jackson. This, and the other *Knock 'em Dead* books, are kept fresh and vibrant thanks to the ministrations of my editor, Ed Walters, the Associate Publisher of Adams Media. Finally, this year I am indebted to Jennifer Lantagne for her indefatigable work on three simultaneous sets of galleys.

Published by Adams Media Corporation
57 Littlefield Street, Avon, MA 02322. U.S.A.
www.adamsmedia.com

ISBN: 1-58062-422-7

Printed in the United States of America.

J I H G F E D C B

Library of Congress Cataloging-in-Publication Data
Yate, Martin John.
Resumes that Knock 'em Dead / Martin Yate. — Rev. and expanded ed.
    p.   cm.
ISBN 1-55850-817-1
    1. Resumes (Employment)   I. Title.
HF5383.Y38   1997
808'.06665—dc21   97-41514
                                                                  CIP

Rear Cover Photo: ARIEL JONES

This book is available at quantity discounts for bulk purchases.
For information, call 1-800-872-5627.

Visit our home page at www.careercity.com

Table of Contents

Introduction . . . . **vii**

Chapter 1: The Marks of a Great Resume **1**
Why you need a resume, what it will mean to the person who eventually reads it, and what this book will do to help you put together one that gets the attention you deserve.

Chapter 2: Three Ways to Sum Yourself Up **5**
The chronological, functional, and combination resumes: what they are and who should use which.

Chapter 3: The Basic Ingredients **15**
What must always go in, what can never go in, and what may be appropriate depending on your background.

Chapter 4: Resumes That Knock 'em Dead **37**
Assembling the raw materials, determining where you want to go, and showing how your experience will meet the employer's needs.

Chapter 5: Writing the Basic Resume **53**
Getting it all down on paper, using the action verbs that make your resume sparkle and shine, and the all-important checklist you must consult before you can say you're done.

Chapter 6: The Final Product **73**
How to choose a word-processing service, what to expect from a professional typesetter, and how to select the best paper, reproduction method, and typeface for your resume.

Chapter 7: Is Your Resume Computer-Friendly? **79**
In the new world age, resumes are increasingly being scanned into computers. Will yours ever be found again?

Chapter 8: Cover Letters **93**
The "rules of the road" for making your letter more than just another piece of mail, the best way to personalize your cover letter, and an invaluable list of sample phrases for use in a wide variety of situations. Also: the Executive Briefing and the Broadcast Letter.

Chapter 9: What Do You Do with It? **109**
Nine sources for interview leads. Why want ads shouldn't be your only source for employment needs. How to do the research, and following up on the best leads.

103402

Chapter 10: The Resumes **117**

Based on real resumes that got real jobs for real people. Which jobs? In alphabetical order:

Accounting Professional 118
Administrative 119
Applications Programmer....................120
Banking Portfolio Manager 121
Broadcast Sales 123
Brokerage Professional........................124
Business Development Manager/
   Consultant....................................126
Buyer 128
Claims Representative 129
Consultant...130
Convention Sales................................131
Corporate Communications 132
Corporate Taxation............................134
Credit Analyst 136
Credit and Collections.........................137
Customer Service Manager 138
Electrical Design Engineer....................139
Electrician 140
Entrepreneurial...................................141
Entry-Level Advertising Sales...............142
Equipment Sales 143
Executive Assistant Legal/Medical.........144
Executive Management 146
Executive Marketing/Sales 148
Finance Executive...............................149
Finance Trust Administration...............151
Health Care Program Administration 152
Health Care Sales 153
Human Resources Generalist 154
Human Resources Professional............156
Human Resources Recruiter.................158

Information Technology Consultant 159
Information Technology Instructor 161
Information Technology Professional ...162
Insurance Claims................................164
Insurance Executive 165
Investment Banking Executive.............167
Jewelry Sales 169
Law Firm Internship 170
Lawyer (Entry-Level) 171
Management Consultant 173
Marketing Analyst...............................174
Marketing Management 175
Medical Technology Sales 177
Music Teacher 179
Nurse 180
Operations and Executive Project
   Management...............................182
Operations Management Investment/
   Securities Industry.......................183
Organizational Management................185
Outside Sales/Account Manager/
   Customer Service 187
Paralegal..188
Pharmaceutical Sales, LPN 189
Probation Officer 190
Project Manager/Programmer Analyst ..192
Property Management.........................194
Public Relations/Media Spokesperson ..195
Publishing/Marketing Professional 196
Real Estate Development.....................197
Retail District Manager........................199
Retail Management 200

Sales and Marketing Executive 201
School Psychologist.............................203
Security/Operations Management 204
Security Services Sales 206
Senior Account Executive 207
Senior International Marketing and
   Business Development Executive.....209
Senior Management Executive 211
Senior Sales and Marketing Manager ...213
Senior Technology Executive .....215 & 217
Software Development.........................219
Stock Trader's Assistant.......................221
Store Manager....................................222
Student System Project Specialist.........223
Supermarket Management...................225
Systems and Networks Manager..........226
Teacher (Entry-Level) 228
Teacher's Aide....................................230
Telecommunications Analyst................231
Telecommunications Management
   Professional.................................232
Telecommunications/Information
   Systems Management....................234
Telemarketing Professional..................235
Tour Director......................................236
Traffic Control
   (Shipping and Receiving).................237
VP of Operations 238
Visual Merchandising Specialist 240
Web Site Designer 242

Appendix **243**

Resumes for Special Situations; Professional Resume Writing Services; Resume Banks; Resources

RESUMES FOR SPECIAL SITUATIONS
James is leaving the military for a
   Finance Executive position 244
Jane is changing careers 245
James is changing careers to
   Human Resources 246
James is an Educator in transition.........247
James is an Electrician changing to a
   career in sales & promotion 248

Jane is changing careers after a
   period of self-employment...............249
James has changed careers many times 250
Jane is a handicapped worker who
   wants to change careers...................251
James is a Technology Expert
   changing to Web Development 252
James is a blue-collar worker and
   wants a white-collar job 253

Jane has had multiple jobs and
   needs to combine her experience 254
Jane is changing careers to become
   a Salesperson..................................255
Jane is a recently divorced homemaker
   reentering the work force 256

PROFESSIONAL RESUME WRITING SERVICES ...257
RESUME BANKS...261
RESOURCES 279

Introduction

Most of the books on writing resumes haven't changed to accommodate today's dynamic work environment. That is the reason for this book: To help "now" people get the very best jobs!

Look at the other resume books on the market; they are full of resume examples with dates going back to what seems, to most job seekers, like the Bronze Age. They use job titles that no longer exist and techniques that no longer work—techniques that in many instances can be downright damaging to your job hunt.

This book is unique in two very important ways.

First, you'll get to read real resumes from real people. Each of the resumes in this book is based on a "genuine article" that worked wonders for its writer. Included are resumes for today's and tomorrow's in-demand jobs, as defined by the Bureau of Labor Statistics and confirmed by the professionals on the front lines: Corporate recruiters and other employment industry professionals across the country. The odds are that you are already working in one of these jobs, or wishing you were.

Also included in the "real-life" section of this book is a selection of resumes from people with special challenges. These reflect the pressures and needs of a modern, profession-oriented society struggling into the information age. Like the resume that got a six-dollar-an-hour factory worker a $70,000-a-year job; or the one that helped a recovering alcoholic and drug-abuser get back on her feet again. There are winning resumes of people recovering from serious emotional challenges and mental problems, of people reentering society after jail, starting over after the divorce, and changing careers. And what's more, these examples have proved themselves effective in every corner of the nation; their writers landed both interviews and jobs.

Second, I explain the ins and outs of putting a resume together as painlessly as possible. I'll show you the three best ways to look at your background and present your resume. Then I'll show you all the available options for inclusion. Why certain things should be in your resume and how they should look, and why other things should never appear. Wherever industry experts disagree, I'll give you both sides of the argument, and my reasoned solution to the dispute. That way you can make a prudent decision about your unique background, based on possession of all the facts and the best advice going. In addition, you will see the infinite variety of styles and approaches that can be used within my guidelines to help you create a truly individual resume.

These two unique concepts, the numerous resume examples, and the nuts-and-bolts sections about resume production and distribution give you everything needed to create a distinctive, professional resume: one that will Knock 'em Dead!

1 | The Marks of a Great Resume

Who needs a resume? Everyone. Certainly you do, unless you are so well known that your reputation is already common knowledge to all potential employers. If that were the case you probably wouldn't be reading this book in the first place.

Anyone, in any job, can be viewed more favorably than his or her competition—if he or she is better organized and prepared, which is what a good resume demonstrates. It's a staunch friend who only speaks well of you and can gain you entrance into undreamed-of opportunities.

Now, no resume ever gets carefully read unless a manager is trying to solve a problem. That problem may be finding a quicker way to manufacture silicon chips. It may be getting the telephone calls answered, now that the receptionist has left. As disparate as these examples might seem, both are still concerned with problem solving. And invariably, the problem that needs a solution is the same: Productivity. The simple question is, "How on earth are we going to get things done quicker/cheaper/more efficiently without a _____?"

Resumes that get acted upon are those that demonstrate the writer's potential as a problem solver.

Your resume must speak loudly and clearly of your value as a potential employee. And the value must be spoken in a few brief seconds, because, in the business world, that's all the attention a resume will get. The resume takes you only the first few paces toward that new job. It gets your foot in the door, and because you can't be there to answer questions, it has to stand on its own.

A resume's emphasis is on what has happened in your business life, what actions you took to make those things happen, and what supportive personal characteristics you brought to the job. It is about how you contributed to solving a business' problems. It has nothing to do with generalizations or personal opinions.

The resume itself came about as a solution to a problem: How does a manager avoid interviewing every applicant who applies for a job? Can you imagine what would happen to a business if everyone who applied for a job was given even a cursory ten-minute interview? The company would simply grind to a halt, then topple into bankruptcy. The solution: Come up with a way to get a glimpse of applicants' potentials before having to meet them face-to-face. The resume appeared and evolved into an important screening and time-saving tool.

While that solved one problem for the employer, it created another for the job applicant: "Considering that my background isn't perfect, how do I write a resume that shows off my best potential?" The first attempt to answer that question is how the gentle art of resume writing came into being.

In the world of recreational reading, resumes are pretty far down on the list. They are usually deadly dull and offer little competition to murder mysteries, tales of international intrigue, and love stories.

Nevertheless, resumes are a required part of every manager's daily reading, and, exactly because they are usually deadly dull, are generally avoided. To combat this deep-seated avoidance, there is a general rule that will help your resume get read and acted upon in the quickest possible time: It needs to be short and long. Short on words, but long on facts and an energy that reflects the real you.

Good resume writing focuses attention on your strengths and shows you as a potential powerhouse of an employee. At the same time, it draws attention away from those areas that lack definition or vigor. You can do this even if you are changing your entire career direction, or starting your life over for other reasons, and I'll show you how.

There is a hidden benefit, too, in the resume-writing process: It focuses your attention and helps you prepare for job interviews. In a very real sense, putting a resume together is the foundation for succeeding at the job interview. Preparation for one is preparation for the other.

For example, the interviewer's command to "tell me about yourself" is one of those tough interview demands that almost all of us have difficulty answering satisfactorily. Were you totally satisfied with your response the last time it came up? I doubt it. You can only answer it well if you have taken the time to analyze and package all your strengths and weaknesses in an organized fashion. It is the only way you will ever learn to speak fluidly about your background and skills in a fashion guaranteed to impress the interviewer. So, why not kill two birds with one stone—prepare for the interview by preparing a resume that will open all the right doors for you.

Interestingly enough, the majority of interviewers accept the contents of a resume as fact. Additionally, a good number of interviewers base all their questions on the resume content: This means that in a very real way you can plan and guide the course of the majority of your interviews by preparing an effective resume.

Those without resumes are forced to reveal their history on a job application form, which does not always allow the perfect representation of skills, and which gives the interviewer no flattering starting point from which to base the interview questions.

In addition to helping you get your foot in the door and easing the course of the interview, your resume will be your last and most powerful advocate. After all the interviewing of all the candidates is done, how do you think the interviewers review and evaluate all the contenders? They go over their notes, application forms, and the resumes supplied by the job candidates. You will want to make yours something powerful and positive.

Finally, the preparation of a good resume has the broad, intangible benefit of personal discovery. You may find, as you answer some of the questions in chapter 4, that your experience is deeper than you imagined, that your contributions to previous employers were more important than you thought. You may look on your career direction in a new light. And you may see your value as a solid employee increase. You will gain confidence that will be important not only for a good performance at the interview; but for your attitude toward the rest of your career.

No sane person will tell you that resume writing is fun, but I will show you the tricks of the trade, developed over the years by executive recruiters and professional resume writers, that make the process easier.

What makes this book truly different is that the resume examples in it are all real resumes from real people, resumes that recently landed them real jobs in "in-demand" professions. They were all sent to me by employment specialists from around the nation. For example, the health care examples were screened initially by professional health care recruiters, and those in the data processing by computer recruiters. These are the pros on the firing line, who know what works and what doesn't in today's business marketplace.

You will find everything you need to make resume writing fast, effective, and painless. Just follow my instructions, and in a few hours you'll have a knock-out resume and never have to read another word about the damn things as long as you live. With that in mind, do it once and do it right—you'll generate a top-flight resume without knocking yourself out!

So now, for your delight and edification, we'll review the marks of a great resume: What type of resume is right for you, what goes in (and why), and what always stays out (and why), and what might go in depending on your special circumstances. This is followed by countless resume examples and a "painting-by-numbers" guide that makes resume writing easy for anyone!

With the changing times and circumstances, there are few rigid rules for every situation. So in those instances where there are exceptions, I'll explain them and your choices. The judgment call will be yours. And when you are finished, you will have one of the very best resumes, one that will be sure to knock 'em dead.

2 | Three Ways to Sum Yourself Up

"Give me a moment of your busy day! Listen to me, I've got something to say!"

That's what your resume must scream—in a suitably professional manner, of course. Not in the manner of the would-be retail clothing executive who had his resume "hand-delivered"…attached to the hand and arm of a store window mannequin.

As it happened, that was only the first surprise in store for the personnel director who received the delivery: The envelope was hand-decorated in gothic script; the cover letter inside was equally decorative (and illegible); the resume writer had glued the four-page resume to fabric, and stitched the whole mess together like a child's book. The crowning glory, however, was yet to come: All the punctuation marks—commas, colons, periods, and the like—were small rhinestone settings. Yes, it got noticed, but its success had to depend entirely on the recipient's sense of humor—which in this case was most noticeable for its absence.

Here's the point: trying to do something out of the ordinary with any aspect of your resume is risky business indeed. For every interview door it opens, at least two more may be slammed shut.

The best (and most businesslike) bet is to present a logically displayed, eye-appealing resume that will get *read*. That means grabbing the reader right away—on that first page. And that's one big reason for short, power-packed resumes.

We all have different backgrounds. Some of us have worked for one company only, some of us have worked for eleven companies in as many years. Some of us have changed careers once or twice, some of us have maintained a predictable career path. For some, diversity broadens our potential, and for some concentration deepens it. We each require different vehicles to put our work history in the most exciting light. The goals, though, are constant:

- To show off achievements, attributes, and cumulation of expertise to the best advantage;
- to minimize any possible weaknesses.

Resume experts acknowledge just three essential styles for presenting your credentials to a potential employer: Chronological, Functional, and Combination (Chrono-Functional). Your particular circumstances will determine the right format for you. Just three styles, you say? You will see resume books with up to fifteen varieties of resume style. Such volumes are, alas, merely filling up space; in the final analysis, each additional style such books mention is a tiny variation on the above three.

The Chronological Resume

This is the most common and readily accepted form of presentation. It's what most of us think of when we think of resumes—a chronological listing of job titles and responsibilities. It starts with the current or most recent employment, then works backward to your first job (or ten years into the past—whichever comes first).

This format is good for demonstrating your growth in a single profession. It is suitable for anyone with practical work experience who hasn't suffered too many job changes or prolonged periods of unemployment. It is not suitable if you are just out of school or if you are changing careers. The format would then draw attention to your weaknesses (i.e., your lack of specific experience in a field) rather than your strengths.

The exact content of every resume naturally varies depending on individual circumstances. A chronological resume usually incorporates six basic components.

- *Contact Information*
- *A Job Objective*
- *A Career Objective*
- *A Career Summary*
- *Education*
- *A Description of Work History*

This last item is the distinguishing characteristic of the chronological resume, because it ties your job responsibilities and achievements to specific employers, job titles, and dates.

There are also some optional categories determined by the space available to you and the unique aspect of your background. These will be discussed in chapter 3.

Chronological

Jane Swift, 9 Central Avenue, Quincy, MA 02169. (617) 555-1212. jswift@careerbrain.com

SUMMARY: Ten years of increasing responsibilities in the employment services industry. Concentration in the high-technology markets.

EXPERIENCE: Howard Systems International, Inc.   1995-Present
Management Consulting Firm
Personnel Manager

Responsible for recruiting and managing consulting staff of five. Set up office and organized the recruitment, selection, and hiring of consultants. Recruited all levels of MIS staff from financial to manufacturing markets.

Additional responsibilities:

- Coordinated with outside advertising agencies.
- Developed P.R. with industry periodicals—placement with over 20 magazines and newsletters.
- Developed effective referral programs—referrals increased 32%.

EXPERIENCE: Technical Aid Corporation   1988-1995
National Consulting Firm. MICRO/TEMPS Division

Division Manager   1993-1995
Area Manager   1990-1993
Branch Manager   1988-1990

As Division Manager, opened additional West Coast offices. Staffed and trained all offices with appropriate personnel. Created and implemented all divisional operational policies responsible for P & L. Sales increased to $20 million dollars, from $0 in 1984.

- Achieved and maintained 30% annual growth over 7-year period.
- Maintained sales staff turnover at 14%.

As Area Manager, opened additional offices, hiring staff, setting up office policies, and training sales and recruiting personnel.

Additional responsibilities:

- Supervised offices in two states.
- Developed business relationships with accounts—75% of clients were regular customers.
- Client base increased 28% per year.
- Generated over $200,000 worth of free trade-journal publicity.

As Branch Manager, hired to establish the new MICRO/TEMPS operation. Recruited and managed consultants. Hired internal staff. Sold service to clients.

EDUCATION: Boston University
B.S. Public Relations, 1987.

The Functional Resume

This format focuses on the professional skills you have developed over the years, rather than on when, where, or how you acquired them. It de-emphasizes dates, sometimes to the point of exclusion. By the same token, job titles and employers play a minor part with this type of resume. The attention is always focused on the skill rather than the context or time of its acquisition.

In many ways, the content of the functional resume is similar to the chronological type. Only the approach is different. It is a case of not so much of what you say, but of how you say it.

This functional format is suited to a number of different personal circumstances, specifically those of:

- Mature professionals with a storehouse of expertise and jobs
- Entry-level types whose track records do not justify a chronological resume
- Career changers who want to focus on skills rather than credentials
- People whose careers have been stagnant or in ebb, who want to give focus to the skills that can get a career under way again, rather than on the history in which it was becalmed in the first place
- Military personnel embarking on a civilian career
- Those returning to the workplace after a long absence
- People closer to retirement than to the onset of their careers

The functional resume does present a major challenge for the writer. Because it focuses so strongly on skills and ability to contribute in a particular direction, you must have an employment objective clearly in mind. When this is achieved, such a resume can be very effective. Without this focus, however, or if you are looking for "a job, any job," this format loses its direction and tends to drift without purpose.

Though a functional resume is a bit more free-form than a chronological one, there are certain essentials that make it work. In addition to contact information and a job and/or career objective, these include the elements that follow.

- *A Functional Summary.* Different skills are needed for different jobs, so the functional summary is where you make the tough decisions to determine what goes in and what stays out. Consider the case of an executive sales secretary bored with her job but challenged by the excitement and money the sales force is enjoying. She will want to emphasize those abilities that lead to success in sales, such as written and verbal communication skills, and time management. On the other hand, she will almost certainly leave out references to her typing and short-hand abilities, because these skills don't contribute to her new goals.

- *Dates.* Strictly speaking, a functional resume needn't give dates. Up until a couple of years ago, you could still sometimes get away with omitting them. That is no longer the case. Today, a resume without dates waves a big red flag at every employer in the land. So, what if your employment history doesn't have all the stability it might? The functional resume is perfect for you, because dates can be deemphasized by their placement. You put them at the end of the resume, or perhaps on a second page, for example, in a small block type; and you use year dates omitting the details of day, week, and month. The idea is to force the reader's attention to your skills, not your history.
- *Education.* The inclusion of education and other optional categories is determined by the space available to you and the unique aspects of your background (see chapter 3).

Functional

Jane Swift
9 Central Avenue
Quincy, MA 02169
(617) 555-1212
jswift@careerbrain.com

OBJECTIVE: A position in Employment Services where my management, sales, and recruiting talents can be effectively utilized to improve operations and contribute to company profits.

SUMMARY: Over ten years of Human Resources experience. Extensive responsibility for multiple branch offices and an internal staff of 40+ employees and 250 consultants.

SALES: Sold high-technology consulting services with consistently profitable margins throughout the United States. Grew sales from $0 to over $20 million a year.

Created training programs and trained salespeople in six metropolitan markets.

RECRUITING: Developed recruiting sourcing methods for multiple branch offices.

Recruited over 25,000 internal and external consultants in the high-technology professions.

MANAGEMENT: Managed up to 40 people in sales, customer service, recruiting, and administration. Turnover maintained below 14% in a "turnover business."

FINANCIAL: Prepared quarterly and yearly forecasts. Presented, reviewed, and defended these forecasts to the Board of Directors. Responsible for P & L of $20 million sales operation.

PRODUCTION: Responsible for opening multiple offices and accountable for growth and profitability. 100% success and maintained 30% growth over seven-year period in 10 offices.

WORK EXPERIENCE:

1995 to Present   HOWARD SYSTEMS INTERNATIONAL, Boston, MA
National Consulting Firm
Personnel Manager

1988-1995   TECHNICAL AID CORPORATION, Needham, MA
National Consulting & Search Firm
Division Manager

EDUCATION: B.S., 1987, Boston University

REFERENCES: Available upon request.

The Combination Chrono-Functional Resume

For the upwardly mobile professional with a track record, this is becoming the resume of choice. It has all the flexibility and strength that come from combining both the chronological and functional formats. If you have a performance record, and are on a career track and want to pursue it, then this is the strongest resume tool available. This format, in addition to contact information and a job objective, incorporates a number of identifying factors, outlined below.

- *A Career Summary.* The combination resume, more often than not, has some kind of career summary. Here you spotlight a professional with a clear sense of self, a past of solid contributions, and a clear focus on future career growth. The career summary, as you might expect, will include a power-packed description of skills, achievements, and personal traits that fairly scream "Success!"
- *A Description of Functional Skills.* This is where the combination of styles comes into play. Following the summary, the combination resume starts out like a functional resume and highlights achievements in different categories relevant to the job/career goals, without any reference to employers.
- *A Chronological History.* Then it switches to the chronological approach and names companies, dates, titles, duties, and responsibilities. This section can also include further evidence of achievements or special contributions.
- *Education.* Then come the optional categories determined by the space available to you and the *unique* aspects of your background.

Combination

Jane Swift
9 Central Avenue
Quincy, MA 92169
(617) 555-1212
jswift@careerbrain.com

OBJECTIVE:

Employment Services Management

SUMMARY: Ten years of increasing responsibilities in the employment services marketplace. Concentration in the high-technology markets.

SALES: Sold high technology consulting services with consistently profitable margins throughout the United States. Grew sales from $0 to over $20 million a year.

PRODUCTION: Responsible for opening multiple offices and accountable for growth and profitability. 100% success and maintained 30% growth over seven-year period in 10 offices.

MANAGEMENT: Managed up to 40 people in sales, customer service, recruiting, and administration. Turnover maintained below 14% in a "turnover business." Hired branch managers and sales and recruiting staff throughout the United States.

FINANCIAL: Prepared quarterly and yearly forecasts. Presented, reviewed, and defended these forecasts to the Board of Directors. Responsible for P & L of $20 million sales operation.

MARKETING: Performed numerous market studies for multiple branch opening. Resolved feasibility of combining two different sales offices. Study resulted in savings of over $5,000 per month in operating expenses.

EXPERIENCE: Howard Systems International, Inc.   1995–Present
Management Consulting Firm
Personnel Manager

Responsible for recruiting and managing consulting staff of five. Set up office and organized the recruitment, selection, and hiring of consultants. Recruited all levels of MIS staff from financial to manufacturing markets.

Additional responsibilities:

- developed P.R. with industry periodicals—placement with over 20 magazines and newsletters.
- developed effective referral programs—referrals increased 320%.

Page 2 of 2, Jane Swift, (617) 555-1212

Technical Aid Corporation   1988-1995
National Consulting Firm. MICRO/TEMPS Division

Division Manager   1993-1995
Area Manager   1990-1993
Branch Manager   1988-1990

As Division Manager, opened additional West Coast offices. Staffed and trained all offices with appropriate personnel. Created and implemented all divisional operational policies. Responsibilities for P & L. Sales increased to $20 million dollars, from $0 to 1984.

- Achieved and maintained 30% annual growth over seven-year period.
- Maintained sales staff turnover at 14%.

As Area Manager, opened additional offices, hiring staff, setting up office policies, and training sales and recruiting personnel.

Additional responsibilities:

- Supervised offices in two states.
- Developed business relationships with accounts—75% of clients were regular customers.
- Client base increased 28% per year.
- Generated over $200,000 worth of free trade journal publicity.

As Branch Manager, hired to establish the new MICRO/TEMPS operation. Recruited and managed consultants. Hired internal staff. Sold service to clients.

EDUCATION: B.S., 1987, Boston University

One of these styles is perfect for you. Pick one, and in the next chapter we'll begin to fill it in with the resume basics.

3 | The Basic Ingredients

It used to be that there were just a few set rules for writing a great resume. Everything was simple—you did this, you didn't do that. Now, however, many of the jobs for which those rules were made no longer exist—so many of the traditional hard and fast rules no longer apply.

New technologies are creating new professions overnight, and, with them, new career opportunities. The content of these new professions and careers is dramatically different from the employment world of a few short years ago. Times and the rules of the game have changed, and these changes require that we adopt a modern and flexible approach to resume writing.

What used to be strictly off-limits in all resumes is now acceptable in many and required in some. (The need for technical jargon to explain skills, for example, comes to mind.) Elements that were once always included, such as the mug shot, are now frowned upon in almost every instance. And so it goes on, creating a fog of confusion for everyone. What are the rules?

Today, writing a resume can be likened to baking a cake. In most instances, the ingredients are essentially the same. What determines the flavor is the order and quantity in which those ingredients are blended. There are certain ingredients that go into almost every resume. There are others that rarely or never go in, and there are those special touches that are added (a pinch of this, a dash of that), depending on your personal tastes and requirements.

Sound complicated? It really isn't. This chapter will explain it all. If a certain ingredient must always go in, you will understand why; the same goes for something that should never appear in your resume. In circumstances where the business world holds conflicting views, these views will be explained so that a reasoned judgment can be made. In these instances you will always get my reasoned opinion, based on my extensive experience and contact in the human resources field.

First, let's look at the ingredients that are part of the mix of every successful resume.

What Must Always Go In

Name

We start with the obvious, but there are other considerations about your name besides remembering to put it on your resume. Give your first and last name only. It isn't necessary to include your middle name(s). My name is Martin John Yate—but my resume says simply Martin Yate, because that is the way I would introduce myself in person. Notice also that it isn't M. J. Yate, because that would force the reader to play Twenty Questions about the meaning of my initials, and the average resume reader isn't looking for light entertainment. Even if you are known by your initials don't put them on your resume. If you use quotation marks or parentheses, those on the receiving end might think it a little strange. Better that it come out at the interview when the interviewer asks you what you like to be called: At the very least you'll have some small talk to break the tense interview atmosphere.

It is not required to place Mr., Ms., Miss, or Mrs. before your name. But what if your first name is Gayle, Carrol, Leslie, or any of the other names that can easily be used for members of either sex? While it isn't strictly necessary, in such instances it is acceptable to put Mr. Gayle Jones, or Ms. Leslie Jackson. The reasoning is based on human frailty and the ever-present foot-in-mouth syndrome: In contacting you to follow up on your resume, your interviewer is likely to make the mistake of asking to speak to Ms. Gayle Jones, or Mr. Leslie Jackson. Though it is a little mistake that is easily corrected, the possible future employer is immediately put in the awkward position of starting the relationship with an apology. If your name falls into the "gender-less" category, avoid the complication and employ a title.

Finally, for those who are the IInd, IIIrd, Junior, or Senior holders of their name: If you always add "Jr." or "III" when you sign your name or if that is the way you are addressed to avoid confusion, go ahead and use it. Otherwise, it is extraneous information on the resume, and therefore not needed.

Address

Always give your complete address. Do not abbreviate unless space restrictions make it absolutely mandatory—you want the post office to have every possible advantage when it comes to delivering those offer letters efficiently. If you do abbreviate—such as with St. or Apt.—be consistent. The state of your residence, however, is always abbreviated to two capitalized letters (for example, MN, WV, LA), according to post office standards. Always include the correct zip code.

The accepted format for laying out your address looks like this:

Maxwell Krieger
9 Central Ave, Apartment 38
New York, NY 23456

Notice that the city, state and zip code all go on the same line, with a comma between city and state.

Telephone Number

Always include your telephone number: Few businesses will send you an invitation for an interview in the mail. Including your area code is important even if you have no intention of leaving the area. In this era of decentralization, your resume might end up being screened in another part of the country altogether!
Examples:

(202) 555-5555
202/555-5555

The inclusion or exclusion of a work telephone number is a little bit more of a problem.

The case for inclusion: Featuring your daytime contact number allows prospective employers to reach you at a time of their convenience.

The case for exclusion: Being pulled out of the Monday meeting every five minutes to take calls from headhunters and *Fortune 500* executives can ruin your whole day. The funny thing about employers is that they always prefer to lose you at their convenience rather than yours. In addition, keeping the company number off the resume adds to its life expectancy. Who needs another detail that may be obsolete in short order?

The solution: Unless your current employer knows of your job search, leave the business number off the resume, but put it in your cover letter. Good cover letters do this with a short sentence that conveys the information and demonstrates you as a responsible employee. For example, something like this can work very well:

"I prefer not to use my employer's time taking personal calls at work, but with discretion you can reach me at 202/555-5555, extension 555, to initiate contact."

E-mail

Your e-mail address has become an integral part of your contact information, as important as your telephone number. In fact, its importance goes beyond that of your phone number. The ability to use a telephone doesn't say anything about your professional skills while an e-mail address implies that you have already adapted to the new technology of the workplace. That's a must for any worthwhile job in the new century. If you have an e-mail address, use it. If you don't, get one— and get with it.

If you are planning on using your e-mail address from work, keep in mind that it increases the odds of your boss learning that you are looking at broader horizons. E-mails leave a trail that an employer can follow, and as many as 35 percent of managers are believed to track their employees' e-mail. So using your company e-mail address is almost as stupid as listing your immediate supervisor as the principal contact for your job hunt.

Using company e-mail outside regular working hours won't work either— the trail is still there for prying eyes to see. And think about what it tells potential employers about how you're likely to act once you're on their payroll!

Job Objective

This section sometimes appears on resumes as:

Position Desired
Job Objective
Objective
Employment Objective

All are acceptable. Regardless of the heading, the job objective has traditionally meant one or two sentences about the kind of job you want and what you can contribute to the company in return for such a job. You will recall from chapter 2 that the use of a job objective in your resume will depend in part on the style of resume you employ to present your qualifications. Remember that the functional resume in particular almost demands one.

That notwithstanding, feelings run strong about whether or not to include a job objective in the resume, so let's review the cases for and against, then reach a considered conclusion.

The case for inclusion: Without a job objective, a resume can have no focus, no sense of direction. And if you don't know where you are going, you can't write a resume, because the body copy has nothing to support. The resume revolves around your objective like the earth around the sun.

The case for exclusion: A job objective is too constricting and can exclude you from consideration from countless jobs you might have been interested in, and for which you are qualified. And after creating a resume with the intent of opening as many doors as possible, you wouldn't want to have half of them slammed shut. Besides, employers are not generally believed to be overly concerned about what you want from them until they have a damn good idea about what they can get out of you.

The solution: You do need an objective, but it needn't fit the traditional definition. The best resumes have objectives written in broad, nonspecific terms. They are often little more than a categorization, such as:

Job Objective: Marketing Management

Sometimes these objectives appear at the top of a resume, as a headline and attention grabber. If they go beyond that, they focus on skills, achievements, and relevant personal characteristics that support the argument.

Job Objective: To pursue an accounting career

STAFF ACCOUNTANT—REAL ESTATE

To obtain a responsible position in a company where my experience, accomplishments, and proficiency will allow me the opportunity for growth.

This last approach is best, because it considers the forces at work in business these days. Including job objectives has as much to do with filing and retrieval systems and computers as it does with people. On the one hand, the resume reader is looking for a problem solver, so, by seeing that you fit into a general area, will want to rush on to the rest of the resume (where there are more specifics). Then what happens? In the best-case scenario, you will get a frantic call asking you to state your terms and a start date right away. But what happens when there isn't a need for your particular talents that day? Your resume gets filed or logged onto the company's database. The folks who file resumes aren't rocket scientists, just overworked functionaries trying to dispose of a never-ending flow of paper. They want to get rid of it as quickly as possible, so they will file your resume according to your instructions. And unless you give it the right help, it may not be filed under the right category; it may never see the light of day again. The broader your objective, the greater frequency with which it will be retrieved and reviewed in the future.

The same argument holds true for resumes sent to employment agencies and executive recruiters, who have been known to keep them on file for as long as ten years.

Just recently, in fact, I heard one of those wonderful tales of an eight-year-old resume that landed a job for its writer because it had a general objective. Why is this relevant? Had the specific job objective of an entry-level professional been on that resume, the writer would never have been considered.

Such considerations are encouraging many job seekers to include brief and nonspecific job objectives in their resumes. You will learn how to come up with the right tone for your specific needs later in the book.

Employment Dates

Resume readers are often leery of resumes without employment dates. If you expect a response, you can increase your odds dramatically by including them—in one form or another.

With a steady work history and no employment gaps you can be very specific (space allowing) and write:

January 11, 1997 to July 4,1998
or
1/11/97 to 7/4/98

or, to be a little less specific:
January 1997–February 1998

But if there are short employment gaps, you can improve the look of things:

1997–1998
instead of
December 12, 1997–January 23, 1998

There is no suggestion here that you should lie about your work history, but it is surprising just how many interviewers will be quite satisfied with such dates. There seems to be a myth that everything written on 20-lb. rag paper needs no further inquiry.

While this technique can effectively hide embarrassing employment gaps, and may be enough to get you in for an interview, you should of course be prepared with an adequate answer to questions about your work history once you sit down with the interviewer. Even if such questions are posed, you will have the opportunity to explain yourself—*mano a mano,* as it were—and that is a distinct improvement over being peremptorily ruled out by some faceless non-entity before you get a chance to speak your piece The end justifies the means, in this case.

Again, if you abbreviate months and years, do so consistently.

Keywords

Just as computers have helped streamline your job-hunting activities, they have done the same for the recruiting work of many human resources departments. One of the changes gaining ground in corporate America is the use of resume screening and tracking systems. Understanding how this technology affects the way your resume is received will dramatically affect your chances for success in your job hunt.

While electronic resume distribution makes your life easier, it's created an avalanche of electronic paper on the other side of the desk. If a company once had to deal with 100 resumes a day, it now probably sees 1,000 or more. Obviously, this incredible increase in volume has to be handled more efficiently. With the high cost of human handling, the wholesale adoption of resume screening and tracking systems by businesses is a given. These systems are already in place in the most forward looking companies—approaching 50 percent of the total. By the time you go through your next job hunt, most likely every business will have them.

When computer screening replaces human judgment, the whole game changes. The computer program can't use human logic (although it is already getting pretty close); instead, the computer searches for keywords that describe the position and the professional skills needed to execute the duties effectively.

Your resume—and a thousand like it—can be scanned for the necessary keywords in seconds. The user receives a list of the resumes that contain the appropriate keywords. The greater the number of relevant keywords in your resume, the higher your ranking. The higher your ranking, the greater the likelihood that your resume will be rescued from the avalanche and passed along to a person for further screening.

In the resume examples you'll see a section that lumps a string of keywords together. A keyword section can be labeled with a variety of names: Special Knowledge, Keyword Preface, Keyword Section, or Areas of Expertise. Here's what the keyword section of a taxation specialist's resume looks like:

AREAS OF EXPERTISE

SBT, C-Corporation and S-Corporation State Income Tax Returns • Vehicle Use Tax Returns • State Income Tax Budgeting and Accrual • Multistate Property Tax Returns • Federal, State and Local Exemption Certificates • State and Local Sales, Use and Excise Tax Management • Tax Audit Management • Tax License and Bonding Maintenance • Certificates of Authority and Annual Report Filing Maintenance • State Sales and Use Tax Assessment • Federal Excise Tax Collection and Deposits • Determination of Nexus • Tax Amnesty Programs

---

A section like this will become mandatory in your resume in the very near future. You would be smart to be ahead of the curve on this one! This keyword section not only dramatically increases your chances of getting the computer's attention, but HR people and line managers appreciate them as a brief synopses of the whole resume.

Job Titles

The purpose of a job title on your resume is not to reflect exactly what you were called by a particular employer, but rather to provide a generic identification that will be understood by as many employers as possible.

A job title should give the employer "something to hang his hat on." So if your current title is "Junior Accountant, Level Three," realize that such internal titling may well bear no relation to the titling of any other company on earth. I remember looking over the personnel roster of a New York bank and learning, to my astonishment, that it had over one hundred systems analysts. (The typical number for an outfit this size is about twelve.) Then I noticed that they had no programmers. The reasoning that I eventually unearthed was remarkably simple. The human resources department, finding people to be title-conscious in this area, obligingly gave them the titles they wanted. (Another perceived benefit was that it confused the heck out of the raiding headhunters, who got disgusted with systems analysts who couldn't analyze their way out of a wet paper bag!)

This generic approach to job titles also holds true as your job takes you nearer the top of the corporate ladder. The senior executive knows that the higher up the ladder, the more rarefied the air and the fewer the opportunities. After all, a company only has one Controller or one VP of Operations. Again, to avoid painting yourself into a career corner, you can be "specifically vague" with job titles like:

Administrative Assistant
instead of
Secretary

Accountant
instead of
Junior Accountant Level II

It is imperative to examine your current role at work, rather than relying on your starting or current title. Job titles within companies change much more slowly than the jobs themselves, so a job change can be the opportunity for some to escape stereotyping and the career stagnation that accompanies it. Take the typist hired three years ago, who has now spent two years with a word processor. Such a person could be identified thus:

Word Processor
instead of
Typist

This approach is important because of the way titles and responsibilities vary from company to company. Often, more senior titles and responsibilities are structured around a person's specific talents, especially so outside the *Fortune 1000*.

There are two situations, however, that don't lend themselves to this technique:

- When you apply for a specific job where you know the title and the responsibilities, and where the position's title is similar but not the same as your own. (Then the exact title sought should be reflected in your resume—as long as you are not being misleading concerning your capabilities.)
- When you apply for a job in certain specific professions, such as health care. (A brain surgeon wouldn't want to be specifically vague by tagging herself as a Health Aide.)

Company Name

The names of employers should be included. There is no need to include street address or telephone number of past or present employers, although it can be useful to include the city and state. The company will find the complete address on your employment application.

When working for a multiple-division corporation you may want to list the divisional employer: "Bell Industries" might not be enough, so you would perhaps want to add "Computer Memory Division." By the way, it is quite all right to abbreviate words like Corporation (Corp.), Company (Co.), Limited (Ltd.), or Division (Div.). Again, be consistent.

Here is how you might combine the job title and company name and address:

> DESIGN ENGINEER.
> Bell Industries, Inc., Computer Memory Div., Mountain View, CA.

The information you are supplying is relevant to the reader, but you don't wish it to detract from space usable to sell yourself. If, for instance, you live in a nationally known city, such as Dallas, you need not add "TX."

There is a possible exception to these guidelines. Employed professionals are justified in omitting current employers when their industry has been reduced to a small community of professionals who know, or know of, each other, and where a confidentiality breach is likely to have damaging repercussions. This usually happens to professionals on the higher rungs of the ladder. Of course, if you don't quite fit into this elite category but are still worried about identifying your firm, you are not obliged to list the name of your current employer.

One approach is simply to label a current company in a fashion that has become perfectly acceptable in today's business climate.

> A National Retail Chain
> An Established Electronics Manufacturer
> A Major Commercial Bank

You will notice that usually a company name is followed by a brief description of the business line:

> A National Retail Chain: Women and junior fashions and accessories.

> An Established Electronics Manufacturer producing monolithic memories.

This requirement is obviated when the writer can get the company's function into the heading.

> A Major Commercial Bank

The writer who can do this saves a line or two of precious space which can be filled with other valuable data.

Responsibilities

This is what is referred to as the meat, or body copy, of the resume, the area where not only are your responsibilities listed, but your special achievements and other contributions are also highlighted. This is one of the key areas that sets the truly great resume apart from the rest. This is a crucial part of the resume; it will be dealt with in detail in chapters 4 and 5.

Endorsements

Remember when you got that difficult job finished so quickly? And all the good things the boss said about your work? Well, in a resume you can very effectively quote him, even if the praise wasn't in writing (though of course it is best to quote directly). A line such as "Praised as 'most innovative and determined manager in the company'" can work wonders.

These third-party endorsements are not necessary, and they most certainly shouldn't be used to excess. But one or two can be a useful addition to your resume. Such quotes, used sparingly, can be very impressive; overkill can make you sound too self-important and reduce your chances of winning an interview.

Such endorsements become especially effective when the responsibilities have been qualified with facts, numbers, and percentages.

Accreditation and Licenses

Many fields of work require professional licensure or accreditation. If this is the case in your line of work, be sure to list everything necessary. If you are close to a particular accreditation or license (a C.P.A., for example), you would want to list it with information about the status:

Passed all parts of C.P.A. exam, September '00 (expected certification February '01).

Professional Affiliations

Your affiliation with associations and societies dedicated to your field shows your own dedication to your career. Membership is also important for networking, so if you are not currently a member of one of your industry's professional associations, give serious consideration to joining. Note the emphasis on "professional" in the heading. An employer is almost exclusively interested in your professional associations and societies. Omit references to any religious, political, or otherwise potentially controversial affiliations. They simply do not belong on a resume; you want yours to reflect a picture of your professional, not your personal, life.

An exception to this rule is in those jobs where a wide circle of acquaintances is regarded as an asset. Some examples would include jobs in public relations, sales, marketing, real estate, and insurance. In that case, include your membership in the Kiwanis or the Royal Lodge of the Raccoons.

By the same token, a seat on the town board, charitable cause involvement, or fundraising work are all activities that show a willingness to involve oneself and can often demonstrate organizational abilities. Space permitting, these are all activities worthy of inclusion because they show you as a sober and responsible member of the community.

These activities become more important as one climbs the corporate ladder of the larger companies. Those firms that take their community responsibilities seriously look for staff who feel and act the same way—an aspect of corporate culture applying itself at the most immediate levels.

Some corporations are committed to the idea that community activities are good public relations. Accordingly, such work may mark an individual for even greater responsibilities and recognition once in the company.

As for method of inclusion, brevity is the rule.

American Heart Association: Area Fundraising Chair

My personal observation is that these activities increase in importance with the maturity of the individual. Employers, quite selfishly perhaps, like to think of their younger staff burning the midnight oil solely for them.

Civil Service Grade

With a civil service job in your background, you will have been awarded a civil service grade. So, in looking for a job with the government, be sure to list it. In transferring from the government to the private sector, you are best advised to translate it into generic terms and ignore the grade altogether, unless you are applying for jobs with government contractors, subcontractors, or other specialized employers familiar with the intricacies of civil service ranking.

Publications and Patents

Such achievements, if they appear, are usually found at the end of the best resumes. Although they serve as positive means of evaluation for the reader, these achievements are of relatively minor importance in many professions.

Nevertheless, both publication and patents are manifestations of original thought and extended effort above and beyond the call of accepted professionalism. They tell the reader that you invest considerable personal time and effort in your career and are therefore a cut above the competition. Publication carries more weight in some industries and professions (where having literary visibility is synonymous with getting ahead); patents are a definite plus in the technology and manufacturing fields. You will notice in the resume examples how the writers list dates and names of publications, but do not usually include copyright information.

"New Developments in the Treatment of Chronic Pain." 1999. *New England Journal of Medicine.*

"Radical Treatments for Chronic Pain." 2000. *Journal of American Medicine.*

"Pain: Is It Imagined or Real?" 1998. *OMNI* Magazine.

Languages

Technology is rapidly changing our world into the proverbial global village. This means that today, as all companies are interested in client-based expansion, a linguistic edge in the job hunt could be just what you need. If you are fluent in a foreign language, you will want to mention it. Likewise if you understand a foreign language, but perhaps are not fluent, still mention it:

Fluent in French
Read and write Serbo-Croatian
Read German
Understand Spanish

Education

Educational history is normally listed whenever it helps your case, although the exact positioning of the information will vary according to the length of your professional experience and the relative strength of your academic achievements.

If you are recently out of school with little practical experience, your educational credentials, which probably constitute your primary asset, will appear near the beginning of the resume.

As you gain experience, your academic credentials become less important, and gradually slip toward the end of your resume. The exception to this is found primarily in certain professions where academic qualifications dominate a person's career—medicine, for instance.

You will notice that all examples for education are in reverse chronological order: The highest level of attainment (not necessarily a degree) always comes first, followed by the lesser levels. In this way, a doctorate will be followed by a master's degree, then a bachelor's. For degreed professionals, there is no need to go back further into educational history. (It is optional to list your prestigious prep school.) Those who attended school but did not graduate should nevertheless list the school in its proper chronological position, but should not draw attention to the fact that they did not receive a degree.

Those who did not achieve the higher levels of educational recognition will list their own highest level of attainment. A word on attainment is in order here. If you graduated from high school, attended college, but didn't graduate, you may be tempted to list your high school diploma first, followed by the name of the college you attended. That would give the wrong emphasis: it says you are a college drop-out and focuses on you as high school graduate. In this instance you would in fact list your college and omit reference to earlier educational history.

While abbreviations are frowned on in most circumstances, it is acceptable to abbreviate educational degrees (Ph.D., M.A., A.B., etc.), simply because virtually everyone understand them.

Those with scholarships and awards will list them, and recent graduates will usually also list majors and minors (space permitting). The case is a little more confused for the seasoned professional. Many human resources professionals say it makes life easier for them if majors and minors are listed, so they can further sift and grade the applicants. That's good for them, but it might not be good for you. All you want the resume to do is get you in the door, not slam it in your face. So, as omitting these minutiae will never stop you from getting an interview, I strongly urge you to err on the side of safety and leave 'em out.

If you are a recent entrant into the workplace, both your scholastic achievements and your contributions have increased importance. Certainly you will list your position on the school newspaper or the student council, memberships in clubs, and recognition for scholastic achievement; in short, anything that demonstrates your potential as a productive employee. As your career progresses, however, prospective employers care less and less about your school life and more and more about your work life. If you have five years of work experience and still feel compelled to list your chairmanship of the school's cafeteria committee, then you are not concentrating on the right achievements.

Changing times have also changed thinking about listing fraternities and sororities on resumes. A case could be made, I think, for leaving them off as a matter of course: If such organizations are important to an interviewer he or she will ask. My ruling, however, is that if the resume is tailored to an individual or company where membership in such organizations will result in a case of "deep calling to deep," then by all means, list. If, on the other hand, the resume is for general distribution, forget it.

Professional Training

Under the educational heading on smart resumes, you will often see a section for continuing professional education, focusing on special courses and seminars attended. Specifically, if you are computer literate, list the programs you are familiar with.

Summer and Part-time Employment

This should only be included when the resume writer is either just entering the work force or re-entering it after a substantial absence. The entry-level person can feel comfortable listing dates and places and times. The returnee should include the skills gained from part-time employment in a fashion that minimizes the "part-time" aspect of the experience—probably by using a Functional resume format.

What Can Never Go In

Some information just doesn't belong in resumes. Make the mistake of including it, and at best your resume loses power. At worst, you fail to land the interview.

Titles: Resume, Fact Sheet, Curriculum Vitae, etc.

Never use any of these variations on a theme as a heading. Their appearance on a resume is redundant: If it isn't completely obvious from the very look of your piece of paper that it is a resume, go back to square one. By the way, there is no difference in meaning among the above terms. "Curriculum Vitae" (or CV, as it is sometimes known) was an early term much favored in English and American academia—basically to prove that the users knew a little Latin. Its use today is outmoded and affected. "Fact Sheet," on the other hand, was a term developed by the employment agencies to imply they were presenting unvarnished facts. The phrase has never caught on.

Availability

Saying anything about your availability for employment on a resume is another redundancy. If you are not available, then why the heck are you wasting everyone's time and slowing down the mails? The only justification of the item's inclusion is if you expect to be finishing a project and moving on at such and such a time, and not before. But your view should be that intelligent human beings always have their eyes and ears open for better career opportunities—because no one else is going to watch out for them. If leaving before the end of a project could affect your integrity and/or references, O.K. There's a lot to be said for not burning your bridges, and as careers progress, it's surprising how many of the same people you bump into again and again.

Let the subject of availability come up at the face-to-face meeting. After meeting you, an employer will often be prepared to wait until you are available, and will probably appreciate your integrity. If, on the other hand, the employer just sees a resume that says you won't be available until next year—well, you'll just never get to a face-to-face meeting in the first place.

Reason for Leaving

There is no real point to stating your reasons for leaving a job on a resume, yet time and again they are included—to the detriment of the writer. The topic is always covered during an interview anyway. Mentioning it in advance and on paper can only damage your chances for being called in for that meeting.

References

It is inappropriate and unprofessional to list the names of references on a resume. You will never see it on a top example. Why? Interviewers are not interested in checking them before they meet and develop a strong interest in you—it's too time-consuming. In addition, employers are forbidden by law to check references without your written consent (thanks to the 1972 Fair Credit and Reporting Act), and they have to meet you first in order to obtain it, right?

Most employers will assume that references are available anyway (and if they aren't available, boy, are you in trouble). For that reason, there's an argument to be made for leaving that famous line—References Available Upon Request—off the end of the resume. I disagree, however. It may not be absolutely necessary to say that references are there for the asking, but those four extra words certainly don't do any harm and may help you stand out from the crowd. Including the phrase sends a little message:

"Hey, look, I have no skeletons in my closet."

A brief but important aside. If you have ever worked under a different surname, you must take this fact into account when giving your references. A recently divorced woman wasted a strong interview performance not too long ago because she was using her maiden name on her resume and at the interview. She forgot to tell the employer that her references would, of course, remember her by a different last name. The results of this oversight were catastrophic. Three prior employers denied ever having heard of anyone by that name the woman's interviewer supplied. She lost the job.

Written Testimonials

Even worse than listing references on a resume is to attach a bunch of written testimonials. It is an absolute no-no. No one believes them anyway.

Of course, that doesn't mean that you shouldn't solicit such references for your files. They can always be produced when references are requested and can be used as a basis for those third-party endorsements we talked about. This will be especially helpful to you if you are just entering the work force, or re-entering after a long absence, because the content of the testimonials can be used to beef up your resume significantly.

Salary

Leave out all references to salary, past and present—it is far too risky. Too high or too low a salary can knock you out of the running even before you hear the starting gun. Even in responding to a help-wanted advertisement that specifically requests salary requirements, don't give them. A good resume will still get you the interview, and in the course of your discussions with the company, you'll certainly talk about salary anyway. If you somehow feel obliged to give salary requirements, simply write "competitive" or "negotiable" (and then only in your cover letter).

Abbreviations

With the exceptions of educational attainments, and those required by the postal service, avoid abbreviations if at all possible. Of course, space constraints might make it imperative that you write "No. Wilshire Blvd." instead of "North Wilshire Boulevard." If that is the case, be sure to be consistent. If you abbreviate in one address, abbreviate in all of them. But bear in mind that you will always seem more thoughtful and professional if everything is spelled out. And anyway, your resume will be easier to read!

Jargon

A similar warning applies to industry slang. Your future boss might understand it, but you can bet your boots that neither his or her boss nor the initial resume screener will. Your resume must speak clearly of your skills to many different people, and one skill that we all need today is a sensitivity to the needs of communication.

If you are in one of the high-technology industries, however, avoiding jargon and acronyms is not only impossible, it is often inadvisable. All the same, keep the nontechnical resume screener in mind before you wax lyrical about bits and bytes.

Charts and Graphs

Even if charts and graphs are part of your job, they make poor use of the space available on a resume—and they don't help the reader. In fact, you should never even bring them out at an interview unless requested. The same goes for other examples of your work. If you are a copywriter or graphic artist, for example, it is all right to say that samples are available, but only if you have plenty of resume space to spare.

Mention of Age, Race, Religion, Sex, National Origin

Government legislation was enacted some years ago forbidding employment discrimination in these areas. If the government had to take action, you know things were bad. Although today it's much better, I urge you to leave out any reference to any of these areas in your resume.

Photographs

In days of old when men were bold and all our cars had fins, it was the done thing to have a photograph in the top right-hand corner of the resume. So, if you are looking for a job in the 1950s, include one; if not, don't. Today, the fashion is against photographs; including them is a waste of space that says nothing about your ability to do a job.

(Obviously, careers in modeling, acting, and certain aspects of the electronic media require photos. In these instances your face is your fortune.)

Health/Physical Description

Who cares? You are trying to get a job, not a date. Unless your physical health (gym instructor, e.g.) and/or appearance (model, actor, media personality) are immediately relevant to the job, leave these issues alone.

Early Background

I regularly see resumes that tell about early childhood and upbringing. To date, the most generous excuse I can come up with for such anecdotes is that the resumes were prepared by the subjects' mothers.

Weaknesses

Any weakness, lack of qualifications, or information likely to be detrimental to your cause should always be canned. Never tell resume readers what you don't have or what you can't or haven't had the opportunity to do yet. Let them find that out for themselves.

Demands

You will never see demands on a good resume. Don't outline what you feel an employer is expected to give or to provide. The time for making demands is when the employer has demonstrated sincere interest in you by extending a job offer with a salary and job description attached. That is when the employer will be interested and prepared to listen to what you want. Until then, concentrate on bringing events to that happy circumstance by emphasizing what you can bring to the employer. In your resume you should, to paraphrase the great man, ask not what your employer can do for you, but rather what you can do for your employer.

Exaggerations

Avoid verifiable exaggerations of your skills, accomplishments, and educational qualifications. Research has now proven that three out of every ten resumes feature inflated educational qualifications. Consequently, verification, especially of educational claims, is on the increase. If, after you had been hired, you were discovered to have told a sly one on your resume, it could cost you your job and a lot more. The stigma of deceit will very likely follow you for the rest of your professional days. On the other hand, I don't notice 30 percent of the work force stumbling around with crippled careers. Matters are tightening up in this area, and ultimately it will be a personal judgment call. Ask yourself, "Do I have a defensible position, should this matter come under scrutiny now or at a later date?"

Judgment Calls

Here are some areas that fall into neither the do nor the don't camp. Whether to include them will depend on your personal circumstances.

Summary

The Summary, when it is included in a resume, comes immediately after the Objective. The point is to encapsulate your experience and perhaps highlight one or two of your skills and/or contributions. You hope, in two or three short sentences, to grab the reader's attention with a power pack of the skills and attributes you have developed throughout your career. Good summaries are short; you don't want to show all your aces in the first few lines! You can see examples of resumes with strong summaries in the resume section of this book.)

On the other hand, many experts feel that the content of the summary must be demonstrated by the body of the resume, and that therefore summaries are pointless duplications and a waste of space. The choice is yours. Used wisely and well, they can work.

Personal Flexibility, Relocation

If you are open to relocation for the right opportunity, make it clear. It will never in and of itself get you an interview, but it won't hurt. On the other hand, never state that you aren't open to relocation. After all, that factor usually comes into play only when you have a job offer to consider. Let nothing stand in the way of a nice collection of job offers!

Career Objectives

These are okay to include at the very start of your career, before your general direction has been confirmed by experience and track record. Inclusion is also acceptable if you have very clearly defined objectives and are prepared to sacrifice all other opportunities. If that is the case, state your goals clearly and succinctly, remembering not to confuse the nature of long-term career objectives with short-term job objectives.

Beware, though, of the drawbacks. First of all, resume readers aren't famous for paying much attention to objectives. Second, I have seen these used on many occasions to make a hiring decision between two candidates. The resumes are compared, A has no objective, B has an objective that doesn't match the initial expectations. Result? A gets the job. Another consideration is that your resume may be on file for years, during which time your objectives are bound to change. You don't need last year's dusty dreams clouding over your bright tomorrows.

Marital Status

If you think mention of your marital status will enhance your chances (if you are looking for a position as a long-distance trucker, marriage counselor, or traveling salesperson, for example), include it. In all other instances leave it out. Legally, your marital status is of no consequence.

Military

Include your good military record with highest rank, especially if you are applying for jobs in the defense sector. Otherwise exclude it: It is no longer any detriment to your career not to have a military history.

Personal Interests

A recent Korn Ferry study showed that executives with team sports on their resumes were seen to be averaging $3,000 a year more than their more sedentary counterparts. Now, that makes giving a line to your hobbies worthwhile, if they fit into certain broad categories. These would include team sports (baseball, basketball), determination activities (running, swimming, climbing, bicycling), and "brain activities" (bridge, chess).

The rule of thumb, as always, is only to include activities that can in some way contribute to your chances. If you can draw a valid connection, include them; if not, don't.

Personal Paragraphs

Here and there throughout the resume section of this book you will see resumes that include—often toward the end—a short personal paragraph that gives you a candid snapshot of the resume writer as a person. Done well, these can be exciting, effective endings to a resume, but they are not to everyone's taste. Typically, they refer to one or two personal traits, activities, and sometimes, beliefs. These are often tied in with skills required for the particular job sought.

The idea is to make the reader say, "Heh, there's a real person behind those Foster Grants, let's get him in here; sounds like our kind of guy." Of course, as no one can be all things to all people, you won't want to go overboard in this area.

4 | Resumes That Knock 'em Dead

It has been theory up to now; this is where the rubber hits the road.

You have a sound idea of why you need a resume; you've had an overview of the different types available to you; and you know what belongs in a powerful resume and what doesn't. We now move from the abstract to the intensely practical side of resume writing.

This is the part of the book that requires you to do some thinking. I will ask questions to jog your memory about your practical experience. The outcome will be a smorgasbord of your most sellable professional attributes. The work we do together in this chapter will not only form the foundation of your resume but prepare you to turn those job interviews into job offers.

People change jobs for a multitude of reasons. Perhaps your career isn't progressing as you want it. Perhaps you have gone as far as you can with your present employer, and the only way to take another career step is to change companies. Maybe you have been in the same job for three or more years, without dramatic salary increases or promotions, and you know that you are going nowhere. You have been stereotyped, classified, and pigeonholed.

Whether you are a fast-tracker, recent graduate, work force reentrant, career changer, or what-have-you, if you are considering new horizons, you must take stock before stepping out.

You need to know where you've been, where you are, and where you're headed. Without this stock taking, your chances of reaching your ultimate goals are reduced, because you won't know how best to use what you've got to get what you want.

Believe it or not, very few people have a clear fix on what they do for a living. Oh, I know; you ask a typist what he or she does, and you get, "Type, stupid." You ask an accountant, and you hear, "Fiddle with numbers, what do you think?" And that is the problem. Most people don't look at their work beyond these simplistic terms. They never examine the implications of their jobs in relation to the overall success of the department and company. Most people miss not only their importance to an employer as part of the business, but also, their importance to themselves. Preparing your resume will give you a fresh and more lucid view of yourself as a professional and your role in your chosen profession.

Employers all want to know the same thing: How can you contribute to keeping their ship afloat and seaworthy? No one is hired merely to be a typist or an accountant—or anything else, for that matter. Companies hire only one type of person—a problem solver. Look at your work in terms of the problems you solve in the daily round, the problems that would occur if you weren't there.

Some people find the prospect of taking stock of their skills to be an ominous one. They feel it means judging themselves by others' standards, by the job title and salary assigned to by someone else. Then, knowing their own weaknesses too well, they look at other people in their position, of whom they see only the exterior, and are awed by those persons' seemingly superior competence, skills, and professionalism.

"Seemingly" is the key word here. You are as good as the next person, and to prove it, all you have to do is look yourself squarely in the eye and learn that you have a great deal more to offer than you may ever have imagined. You have solved problems. That's what this chapter is all about.

The Secret of Resume Writing

As a resume writer, you have a lot in common with journalists and novelists. Beginners in each field usually bring some basic misconceptions about how writing is done: I always thought that Stephen King or James Clavell sat down, wrote "Page 1," then three weeks later wrote "The End," and placidly returned the quill to the inkwell. In fact, many professional writers—and resume writers—have more in common with sculptors. What they really do to start the creative process is to write masses of notes. This great mass is the raw material, like a block of stone, at which you chip away to reveal the masterwork that has been hiding there all along.

The key is that the more notes you have, the better. Just remember that whatever you write in the note-making part of your resume preparation will never suffer public scrutiny. It is for your private consumption; from these notes, the finished work of art will emerge for public view.

This chapter is going to help you write those notes, as you recapture all those forgotten moments of glory that employers love to hear about.

The only difficult step to take is the first one. So pick up a pen and some paper, and plunge ahead right now; without even pausing for breath.

Questionnaire, Part One: Raw Materials

This questionnaire is set up to follow your entire career. In answering the questions as completely as you can, you are creating the mass of raw material from which you will sculpt the final work of art.

1. *Current or Last Employer:* This includes part-time or voluntary employment if you are a recent graduate or about to reenter the work-force after an absence. Try looking at your school as an employer and see what new information you reveal about yourself.
   Starting Date:
   Starting Salary:
   Leaving Date:
   Leaving Salary:
2. *Company Description:* Write one sentence that describes the product(s) your company made or the service(s) it performed.
3. *Title:* Write your starting job title (the one given to you when you first signed on with the company). Then write a one- or two-sentence description of your responsibilities in that position.
4. *Duties:* What were your three major duties in this position?
5. *Methods, Skills, Results:* Now, for each of the above three duties, answer the following questions:

   What special skills or knowledge did you need to perform this task satisfactorily?

   What has been your biggest achievement in this area? (Try to think about money saved or made, or time saved for the employer. Don't worry if your contributions haven't been acknowledged in writing and signed in triplicate, as long as you know them to be true without exaggeration.)

What verbal or written comments were made about your contributions in this area, by peers or managers?

What different levels of people did you have to interact with to achieve your job tasks? How did you get the best out of superiors? Co-workers? Subordinates?

What aspects of your personality were brought into play when executing this duty? (For example, perhaps it required attention to detail, or determination, or good verbal and writing skills. Whatever, jot them all down.)

To help you address that last issue (it's a vitally important one), you should look over the following list of a number of personality traits that are in constant demand from all employers.

Analytical Skills: Weighing the pros and cons. Not jumping at the first solution to a problem that presents itself.

Chemistry: Your willingness to get along with others and get the job done.

Communication Skills: More than ever, the ability to talk with and write effectively to people at all levels in a company is a key to success.

Confidence: Poise, friendliness, honesty, and openness with all employees—high and low.

Dedication: Doing whatever it takes to get the job done.

Drive and Determination: A desire to get things done. Goal-oriented. Someone who does not back off when a problem or situation gets tough.

Economy: Most problems have an expensive solution and an inexpensive one that the company would prefer to implement.

Efficiency: Always keeping an eye open for inefficient uses of time, effort, resources, and money.

Energy: Extra effort in all aspects of the job, the little things as well as the important matters.

Honesty/Integrity: Responsibility for all your actions—both good and bad. Always making decisions in the best interests of the company, rather than on whim or personal preference.

Listening Skills: Listening, rather than just waiting your turn to speak.

Motivation: Enthusiasm, finding reasons to accept challenges rather than avoid them. A company realizes that a motivated person accepts added challenges and does that little bit extra on every job.

Pride: Pride in a job well done. Paying attention to detail.

Reliability: Follow-through, a willingness to keep management informed, and a predisposition toward relying on oneself—not others—to see your job done.

Sensitivity to Procedures: Following the chain of command, recognizing that procedures exist to keep a company functioning and profitable. Those who rush to implement their own "improved procedures" wholesale, or organize others to do so, can cause untold chaos in an organization.

6. *Supporting Points:* If you asked for a promotion or a raise while in this position, what arguments did you use to back up your request?

7. *Most Recent Position:* Write down your current (or last) job title. Then write a one- or two-sentence description of your responsibilities in that position, and repeat steps three through six. In this step it is assumed that you have a title and responsibilities that are different from those you had when you first joined the company. If this is not the case, simply ignore this step. On the other hand, many people have held three or four titles with a specific employer, and gained breadth of experience with each one. In this instance, for each different intermediary title, repeat steps one through six. The description of responsibilities should be reserved for your departing (or current) title.

8. *Reflecting on Success:* Make some general observations about work with this employer. Looking back over your time with this employer, what was the biggest work-related problem that you had to face? What solution did you find? What was the result of the solution when implemented? What was the value to the employer in terms of money earned or saved and improved efficiency? What was the area of your

greatest personal improvement in this job? What was the greatest contribution you made as a team player? Who are the references you would hope to use from this employer, and what do you think they would say about you?

9. *Getting All the Facts:* Repeat the last eight steps for your previous employer, and then for the employer before that, and so forth. Most finished resumes focus on the last three jobs, or last ten years before that, and so forth. In this developmental portion of the process, however, you must go back in time and cover your entire career. Remember that you are doing more than preparing a resume here: you are preparing for the heat of battle. In the interview preparation, throughout any telephone screening interviews, and especially before that crucial face-to-face meeting, you can use this Questionnaire to prepare yourself for anything the interviewer might ask. One of the biggest complaints interviewers have about job candidates, and one of the major reasons for rejection, is unpreparedness: "You know, good as some of this fellow's skills are, something just wasn't right. He seemed—slow somehow. You know, he couldn't even remember when he joined his current employer!" You won't have that problem.

Questionnaire, Part Two: Details, Details, Details

The hard work is done and it's all downhill from here. Just fill in the facts and figures relating to the following questions. Obviously, not everything will apply to you. The key is just to put it all down; you can polish it later.

Military History

Include branch of service, rank, and any special skills that could further your civilian career.

Educational History

Start with highest level of attainment and work backward. Give dates, schools, majors, minors, grade-point averages.

Specify any scholarships or other special awards.

List other school activities, such as sports, societies, social activities. Especially important are leadership roles: Any example of how you "made a difference" with your presence could be of value to your future. Obviously, this is important for recent graduates with little work experience.

Languages

Specify fluency and ability to read and write foreign languages.

Personal Interests

List interests and activities that could be supportive to your candidacy. For example, an internal auditor who plays chess or bridge would list these and probably use them in a resume, because they support the analytical bent so necessary to work.

Technological Literacy

In this new era of work every potential employer is concerned about your ability to work with new technologies. If you are computer and Internet literate, let's hear the details. If not, it's time to catch up with today's technology—before you get left behind with the industrial era dinosaurs.

Demonstrating that you have up-to-date knowledge and are comfortable with computers and the Internet, along with understanding how they apply to your specific profession, are key to your professional survival. You should be able to identify the equipment and applications you need to function effectively in your field.

Patents

Include patents that are both pending and awarded.

Publications

If you have published articles, list the name of the publication, title of article and the publication date. If you have had books published, list the title and publisher.

Professional Associations

Include membership and the details of any offices you held.

Volunteer Work

Also include any volunteer work you performed. It isn't only paid work experience that makes you valuable.

Miscellaneous Areas of Achievement

All professions and careers are different. Use this section to itemize any additional aspects of your history where you somehow "made a difference" with your presence.

Questionnaire, Part Three: Where Are You Going?

Knowing where you want to go will determine both the wording and the layout of your resume. There is an old saying that if you don't know where you are going, you have no hope of getting there. Remember that there is a difference between valid objectives and pipedreams. Dreams aren't bad things to have, but they mustn't be confused with making a living.

Your first step is to write down a job title that embraces your objectives. Having taken this simple step, you need to note underneath it all the skills and qualifications needed to do that job successfully. List them like this:

Job Title
1. First skill
2. Second skill
3. Third skill
4. Fourth skill
5. Fifth skill

But remember that your thoughts on what it takes may not jibe with the employer's thoughts. And what if you are simply not sure what it takes to do the job at all? Simple. Take a trip to the library and ask to see a copy of the *Dictionary of Occupational Titles*. It gives you endless job titles, as you might expect, and brief job descriptions. Make notes by all means, but don't copy it out word for word. The book is full of dead prose that's copper-bottom guaranteed to send the average resume reader to sleep in three seconds flat. You want to avoid letting any of this soporific stuff sneak into the final draft of your resume.

When you have decided on an objective, and defined what it takes to do that job, go back through the first part of the questionnaire and flag all the entries you can use to build a viable resume. Just underline or highlight the appropriate passages for further attention when the time comes for putting pen to paper.

The chances are that you will find adequate skills in your background to qualify you for the job objective. And remember: Few people have all the qualifications for the jobs they get!

If you still aren't sure, develop a "Matching Sheet" for yourself. List the practical requirements of your job objective on one side of a piece of paper and match them on the other side with your qualifications. A senior computer programmer, looking for a step up to a systems analysis position with a new job in financial applications, might develop a Matching Sheet that looks like this:

Job Needs	My Experience
Mainframe IBM experience	6 yrs. experience
IBM COBOL	COBOL, PL/1, Assembler
Financial experience	6 yrs. in banking
Sys. dev. methodology	Major sys. dev., 3 yrs.
Communication	Ongoing customer service
	work OS/MVS, TSO/SPF,
	CICS, SNAOS/MVS, TSO/SPF,
	ROSCOE, IMS, DB/DC, SAS

But what about the junior accountant who had VP of finance as a goal? Naturally, at this stage, many of the needed skills—and much of the experience—aren't in place. If you fall into this category, don't worry. You just happened upon a career objective rather than a job objective. To solve the dilemma, list all the title changes between your present position and your dream job. This will show you how many career steps stand between you and your ultimate goal. Your job objective is simply the title above your own, the first achievable stepping stone toward the ultimate goal.

At best, job and career objectives are simply a tool to give you focus for writing the resume, and to give the reader something to take sightings on. The way the world is changing, by the time you can reasonably expect to reach your ultimate career goal, that particular position may not even exist.

Be content with a generalized objective for the next job. And don't be afraid of that objective—you aren't taking holy orders, you're identifying a job you'd like to win. Who knows what the next few years will hold for you?

Sample Questionnaire

This sample questionnaire was filled out by a fellow professional using the questionnaire guidelines on pages 39–45. Actual resume examples based on the following information—chronological, functional, and combination formats—can be found on pages 7–13.

1. Current or Last Employer:
   This includes part-time or voluntary employment if you are a recent graduate or about to reenter the work force after an absence. That does not mean you should ignore this section: Try looking at your school as an employer and see what new information you reveal about yourself.

   BRANCH MANAGER
Starting Date	*11/92*
Starting Salary	*$13,000*
Leaving Date	*8/95*
Leaving Salary	*$26,000*

   AREA MANAGER
Starting Date	*8/95*
Starting Salary	*$31,200*
Leaving Date	*8/98*
Leaving Salary	*$41,600*

   DIVISION MANAGER
Starting Date	*8/98*
Starting Salary	*$62,400*
Leaving Date	*3/00*
Leaving Salary	*$62,400*

2. Write one sentence that describes the products your company made or the services it performed.

   BRANCH MANAGER through DIVISION MANAGER: MICRO/TEMPS sold software consulting services to the computer-user industry.

3. List your starting job title (the one given to you when you first signed on with the company). Then write a one- or two-sentence description of your responsibilities in that position.

BRANCH MANAGER
Started a new division of the Technical Aid Corporation called MICRO/TEMPS. Was responsible for developing a client and applicant database, while showing a profit for the division.

AREA MANAGER
Opened an additional office in the Washington area. Was accountable for the profitability of both the Boston and Washington offices.

DIVISION MANAGER
Responsible for market studies for future branches to be opened. Directly involved in choosing new locations, opening office, training staff and having the office profitable in less than one year's time.

4. What were your three major duties in this position?

BRANCH MANAGER
A) Selling software services to clients.
B) Interviewing applicants and selling them on consulting.
C) Setting up interviews for applicants and clients to meet.

AREA MANAGER
A) Training sales and recruiting staff.
B) Developing and implementing goals from forecasts.
C) Interfacing with other divisions in order to develop a working relationship between different divisions.

DIVISION MANAGER
A) Hired and trained Branch Managers for all new offices.
B) Developed P & L forecasts for the B.O.D.
C) Developed and implemented division policies.

5. Now, for each of the above three duties, answer the following questions:

What special skills or knowledge did you need to perform this task satisfactorily?

BRANCH MANAGER
A) Knowledge of the computer industry.
B) Key contacts in the Massachusetts computer industry.

AREA MANAGER
A) Knowledge and experience developing a branch.
B) Experience training sales and recruiting staff.

DIVISION MANAGER
A) Knowledge and understanding of developing a profitable division.
B) Knowledge and experience hiring and training branch managers.

What has been your biggest achievement in this area? (Try to think about money saved or made, or time saved for the employer. Don't worry if your contributions haven't been acknowledged in writing and signed in triplicate, so long as you know them to be true without exaggeration.)

BRANCH MANAGER
Successfully developed a new division of the Technical Aid Corporation. Now generating $18,000,000 in revenues.

AREA MANAGER
Successfully opened new branches for the division and hired and trained the staff.

DIVISION MANAGER
Built division to $20 million in annual sales.

What verbal or written comments were made about your contributions in this area, by peers or managers?

BRANCH MANAGER
Hard-working, stay-at-it attitude.

AREA MANAGER
Hires good people and knows how to get the best out of them.

DIVISION MANAGER
Her division always makes the largest gross profit out of any of the divisions.

What different levels of people did you have to interact with to get this particular duty done? How did you get the best out of each of them?

BRANCH MANAGER
A) *Superiors—Listened to their ideas and then tried to show them I could implement them.*
B) *Co-workers—Shared experiences and company goals—set up some competition.*
C) *Subordinates—Acknowledged their responsibilities as very important for the team.*

AREA MANAGER
A) *Superiors—Explained situations clearly and made them understand our options.*
B) *Co-workers—Challenged to reach goals.*
C) *Subordinates—Complimented when and where it was necessary.*

DIVISION MANAGER
A) *Superiors—Asked for their experience and advice in difficult situations.*
B) *Co-workers—Set up and accepted contest between managers.*
C) *Subordinates—Made them feel they were extremely important as a member of the team.*

What aspects of your personality were brought into play when executing this duty?

PERSONALITY: BRANCH MANAGER TO DIVISION MANAGER
strong willpower
stick-to-it attitude
high achiever
aggressive
high goal setter

6. If you asked for a promotion or a raise while in this position, what arguments did you use to back up your request?

   BRANCH MANAGER—Increase in sales.
   AREA MANAGER—Increase in responsibility.
   DIVISION MANAGER—Increase in gross profit and responsibilities.

7. Write down your current (or last) job title. Then write a one- or two-sentence description of your responsibilities in that position, and repeat steps 3 through 6.

   Current title—*Personnel Manager*

   Step 3: Description of responsibilities. *Hiring all internal staff of technical managers and sales people, additionally responsible for hiring all external consultants.*

   Step 4: Three major duties:
   A) *Hiring of all internal and external consultants*
   B) *Setting up wage and salary guidelines*
   C) *Establishing the Boston office so it could become profitable quickly*

   Step 5: Skills or knowledge needed:
   A) *Ability to source qualified candidates*
   B) *Experience in start-up situation*
   C) *Knowledge of the Boston marketplace*

   Biggest achievement: *Helped in making the branch profitable in nine months.*

   Verbal or written comments: *A no-nonsense kind of person, aggressive and hard-working; good at getting the best out of people.*

   Superiors: *Was up front with any problems and clearly and concisely laid out all the alternatives.*

   Co-workers: *Set up good networking of communications to have information flow quickly and easily.*

Subordinates: *Made them aware that we all had a lot to do, but that we were all important.*

Step 6: Raise or promotion.
Increase in sales figures and was responsible for hiring more consultants than we had originally discussed.

8. Make some general observations about work with this employer.
Looking back over your time with this employer, what was the biggest work-related problem that you had to face?
They wanted to grow rapidly, but didn't want to invest the money it took to recruit and attract good consultant talent.

What solution did you find?

Got consultants through Boston Computer Society and other related organizations, and set up a very aggressive referral program.

What was the result of the solution when implemented?

We started to attract quality consultants, and our name was beginning to circulate.

What was the value to the employer in terms of money earned or saved and improved efficiency?

Company did not spend a lot of money on recruiting efforts and was able to attract quality people.

What was the area of your greatest personal improvement in this job?

Made many key contacts in some excellent organizations.

What was the greatest contribution you made as a team player?

Brought internal staff members closer together as a working team.

Who are the references you would hope to use from this employer, and what do you think they would say about you?

Ken Shelly—He was one of our first external consultants hired. He would probably say that I identified some key consultants for this project at Sheraton, and that he could always rely on me to help him no matter what.

Dave Johnson—He was our technical manager. He would say that I did my job extremely well considering the little resources I had, and that I identified many quality applicants. He would also say that I knew how to find even difficult people.

5 | Writing the Basic Resume

Advertisements and resumes have a great deal in common.

You will notice the vast majority of advertisements in any media can be heard, watched, or read in under thirty seconds. That is not accidental. The timing is based on studies relating to the limit of the average consumer's attention span.

And that is why you sometimes notice that both resumes and advertisements depart from the rules that govern all other forms of writing. First and last they are an urgent business communication, and businesses like to get to the point.

Before getting started, good advertising copywriters imagine themselves in the position of their target audience. They imagine their objective—selling something. Then they consider what features their product possesses and what benefits it can provide to the purchaser.

You will find a similar procedure beneficial in your own writing. Fortunately, your approach is simplified somewhat, because you can make certain generalizations. You can assume, for instance, that the potential employer has a position to fill and a problem to solve, and that he or she will hire someone who is able to do the job, who is willing to do it, and who is manageable.

For the next fifteen minutes, imagine yourself in one of your target companies. You are in the personnel department on resume detail. Fortunately it is a slow morning, and there are only thirty that need to be read. Go straight to the example section now and read thirty resumes without a break, then return to this page.

Now you have some idea of what it feels like. Except that you had it easy—the resumes you read were good, interesting ones; resumes that got real people real jobs. Even so, you probably felt a little punch drunk at the end of the exercise. But I know that you learned a very valuable lesson: Brevity is to be desired above all other things.

Preparation

Collect an old resume, some generic job descriptions, and of course, the completed Questionnaire. Then get comfortably set up at your computer (or with a pad of paper if it makes you more comfortable) and you're ready to go!

Now, just write. Don't even try for style or literacy—you can tend to that later. Think of yourself as speaking on paper. You'll find your personal speech rhythms will make for a lively resume, once they have been edited.

Choose a Layout

You have seen the basic examples of chronological, functional, and combination resumes in chapter 2, and certainly you have browsed through the dozens of actual resumes. Find one that strikes your fancy and fits your needs, and use it as your model. It need not reflect your field of professional expertise. Obviously, you will have to tinker with any model, adding or deleting jobs and making other subtle adjustments as necessary, to fashion it for your background.

This first step is just like painting by numbers. Go through the model and fill in the obvious slots—name, address, telephone number(s), e-mail address, employer names, employment dates, educational background and dates, extramural activities and the like. Shazam! Now the first half of your resume is complete.

Filling in the Picture: Chronological Resumes

Objectives

You can have a simple nonspecific objective, one that gives the reader a general focus, such as, "Objective: Data Processing Management." It gets the message across succinctly; and if there is no immediate need for someone of your background, it encourages the employer to put your resume in the file where you feel it belongs. That's important, because even if you are not suitable for today's needs, there's a good chance that the resume will be pulled out when such a need does arise.

If you choose to use an expanded, detailed objective, refer to chapter 3. You will of course:

- Keep it short, just one or two sentences.
- Express your objective in the fewest possible words that can bring a picture to the reader's mind.
- Not get too specific—no one is that interested.
- Focus the objective on what you can do for the company and avoid mention of what you want in return.
- State exactly the job title you seek, if the resume is in response to a specific advertisement.
- Keep your objectives general to give yourself the widest number of employment options, if the resume will be sent out "blind" to a number of companies.

Of course, with your resume produced on a computer, your objective can go through subtle variations for each specific job.

If you want to use both a nonspecific and a detailed objective, headline the resume with the nonspecific title, and then follow with the more detailed one.

Company Role

Now, for each employer, edit your response from step two of the Questionnaire, which outlines that company's services or products. Make it one short sentence: Do not exceed one line or ten words.

Job Titles

Remember what we said in chapter 3. There is nothing intrinsically wrong with listing your title as "Fourth-Level Administration Clerk, Third Class," as long as you are prepared to wait until doomsday for it to be considered by someone who understands what it means and is able to relate it to current needs. With this in mind:

- Be general in your job title. All companies have their particular ways of dispensing job titles, and they all vary. Your title with employer A will mean something entirely different to employer B, and might not make any sense at all to employer C.

- Whenever possible, stay away from designations such as trainee, junior, intermediate, senior—as in Junior Engineer—and just designate yourself as Engineer, Designer, Editor, or what have you.

Responsibilities

In a chronological resume, the job title is often followed by a short sentence that helps the reader visualize you doing the job. Get the information from the completed questionnaire and do a rough edit to get it down to one short sentence. Don't worry about perfection now; the polishing is done later.

The responsibilities and contributions you list here are those functions that best display your achievements and problem-solving abilities. They do not necessarily correspond with how you spent the majority of your working day, nor are they related to how you might prefer to spend your working day. Problems sometimes arise by mistakenly following either of these paths. It can perhaps best be illustrated by showing you part of a resume that came to my desk recently. It is the work of a professional who listed her title and duties for one job like this:

> Sales Manager: Responsible for writing branch policy, coordination of advertising and advertising agencies. Developed knowledge of IBM PC. Managed staff of six.

Is it any wonder she wasn't getting responses to her resume-mailing campaign? Here, she has explained where she was spending her time when the resume was created. The explanation, however, has nothing to do with the major functions of her job. She has mistakenly listed everything in the reverse chronological order, not in relation to the items' relative importance to a future employer. Let's look at what subsequent restructuring achieved:

> Sales Manager: Hired to turned around stagnant sales force. Successfully recruited, trained, managed and motivated a consulting staff of six. Result: 22 percent sales gain over first year.

In the rewrite of this particular part of the resume, notice how she thought like a copywriter and quickly identified the problem she was hired to solve.

> Hired to turn around stagnant sales force. (Demonstrates her skills and responsibilities.)

> Successfully recruited, trained, managed and motivated a consulting staff of six. Result: 22 percent sales gain over first year. (Shows what she subsequently did about them, and just how well she did it.)

By doing this, her responsibilities and achievements become more important in the light of the problems they solved.

Some More about Contributions

Business has very limited interests. In fact, those interests can be reduced to a single phrase: Making a profit. Making a profit is done in just three ways: By saving money in some fashion for the company; by saving time through some innovation at the company, which in turn saves the company money and gives it the opportunity to make more money in the time saved; or by simply making money for the company.

That's all there is to any business, when you reduce things to their simplest forms.

That does not mean that you should address only those points in your resume and ignore valuable contributions which cannot be quantified. But it does mean that you should try to quantify as much as you can.

If you find it difficult to recall and prioritize your responsibilities at a given company, go to the library and consult the *Directory of Job Descriptions*. But, as I have said before, be careful. If you do resort to this as a memory jogger be careful not to copy out the appropriate entry in its entirety—the prose is deadly boring.

Achievements

Your achievements will be listed in step five of the first part of the Questionnaire. The achievements you take from step five will not necessarily be the greatest accomplishments that can help you reach your stated (or unstated) employment objective. Concentrate solely on those topics that relate to your objectives, even if it means leaving out some significant achievement; you can always rectify the situation at the interview.

Pick two to four accomplishments for each job title and edit them down to bite-size chunks that read like a telegram. Write as if you had to pay for each entry by the word—this approach can help you pack a lot of information into a short space. The resulting abbreviated style will help convey a sense of immediacy to the reader.

Responsible for new and used car sales. Earned "Salesman of the Year" awards, 2000 and 2001. Record holder for:

- Most Cars Sold in One Month
- Most Cars Sold in One Year
- Most Board Gross in One Month
- Created an annual giving program to raise operating funds. *Raised $2,000,000.*
- Targeted, cultivated, and solicited sources including individuals, corporations, foundations, and state and federal agencies. *Raised $1,650,000.*
- Raised funds for development of the Performing Arts School facility, capital expense, and music and dance programs. *Raised $6,356,000.*

Now, while you may tell the reader about these achievements, you should never explain how they were accomplished. After all, the idea of the resume is to pique interest and to raise as many questions as you answer. Questions mean interest, and getting that interest satisfied requires talking to you!

You probably have lots of great accomplishments to share with the reader that will tempt you to add a second page, or even a third. Your resume, however, is designed to form the basis for tantalizing further discussions, so just be content with showing the reader a little glimpse of the gold vein—and let him or her discover the rest of the strike later. Very often the information discovered by the interviewer's own efforts takes on greater value than information offered free of charge on paper. Also, you have saved some of your heavy firepower for the interview, so that the meeting will not be an anticlimax for the interviewer. And that, in turn, will lend you some leverage and control in the discussions.

Prioritize the listing of your accomplishments as they relate to your job objective, and be sure to quantify your contributions (that is, put them into tangible, profit-oriented terms) wherever possible and appropriate.

Now is the time to weave in one or two of those laudatory quotes (also from step five). Don't include every one, but do incorporate enough to show that others think well of you.

- Sales volume increased from $90 million to $175 million. Acknowledged as "the greatest single gain of the year."
- Earnings increased from $9 million to $18 million. Review stated, "always a view for the company bottom line."
- Three key stores were each developed into $30-million units. Praised for "an ability to keep all the balls in the air, all the time."

Functional or Combination Resumes

These resumes are similar to chronological ones in content; often it's just the order of information that is different. Employers and employment dates are downplayed by relegating them to the end of the paragraphs, or to the bottom of the resume. Job titles and job responsibilities for specific jobs are sometimes omitted altogether.

In a functional or combination resume, you will have identified the skills and attributes necessary to fulfill the functions of the job objective, and will highlight the appropriate attributes you have to offer. In this format, you will have headings that apply to the skill areas your chosen career path demands, such as: Management, Training, Sales, etc. Each will be followed by a short paragraph packed with selling points. These can be real paragraphs, or the introductory sentence followed by the bullets usually recommended for the chronological formats. Here are examples of each style.

COLLECTIONS:
Developed excellent rapport with customers while significantly shortening pay-out terms through application of problem-solving techniques. Turned impending loss into profit. Personally salvaged and increased sales with two multi-million dollar accounts by providing remedial action for their sales/financial problems.

COLLECTIONS:
Developed excellent rapport with customers while
significantly shortening pay-out terms:

- Evaluated sales performance, offered suggestions for
  financing/merchandising.
- Performed on-the-spot negotiations; turned impending
  loss into profit.
- Salvaged two multi-million-dollar problem accounts by
  providing remedial action for their sales/financial
  problems. Subsequently increased sales.

Keep each paragraph to an absolute maximum of four lines. This ensures
that the finished product has plenty of white space so that it is easy on the
reader's eye.

Editing and Polishing

Sentences gain power with verbs that demonstrate an action. For example, one
client—a mature lady with ten years at the same law firm in a clerical
position—had written in her original resume:

I learned to use a computer database.

After discussion of the circumstances that surrounded learning how to use
the computer database, certain exciting facts emerged. By using action verbs
and an awareness of employer interests, this sentence was charged up, given
more punch. Not only that, for the first time the writer fully understood the
value of her contributions, which greatly enhanced her self-image:

I analyzed and determined need for automation of an
established law office. Responsible for hardware and
software selection, installation and loading. Within one year, I
had achieved a fully automated office.

Notice how the verbs show that things happen when you are around the
office. These action verbs and phrases add an air of direction, efficiency and

accomplishment to every resume. They succinctly tell the reader why you did and how well you did it.

Now look at the above example when a third party endorsement is added to it:

> I analyzed and determined need for automation of an established law office. Responsible for hardware and software selection, installation and loading. Within one year, I had achieved a fully automated office. Partner stated, "You brought us out of the dark ages into the technological age, and in the process neither you nor the firm missed a beat!"

Keywords

With the advent of electronic resume screening tools, it's become more and more important to use specific keywords in your resume. Internal job descriptions are usually built of nouns and verbs that describe the skill sets required for the job. Your resume should be built the same way, with nouns that identify the skill sets and verbs/action phrases that describe your professional behavior and achievements with these skill sets.

This is an important distinction in the initial screening process. Screening software focuses on the skill sets, which invariably are nouns. If you are a computer programmer the screening device might search for words like HTML; if you are an accountant it might search for words like "financial analysis." Only when the computer has identified those resumes that include matching skills do human eyes enter into the picture; and only then can the verbs/action phrases that describe your competencies and achievements have the desired impact. With an electronic resume, the nouns/skill sets are the skeleton, while the verbs/action phrases are designed to put flesh on the bones—for human eyes hungry for talent.

For our purposes the keyword nouns are the words commonly used to describe the essential skill sets and knowledge necessary to carry out a job successfully. They are likely to include:

- Skill sets/abilities/competencies
- Application of these skills sets
- Relevant education and training

As you complete the self-analysis questionnaire on pages 39–45, you will identify keywords in all of these areas.

You may also want to study the keywords that appear frequently in help wanted ads and electronic job postings. If you do, you'll notice that different words (synonyms) are used to describe the same job or skill set. For example, one job posting might outline a need for a secretary, while another nearly identical job posting might identify the job title as administrative assistant.

Now, bring on the electronic screening tools. If you identify yourself as a secretary, a computer searching for an administrative assistant might pass you over. So if you are a secretary, you might also want to include the phrase "administrative assistant" in your resume. Likewise, an attorney might want to include "lawyer"; someone in HR management might want to include "personnel administration." You get the idea.

You'll want to weave these synonyms for job titles and skill sets into the main body of your resume as much as possible. However, that won't always be possible. The logical flow of your resume—or insufficient space—might prevent you from using the keywords in place. That's where a separate keyword section comes in handy. It is the perfect spot to list the technical acronyms and professional jargon that you can't fit into the body copy.

Here's an example of a keyword box from a sales management professional:

SPECIFIC KNOWLEDGE AND SKILLS

- Market Trend Analysis
- Profit & Loss
- Multi-Site Management
- Needs Analysis
- Budget
- Employee Motivation
- Business Savvy
- Sales
- Performance Evaluations
- Contract Negotiation
- Technical Expertise
- Team Training

This innovation in resume writing allows you to add a host of additional information to your resume in a highly space-efficient way—usually in 20 or 30 words.

Using a keyword section will increase the odds of an electronic screening agent making multiple matches between your resume and an open job requisition. Neither will it offend human eyes, which will view the list of keywords as an expansion of the body copy—and a ready source for topics for discussion.

This compels me to offer you a warning: Don't use keywords to extend the "reach" of your resume. You must have real experience in each of the areas you include. Including keywords for areas where you have no professional expertise may get you a telephone conversation with an employer, but it will also quickly reveal you as an impostor. End of story.

Where does the keyword section go? As far as the computer is concerned it doesn't matter. The computer doesn't care about the niceties of layout and flow. However, human eyes will also see the keyword section so there is a certain logic in putting it front and center, after any summary or objective or immediately after the contact information. The keyword section acts as a preface to the body copy, in effect saying, "Hey, here are all the headlines. The stories behind them are immediately below." To put it another way, the keyword section acts as a table of contents for your resume, with the body—with its action words and phrases—explaining and expanding on the list of topics.

Your keyword section can be as long as you require, though they typically don't run longer than 40 items and usually are a little shorter. There's no need to use definite or indefinite articles or conjunctions. Just list the word, starting with a capital and ending with a period: "Forecasting," or a phrase, such as "Financial modeling."

You can also think of your keyword section as an electronic business card that allows you to network with computers!

Action Verbs

Here are over 175 action verbs that will see which ones you can use to give punch to your resume writing.

accepted
accomplished
achieved
acted
adapted
addressed
administered
advanced
advised
allocated
analyzed
appraised
approved
arranged
assembled
assigned
assisted
attained
audited
authored
automated
balanced
budgeted
built
calculated
catalogued
chaired
clarified
classified
coached
collected
compiled
completed
composed
computed
conceptualized
conducted

consolidated
contained
contracted
contributed
controlled
coordinated
corresponded
counseled
created
critiqued
cut
decreased
defined
delegated
demonstrated
designed
developed
devised
diagnosed
directed
dispatched
distinguished
diversified
drafted
edited
educated
eliminated
emended
enabled
encouraged
engineered
enlisted
established
evaluated
examined
executed
expanded

expedited
explained
extracted
fabricated
facilitated
familiarized
fashioned
focused
forecast
formulated
founded
generated
guided
headed up
identified
illustrated
implemented
improved
increased
indoctrinated
influenced
informed
initiated
innovated
inspected
installed
instigated
instituted
instructed
integrated
interpreted
interviewed
introduced
invented
launched
lectured
led

maintained
managed
marketed
mediated
moderated
monitored
motivated
negotiated
operated
organized
originated
overhauled
oversaw
performed
persuaded
planned
prepared
presented
prioritized
processed
produced
programmed
projected
promoted
proposed
provided
publicized
published
purchased
recommended
reconciled
recorded
recruited
reduced
referred
regulated
rehabilitated

remodeled
repaired
represented
researched
resolved
restored
restructured
retrieved
revamped
revitalized
saved
scheduled
schooled
screened
set
shaped
solidified
solved
specified
stimulated
streamlined
strengthened
summarized
supervised
surveyed
systemized
tabulated
taught
trained
translated
traveled
trimmed
upgraded
validated
worked
wrote

Use these words to edit and polish your work, to communicate, persuade, and motivate the reader to take action.

This stage is most challenging, because many people in different companies will see and evaluate your resume. Keep industry "jargon" to a minimum; there will be some who understand the intricacies and technicalities of your profession, and some who don't. And you need to share your technical or specialist wisdom with the nonspecialists, too.

Varying Sentence Structure

Most good writers are at their best when they write short punchy sentences. Keep your sentences under about twenty words; a good average is around fifteen. If your sentence is longer than the twenty mark, either shorten it by restructuring, or make two sentences out of the one. The reader on the receiving end has neither the time nor the inclination to read your sentences twice to get a clear understanding.

At the same time, you don't want the writing to sound choppy, so vary the length of sentences when you can. You can also start with a short phrase and follow with a colon:

- Followed by bullets of information,
- each one supporting the original phrase.

All these different techniques are designed to enliven the reading process. Here's an example of how the above suggestions might be put into practice.

Analyzed and determined need for automation of an established law office:

- Responsible for hardware and software selection;
- Coordinated installation of computer database and six work stations;
- Operated and maintained equipment, and trained other users;
- Achieved full automation in one year.

Partner stated, "You brought us out of the dark ages, and neither you nor the firm missed a beat!"

Just as you use short sentences, use common words. They communicate quickly and are easy to understand. Stick to short and simple words wherever possible without sounding infantile. Of course, you need action words and phrases. But the real point is to stay away from obscure words.

Short words for short sentences
help make short, gripping paragraphs:
Good for short attention spans!

Within your short paragraphs and short sentences, beware of name and acronym dropping, such as "Worked for Dr. A. Witherspoon in Sys. Gen. SNA 2.31." This is a good way to confuse (and lose) readers. Such coinage is too restricted to have validity outside the small circle of specialists to whom they speak. Your resume deserves the widest possible readership. Apart from the section on the resume that includes your educational qualifications, stay away from jargon unless you work in a highly technical field.

Voice and Tense

The voice you develop for your resume depends on a few important factors: getting a lot said in a small space; being factual; and packaging yourself in the best way.

The voice you use should be consistent throughout the resume. There is considerable disagreement among the experts about the best voice, and each of the leading options have both champions and detractors.

Sentences can be truncated (up to a point) by omitting pronouns—I, you, he, she, it, they—and articles—a or the. In fact, many authorities recommend the dropping of pronouns as a technique that both saves space and allows you to brag about yourself without seeming boastful. It gives the impression that another party is writing about you. Many people feel that to use the personal pronoun ("I automated the office") is naïve and unprofessional. These experts suggest you use either the third person ("He automated the office") or leave the pronoun out altogether ("Automated office").

At the same time, there are others who recommend that you write in the first person because it makes you sound more human. Use whatever style works best for you. If you do use the personal pronoun, though, try not to use it in every sentence—it gets a little monotonous and takes up valuable space on the page.

A nice variation I have seen is a third-person voice used through the resume and then a final few words in the first person appended to the end of the resume, to give an insight into your values. Here is an example:

Regular third person:
James Sharpe is a professional who knows Technical Services from the ground up. He understands its importance in keeping a growing company productive, and takes pride in creating order in the chaos of technology.

Abbreviated third person:
Responsible for machine and system design, production scheduling, procurement and quality control. Redesigned conveyors and simplified maintenance while improving quality. Instituted a system of material control to account for all materials used.

First person:
I am accustomed to accepting responsibility and delegating authority, and am capable of working with, and through people at all levels. Am able to plan, organize, develop, implement, and supervise complex programs and special projects. All of this requires a good sense of humor and a personal dedication to producing timely, cost-effective results.

Many people mistake the need for professionalism in a resume with stiff-necked formality. The most effective tone is one that mixes both the conversational and the formal, just the way we do in our offices and on our jobs. The only overriding rule is to make it readable, so that another person can see the human being shining through the pages.

Length

The accepted rules for length are one page for every ten years of your experience. If you have more than twenty years under you belt, however, you won't want to appear to be too steeped in the annals of ancient history, and so will not want to exceed the two-page mark.

Occasionally a three- or four-page resume can be effective, but only when:

- You have been contacted directly by an employer about a specific position and have been asked to prepare a resume for that particular opportunity.
- An executive recruiter who is representing you determines that the exigencies of a particular situation warrant an extensive dossier. Usually, such a resume will be prepared exclusively by the recruiter.

You'll find that thinking too much about length considerations while you write will hamper you. Think instead of the story you have to tell, then layer fact upon fact until it is told. When that is done, you can go back and ruthlessly cut it to the bone.

Ask yourself these questions:

- Can I cut out any paragraphs?
- Can I cut out any sentences?
- Can I cut out any superfluous words?
- Where have I repeated myself?

If in doubt, cut it out—leave nothing but facts and action words!

And if you find at the end that you've cut out too much, you'll have the additional pleasure of reinstating text!

The Proofreading Checklist for Your Final Draft

There are really two proofing steps in the creation of a polished resume. The first you do at this point, to make sure that all the things that should be in are there—and that all the things that shouldn't, aren't. The final proofing is addressed later in the book.

In the heat of the creative moment, it's easy to miss critical components or mistakenly include facts that give the wrong emphasis. Check your resume against these points:

Contact Information

- Is the pertinent personal data—name, address, personal telephone number, and e-mail address—correct? (You will want to make sure that this personal data is on every page.)
- Is your business number omitted unless it is absolutely necessary and safe to include it?

Objectives

- Does your objective briefly state your employment goals without getting too specific and ruling you out of consideration for many jobs?
- If you gave a detailed objective (up to—but no more than—two sentences), does it focus on what you can bring to the employer, rather than what you want from the employer?
- Is your stated objective supported by the facts and accomplishments stated in the rest of your resume?

Summary

- If you choose to include a summary, is it no more than two or three sentences long?
- Does it include at least one substantial accomplishment that supports your employment goals?
- Does it include reference to some of your personality or behavioral traits that are critical to success in your field?

Keywords

- If you include a keyword section, this is probably the place to put it.
- Do you have experience in each of the areas you've listed?
- Can you illustrate your experience in conversation?
- Does it include commonly used synonyms for your skill sets that you have not already used in the body of the resume?
- Is the spelling and capitalization correct? (It's easy to make mistakes here especially with acronyms.)
- Are there any other justifiable keywords you should add?

Body of Resume

- Is your most relevant and qualifying work experience prioritized throughout the resume to lend strength to your application?

- Have you avoided wasting space with inessential employer names and addresses?
- Have you been suitably discreet with the name of your current employer?
- Have you omitted any reference to reasons for leaving a particular job?
- Have you removed all references to past, current, or desired salaries?
- Have you removed references to your date of availability?

Education

- Is education placed in the appropriate position? (It should be at the beginning of the resume if you have little or no work experience; at the end if you are established in your field and your practical experience now outweighs your degree.)
- Is your highest educational attainment shown first?
- Have you included professional courses that support your candidacy?

Chronology

- If you've done a chronological resume, is your work history stated in reverse chronological order, with the most recent employment coming at the head of the resume?
- Within this reverse chronology, does each company history start with details of your most senior position?
- Have you avoided listing irrelevant responsibilities or job titles?
- Does your resume emphasize the contributions, achievements, and problems you have successfully solved during your career? Is this content made prominent by underlining, bolding, italicizing, etc.?
- Does the body copy include at least one, and possibly two or three, laudatory third-party endorsements of your work?
- Have you avoided poor focus by eliminating all extraneous information? (This category includes anything that doesn't relate to your job objective, such as captaining the tiddlywinks team in kindergarten.)
- Have you included any volunteer or community service activities that can lend strength to your candidacy?
- Is the whole thing long enough to whet the reader's appetite for more details, yet short enough not to satisfy that hunger?
- Have you left out lists of reference and only included mention of the availability of references (if, of course, there is nothing more valuable to fill up the space)?

- Have you avoided treating your reader like a fool by highlighting the obvious (i.e., heading your resume, "RESUME")?

Writing Style

- Have you substituted short words for long words? And one word where previously there were two?
- Is your average sentence ten to twenty words? Have you made sure that any sentence of more than twenty words is shortened or broken into two sentences?
- Have you kept every paragraph under five lines, with many paragraphs considerably shorter?
- Do your sentences begin, wherever possible, with the powerful action verbs and phrases from earlier in the chapter and from the resume examples?
- If you are in a technical field, have you weeded out as much of the jargon as possible?

Crossing the T's, Dotting the I's

Before your resume is finished, you have to make sure that your writing is as clear as possible. Three things guaranteed to annoy resume readers are incorrect spelling, poor grammar, and improper syntax. Go back and check all these areas. If you feel uneasy about your resume's syntax, you had better get a third party involved.

An acquaintance of mine recently came up with an eminently practical solution to the "style" problem. She went around to the local library, waited for a quiet moment, and got into conversation with the librarian, who subsequently agreed to give her resume the old once-over for spelling, grammar, and syntax. You say you're on bad terms with the library because of all those overdue books? Surely you know someone whose opinion you trust in these matters. Enlist him or her. The point is that you must do everything you can to make the resume a "perfect" document before it is sent out.

It simply isn't possible for even the most accomplished professional writer to go directly from final draft to print, so don't try it. Your pride of authorship will blind you to the blemishes, and that's a self-indulgence you can't afford.

You need some distance from your creative efforts to gain detachment and objectivity. There is no hard and fast rule about how long it takes to come up with the finished product. Nevertheless, if you think you have finished, leave it alone as long as you can—at least overnight. Then you can come back to it fresh and read almost as if it were meeting your eyes for the first time.

More Than One Resume?

Do you need more than one type of resume? It depends. Some people have a background that qualifies them for more than one job. If this applies to you, the process is as simple as changing your objective for various employers and rewriting along the lines directed in this chapter.

There is a case for all of us having resumes in more than one format. I was once engaged in an outplacement experiment for a group of professionals. With just a little extra work, we developed chronological, functional, and combination resumes for everyone. The individuals concerned sent out the resume of their choice. Then, in those instances where there was no response, a different version of the resume was sent out. The result from just a different format: 8 percent more interviews.

What's Next?

Almost home now. Save your notes, early drafts, and, of course, the completed Questionnaire. This "legwork" represents essential material you'll need in updating or revising future versions of your resume.

6 | The Final Product

When it comes to clothes, style has a certain look. It has a feel that everyone recognizes but few can define accurately. Fortunately, with resumes, the situation is considerably simplified. There are definite rules to follow.

What Do You Mean I Need TWO Resumes?

One of these rules is that in today's job market you can't get by with just one perfect resume any more. Why not? Because an astounding 78 percent of resumes are read not by humans but by machines. Your resume may be an aesthetic marvel, beautiful to behold, but if it goes into the computer as gobbledy-gook, it won't do you much good. That's why you need two. This chapter will cover "the traditional" resume—the resume designed for human eyes. The other kind, the "computer-friendly" resume, is custom-designed to get through a computer scanner with data intact. It is such a hot topic in today's job market that I have devoted a separate chapter to it (see chapter 7, "Is Your Resume Computer-Friendly?"). Of course, the two kinds of resume do have certain basics in common. Let's start with those.

The Circular File

A lot of resumes get trashed without ever being properly read.

The average resume arrives on a desk with dozens of others, all of which require screening. Stand in the shoes of a day-in, day-out resume reader, and you can expect that your resume will get a maximum of thirty to forty seconds of initial attention. And that's only if it's laid out well and looks clear.

What are the biggest complaints about those resumes that reach the trash can in record time?

Impossible to read. They have too much information crammed into the space and are therefore very difficult to read and hard on the eyes.

No coherence. Their layout is unorganized, illogical, and uneven. In other words, they look shoddy and slapdash—and who wants an employee like that?

Typos. They are riddled with misspellings.

Here are some tips garnered from the best resumes in America that will help yours rise above the rest.

Get Your Computer Ready!

If you plan to be employable in the year 2001, you'd better wake up and smell the coffee—computer literacy is a must. Typing on typewriters doesn't cut it any more. Typing your resume or using a typing service is the equivalent of carving your resumes in tablets of stone. It looks old-fashioned, and it must be done from start to finish every time you need to send one to someone else or customize it for another purpose. If you cannot now prepare your resume in a computer, engage the services of a good word-processing outfit while you get up to speed.

Hard Copy

Not all printers are created equal. When you use a computer or a word-processing service, insist that your letters be printed on a letter-quality printer or a laser printer; either of these will give you high-quality print.

Fonts

A laser printer gives you a vast choice of print styles and quality fonts. Business is rapidly coming to accept the likes of Bookman, New York, and Palatino as the norm. By the way, when choosing your font, stay away from heavy and bold for your body copy (although you may choose to take a more dramatic approach with key words or headlines). Bold type takes up too much space, and if it needs to be copied on the receiving end, it can blur and look dreadful. Avoid "script" faces similar to handwriting; while they look attractive to the occasional reader, they are harder on the eyes of the person who reads any amount of business correspondence. Capitalized copy is tough on the eyes too; we tend to think it makes a powerful statement when all it does for the reader is cause eye strain.

How to Brighten the Page

Once you decide on a font, stick with it, because more than one on a page looks confusing. You can do plenty to liven up the visual impact of the page within the variations of the font you have chosen.

Most fonts come in a selection of regular, bold, and italic. Good traditional-style resumes try to take advantage of this—they can vary the impact of key words with italics, underline important phrases, or use boldface or capital letters in titles for additional emphasis. (Computer-friendly resumes, by contrast, keep type variations to a minimum.)

You will notice from the examples in this book that the best resumes pick two or three typographical variations and stick with them. For example, a writer who wants to emphasize personality traits might italicize only those words or phrases that describe these aspects; this way the message gets a double fixing in the reader's mind.

Proofing

When you have the printed resume in hand, you *must* proofread it. Check everything, from beginning to end.

- Is everything set up the way you want it?
- Are there any typographical errors?
- Is all the punctuation correct?
- Has everything been underlined, capitalized, bolded, italicized, and indented, exactly as you specified?

Once you read the resume, try your best to get someone else to review it as well. A third party will always provide more objectivity than you can, and can catch errors you might miss.

Appearance Checklist

- Have you remembered that the first glance and the first feel of your resume can make a powerful impression?
- Have you used only one side of the page?
- If you have employed more than one page for your resume, did you check to make sure that your name, address, and telephone number are on every page?
- If more than one page, did you paginate your resume ("1 of 2" at the bottom of the first page, and so on)?

Choosing Your Paper

Quality and care have a look and a feel to them that are loud and clear. Quality paper always makes a favorable impression on the person holding the page.

Beyond the aesthetics, there are plenty of reasons to use quality paper for your copies. The right paper will take the ink better, giving you clean, sharp print resolution.

While you should not skimp on paper cost, neither should you be talked into buying the most expensive available. Indeed, in some fields (health care and education come to mind), too ostentatious a paper can cause a negative impression. The idea is to create a feeling of understated quality.

Paper can come in different weights and textures. Good resume-quality paper has a weight designation of between 16 and 25 lbs. Lighter, and you run the risk of appearing nonchalant, unconcerned about the personal "I-printed-this-especially-for-you" aspect of the resume. Heavier, and the paper is unwieldy, like light cardboard.

As for color, white is considered to be the prime choice. Cream is also acceptable, and I'm assured that some of the pale pastel shades can be both attractive and effective. Personally, I think that most professionals just don't show up in the best light when dressed in pink—call me old-fashioned if you will.

Such pastel shades were originally used to make resumes stand out. But now that everyone is so busy standing out from the crowd in Magenta and Passionate Puce, you might find it more original to stand out in white or cream. Both colors reflect the clean-cut, corporate conservatism of our time. White and cream are straightforward, no-nonsense colors.

Cover letter stationery should always match the color and weight of your resume. To send a white cover letter—even if it is written on your personal stationery—with a cream resume is gauche, and detracts from the powerful statement you are trying to make.

A good idea, in fact, is to print some cover-letter stationery when you produce your finished resume. The letterhead should be in the same font and on the same kind of paper, and should copy the contact data from your resume.

Copies

Every resume should be printed on standard, 8½" x 11" (letter-size) paper. If the original is set up like this, you will be able to take it to a good-quality copy shop for photocopying. Technology has improved so much in this area that as long as the latest equipment is used, you should have no problems. (Bear in mind, though, that the computer-friendly resume is always an original—to ensure a clean scan.)

If you choose to have your resume printed—rather than photocopied—for whatever reason, you must go to a multi-lith or photo-offset printer. Both produce really smart, professional copies. Of the two—unless you are printing more than two-hundred copies—photo-offset will be proportionately more expensive. Shop around for prices, as printers vary quite dramatically in their price structures. While you are shopping, ask to see samples of their resume work—they are bound to have some. If not, keep shopping.

Word-processing services can produce not only the resume and cover letter stationery but also the required number of copies of both, as can a multi-lith or offset printer. There are both local and national companies that can provide these services.

The Final Checklist

- Have you used a good-quality paper, with a weight of between 16 and 25 lbs.?
- Does the paper size measure 8½" x 11"?
- Have you used white, off-white, or cream-colored paper?
- If your resume is more than one page, have you stapled the pages together (one staple in the top left-hand corner)?
- Is your cover letter written on stationery that matches your resume?

7 | Is Your Resume Computer-Friendly?

Computers have infiltrated human resources offices across America. Here's how they'll affect your job search.

PART ONE:
Is Your Resume Scanner-Friendly?

Review Your Resume

You say you already have a great resume. After all, it helped you land your most recent job, and the one before that, and the one before that. Now all you have to do is update it—add your latest job title, your responsibilities, the beginning and end dates of your employment, special projects you worked on, advanced training you received, and the like—and your resume will be ready to send in the mail, or put into your briefcase.

Right?

Well, it may not be that simple. If your resume looks exactly as it did a few years ago, then merely updating the information and keeping the old format may not be good enough. The resume that opened corporate doors for you five years ago, or even last year, may not work for you now. In fact, it *may not even get read.*

Resumes in the Computer Age

Computers are being used to scan and store your resume electronically; they are being used to read help-wanted advertisements on Web site databases, and to search the resume banks on those same Web sites. In fact, the next HR professional to scan your resume is likely to be a PC or Mac instead of a mortal. The problem is that computers look at things differently than we do, which creates the new challenge of making your resume attractive to digital eyes.

Since the mid-1980s, when the technology was first introduced, the number of companies using computer-based automated tracking systems has climbed steadily. The technology has become so pervasive that by mid-1997, 85 percent of companies surveyed had some sort of automated resume-tracking system in place.

The Way It Was

It seems like only yesterday that most companies manually read, assessed, coded, and filed all of the resumes they received. When a position opened up, an HR representative would look through all the files for likely prospects. The most promising candidates would then be invited for an interview.

In its day, this was a pretty good system. It was especially nice when you, the applicant, made the short list of prospects. Of course, sometimes the manual system didn't work in your favor. Once in a while, an HR professional who didn't like your choice of stationery, or thought that your alma mater wasn't covered in quite enough ivy, would code your resume unfavorably or even put it in the circular file. Or perhaps a recruiter thought of you immediately when a job opened up, but couldn't lay his hands on your resume quick enough to call you before the position was filled—perhaps because another supervisor, who was winging her way to Europe, had the resume in her briefcase.

Often, under the manual tracking system, resumes were misplaced, miscoded, or misfiled, never to be found again. Frequently, a perfectly good resume was buried under so much paper that it just wasn't worth anybody's trouble to unearth it. It used to be common to trash all resumes every six months.

The problems with manual resume tracking became especially apparent when corporate cutbacks caused companies to reduce their HR staff. With three people doing the job of ten, it simply wasn't possible to access, code, file, and retrieve resumes in an orderly, effective fashion. Corporations sometimes missed their chance to hire the best candidate for the job because the appropriate resume didn't make it to the top of the heap, out of the file cabinet, or sometimes even out of the envelope.

So What's New?

These days, solicited and unsolicited resumes alike are increasingly likely to be filed in electronic databases rather than in metal cabinets. Under this system, no matter how large the computerized stack of resumes, any computer user can pull up appropriate ones with a few keystrokes or clicks of a mouse. The challenge for you is to get your resume into a shape and style that:

- Can be scanned, digitized, and stored electronically, once received through the mail.
- Can be transmitted, via e-mail, to specific individuals or companies.
- Can be loaded onto public resume databases.

In the first instance, your printed/hard copy resume would wing through the mail to a company. There, a functionary in the HR department runs it through a scanner; this digitizes your resume and allows it to be stored electronically in the company's database.

In the second instance, you create a digitized resume yourself. You use this electronic/digitized version of your resume to e-mail to companies at their Web sites, to specific executives at their e-mail addresses, and to log it into the proliferating array of resume banks. We'll discuss digitized resume formats in greater detail later in this chapter.

The Computer Recruiter

What should you know about the technology that just might be responsible for deciding whether or not you're invited to that next job interview?

Like their human counterparts, computers have their good traits and their bad. The good part is that computers don't care what school you went to, whether or not you're married, or how old you are. In a computerized search for qualified candidates, there's no room for human prejudice or error. Your name either pops up or it doesn't. Either way, it's nothing personal; it's strictly an automated decision. The bad news is that, if you're using a traditional resume that isn't computer-friendly (and, as you'll see, most traditional resumes aren't), your name probably won't pop up. A resume that was perfectly fine before automated tracking and the advent of the Internet will most likely leave you in the dust today.

New Resume Rules

If you want to impress a human recruiter before he or she even reads your resume, make sure that your envelope matches your stationery, that the address is well-typed, and that the layout catches the eye. Similarly, if you want to impress a computerized recruiter, you want to first be confident that optical character recognition (OCR) software can properly read the font in which your resume was written. This is because resumes are scanned, not typed, into databases. A computer can scan a resume in a couple of minutes. The danger is that if your resume was constructed to fit the old rules of resume writing (the more eye-catching, the better), the scanner and OCR software may get confused and miss some critical information.

The human resources person who is assigned to check the resume once it's scanned may or may not have the time, or the know-how, to undo the damage; he or she may not even notice that critical elements are missing or distorted. It's therefore your responsibility to make sure the computer scans your resume properly. The rules that apply to making your resume scannable will also apply to the creation of your electronic resume; again, we'll discuss this later in the chapter.

Keep It Simple

Here's how you can help the computer (that is, the scanner and OCR software) do its job.

- Always send a clean, crisp, original resume. Even photocopies that look fine to your eye may be too fuzzy to scan.
- Put your name on the first line of your resume, with nothing else before it. If you put your address first, then your new moniker might well be "555 Bayville Drive!"
- When choosing a font, stick to common ones, such as Times, Universe, Palatino, Optima, Courier, Futura, ITC Bookman, and New Century Schoolbook. Avoid exotic or serif fonts that the OCR software might confuse or might not recognize.
- Keep the point sizes between 10 and 14. Type that is too large or too small may not scan properly.
- If you want to use boldface, save it for headings. While most OCR software can read boldface, some can't, so don't take the risk of using it for your name, address, telephone number, or e-mail address.
- Leave out decorative lines, particularly vertical lines. Or, if you use them, do so judiciously, leaving at least a quarter of an inch of space around

them. Otherwise, you're liable to confuse the software, which often can't tell the difference between lines and letters.

Here are some things that are guaranteed to make your resumes computer-*unfriendly* and that you should always avoid:

- Double columns and other complicated layouts. The scanner can only read from left to right—and it's not going to appreciate your creativity.
- Colored paper. Use white or light beige paper; save the pink and blue stuff for personal letters announcing your new job. A key to scannability is to get the greatest possible amount of contrast between the background and the letters.
- Odd-sized paper. You should always use 8½ x 11-inch sheets.
- Graphics, shading, ellipses, brackets, or parentheses.
- Italics, script, or underlining.
- Compressing letters. It isn't worth cramming a lot of information onto one page if the computer can't scan it.
- Stapling, folding, or faxing your resume. Send your resume, unstapled and unfolded, in a 9 x 12-inch envelope—or hand-deliver it.

Getting the Computer's Attention

If you've taken care to update your resume so that the computer can read it, the next step is to be sure the computer can find you when it's looking for somebody with your skills.

A computer isn't able to interpret your resume and make judgments about your suitability—you have to convince it. And the way to do that is by using keywords.

Here's the Key

A keyword is a word or phrase the software will search for when looking for job candidates. It is any label that can be used to describe you, or the job. The keywords are first chosen by the software user.

Also known as "talents," keywords are not action words like "oversaw," "initiated," and "installed," with which we've all saturated resumes in the past. They are nouns used to label the job and yourself. They encompass technical jargon, specific skills that relate to the job, degrees you hold, job titles, personal traits, and other buzzwords.

If you're in doubt about which keywords to include on your resume, then check the classifieds for positions similar to the one you're looking for, and take note of which nouns crop up repeatedly—skills, traits, and so on. Keep a running list of possibilities from which you can pick and choose, depending on the job you're applying for. Also, be open to collecting new keywords while reading the want ads (or during interviews) to add to your resume. If employers are looking for an Engineer of Excellence with a diploma in Delightfulness who can attack a Wonderwidget to a Maximachine, then those are your keywords!

How to Use Keywords

Of course, it behooves you to make sure that your keywords describe who you are and what you know, and that you're not just fudging it. Telling the computer anything it might want to hear, regardless of whether it's fact or fiction, isn't the best policy. At worst, you could tip off a prospective employer who might wonder why somebody with an engineering degree is also an expert in education, psychology, business, theater, law, and medicine.

Scanning software has limits on how many keywords it can retain, so keep the list down to a reasonable length—say, eighty words or so. And make sure the most important words go first. The scanning software won't weight your placement of keywords, but the subsequent human eyes will.

The art of making computer-friendly resumes is still brand new, and we are all feeling our way, to a certain extent. One neat technique that people are just starting to use (and are apparently finding very effective) is to place a box filled with applicable keywords/talents that might not appear in the body of your resume either near the top or at the bottom of your resume. There is absolutely no hard and fast rule on this yet, but you might find including it at the bottom of a resume less intrusive. For example, here's the talent box used by a HR professional who was able to reveal an additional bunch of skills, and make her resume more computer-friendly.

> Talents: team leader, people and communication skills, hardware needs evaluation, database management, client orientation, word-processing, spreadsheets, arbitration, manual writing, union negotiation, downsizing.

Part Two: Is Your Resume Internet-Friendly?

Is the Internet the answer to a job seeker's prayer, or the emperor's new suit of clothes? Some tout it as a speedy way to end your job hunt, since it gives you global exposure. ("But," you say,"I only want to work in Michigan!") Others discount the Internet, claiming you have about one chance in a hundred of getting a job this way. Neither view is right; the issue isn't that simple or clearcut, since little in the modern world of work is unarguably right or wrong.

The most practical way to look at the Internet, in the context of your job hunt, is as a means of communication that simply gives you a handful of new ways to get in contact with potential employers and headhunters. You can:

- Meet and talk electronically with other job hunters, or even job hunting and career experts.
- Network with your professional peers in newsgroups. Newsgroups are ongoing discussion groups with a narrow focus aimed at people who share a common interest. There are newsgroups for every profession, from accountants to zoologists.
- Approach potential employers through their own Web sites. This method may get your resume closer scrutiny, since the flow of applicants online is lighter than through traditional methods. By the same token, you might also get a much swifter response, since your manipulation of the new technology can tag you as a potentially more desirable employee. Remember that even if a company has job openings but isn't advertising specifically for your skill sets, you can still query it.
- Scan the job banks. These are nothing more than the help-wanted section of newspapers published in an electronic medium. Instead of reading the ads for an hour, your computer can generate matching jobs in seconds or minutes, which makes life easier for you.
- Load your resume into a resume bank, which functions just like HELP AVAILABLE ads in your local newspaper. Although in the past I have been strongly against advertising your availability in print, since no employer or headhunter has the time or inclination to read these ads, using this same technique in this new medium changes the picture in

two ways. First, the VP of Human Resources for your local First National Bank is still unlikely to peruse these data banks, but he now has electronic servants who will. Second, headhunters do scan the resume banks as yet another way of digging up that hard-to-find professional for a client.

The electronic world can give you a number of practical ways to pursue your job hunt. But keep in mind that the headhunters use this new medium as just another way of completing a job search—and you should do the same.

The rest of this chapter will concern itself with how electronic resumes can help you in your job search.

The Technical Side of an Electronic Resume

The oldest, most common, and soon-to-be outmoded method of compiling an electronic resume is to write and save it in a text format (often referred to as ASCII). The benefit of this format is that there are no formatting commands, so anyone can read the document, regardless of the software application/program they are using. You can also cut and paste parts of a text document into the information boxes you'll find on many resume bank Web sites. To create a text/ASCII format resume, create a new resume in whatever application that you are using (or make a copy of an existing one). Then, as you exit the document, us the "Save As" option to save it in text/ASCII format. Depending on the application you are using, the computer may advise you that your actions will destroy the formatting; ignore the warning and save it as text/ASCII anyway.

After this, your resume will now look like a dog's dinner. Unfortunately, there are only a few things you can do to improve the look of a text resume. You can use a text editor to edit your resume to look more like your real resume. Since e-mail allows no more than seventy characters to a line, you will most likely have to reformat your document. Similarly, if you have created space on your resume using the tab key, you'll want to redo it using the space bar instead. Apart from these guidelines, the dos and don'ts are the same that apply to making your resume scanner-friendly, which were addressed earlier in the chapter.

HTML

HTML is the acronym for Hypertext Markup Language, the wave of the electronic resume future. HTML allows you to create sharply designed and formatted resumes. It does this by placing your wording between tags, parenthesis, and slashes that indicate certain kinds of formatting. These tags allow another person's (read: human resource recruiter) electronic browser to translate the accompanying data into words, graphics, format, and even color, either on a screen or as a printout. This makes HTML extremely useful in electronic resume writing since, when printed, your electronic resume will stack up against traditionally printed and mailed resumes.

HTML uses two different types of tags: those that identify and format the content of your resume so that it looks good, and those that allow you to condense your resume into its critical essentials, so that the search engines other people use when searching the resume databases will pick you out of the crowd. These condensed essentials, called metatags, will not be seen on your actual resume, and are only visible to the search engine (read: the software that searches the resume database). While HTML coding might only seem like a good idea for computer science majors, it is in fact getting easier and easier to create your own HTML resume. (You might even remember, if not admit to, an era when "WYSIWYG" seemed equally obscure.) Many current word processors allow you to save text in HTML format, and software developers have made a whole bunch of tools available to HTML wanna-bes.

Final Considerations

One issue to consider is that of confidentiality. As with any distribution medium, once the resume is out of your hands, you no longer have control over what happens to it. So it's wise to evaluate the relative compatibility of your needs and how they match the operational realities of the different databases.

For example, if you don't want people to know where you live, or to be able to contact you directly at home or work (it's never a good idea to have a work contact number on a resume), act accordingly. Get a voice mail service for telephone calls. Don't imagine for a moment that recruiters are going to use your e-mail address, though; if you look like a good fit, the phone is still the quickest means of cutting to the chase. Conversely, if e-mail is your only means of contact, you can expect to miss hearing about a few opportunities. And just as you would never use your current employer's time or phone to pursue a job contact, don't use their e-mail either. Depending on where you live, it is quite legal for an employer to monitor your e-mail.

If you are employed, identify your current employer as "a major bank," "a mid-sized service company," or "an international pharmaceutical conglomerate." Not only will you not get unwanted calls at work, but you won't run the risk of your current boss learning of your search before it suits your needs.

Other confidentiality considerations can be answered at each individual site. When you get to a particular Web site, one of the first things you will do is to look for FAQs (frequently asked questions) to find out:

- Who can access this database?
- Can you block access to certain employers or people?
- Are you notified when someone downloads your resume?

Apart from the confidentiality issue, you will want to know if you can get access to your resume to update it, change it, or delete it. If not, you'll want to know the procedure for achieving each of these ends. Some resume banks will charge you for updates.

Internet Myths

This question of updating your resume brings us to three areas of Internet lore you need to be aware of:

1. You will be told that a *good* database will delete your resume after three to six months if you don't update it. This is absolute drivel! Constant resume updating is driven by commercial concerns. No one on God's earth needs a resume updated every ninety days! The other argument for deleting resumes that aren't updated is that, once employed, you won't want to get calls from other employers. Again, absolute drivel! Happily employed or not, wouldn't you rather hear about exciting new jobs that fit your skill sets, and have the opportunity to pursue or reject them, *rather than never hear about them at all?* Of course you'll want to hear about every opportunity, if not for today, then for tomorrow, if your current employment no longer suits your career needs, or your company is about to downsize. You want to get your resume out there, period! And there's no reason to limit your resumes to services that limit your exposure.

2. You will be told that a one-page resume is no longer the rule. Now, while one of the strengths of the Internet as a publishing medium is that space is limitless, that does not in any way affect the dictum that when it comes to resumes, shorter is better. Yes, your resume can be longer, but that won't stop human eyes from getting bored by the end of page two, just as resume screeners have always done. So no matter who tells you this, use your common sense and keep it short and succinct.

3. You will also be told to put your resume on only two to four resume databases, because employers are frustrated at finding the same candidates at every database they check. Excuse me? Am employer can check a hundred databases, but you can only use a maximum of four? Here are the facts: as an employer, if I like your background, I'll be happy to find you. If I like your background and I find you in a number of places, it will make recruiting you more difficult since I'll likely have more competition from other employers. On the other hand, if I keep finding your resume and you *don't* match my needs, it shouldn't matter if I find you in two or two hundred databases.

If you want to take advantage of the Internet as a means of resume creation and/or distribution, there are services out there that will take care of this business for you for a fee. If you choose to do this, there are a handful of questions you'll need to answer for yourself to make an informed decision.

- Exactly what is the service? Will they write the resume for you? Will it be in text, HTML, or multimedia? (You really don't need multimedia unless you are in graphic design and want to show your command of the new technology, in which case you'll have to walk the walk and talk the talk. On the other hand, HTML is state of the art and will show you in your best light.)
- How much will everything cost?
- Is there a charge to edit or update your resume once it is created, or to create a slightly different resume that emphasizes other skill sets? Once you have been in the job market for a few years, you're probably qualified for more than one job, which means that you'll need a separate resume that will highlight those skills.
- How is your resume marketed? Find out how many sites the company will post your resume on, and whether or not they will repost it if that site trashes your resume after a predetermined period of time.
- What, if anything, will you be charged if you get a job as a result of the service?

To get you started with these services, try:

- Resumes on the Web   *www.resweb.com*
- Job Center   *www.jobcenter.com*
- Resume Creator   *www.ipt.com/internetworking/create.htm*
- The Resume Place   *www.resume-place.com/jobs*
- Job Lynx   *www.joblynx.com*
- AAA Resume Posting   *www.infi.net/-resume*
- Superior Resumes, Inc.   *www.mindtrust.com*

Internet Resume Etiquette

Sending out your resume through another medium (e-mail rather than regular mail) requires that you adhere to a few simple rules if you want that resume to be seen and acted upon.

1. While some companies will advertise their positions electronically, they don't all accept electronic resume submissions. So when you see a position and want to apply for it, read the instructions carefully and follow them.
2. If you are applying for a job listed in a job bank, it will always be headed with a job title, and will often have a reference number as well. Be sure to use these in your cover letter. For example:

Ref: Internal Auditor, Ref #123, Monster Board Job Bank

Make reference to the same in the first paragraph of your cover letter. For example:

Dear Ms. Jones:

I have long admired the work of Pzifer, Inc., so when I came across your job posting for an Internal Auditor (Ref #123) on the Monster Board Job Bank, it took me two seconds to decide I had to throw my hat in the ring.

3. When you send a resume in more traditional circumstances, you will typically send two documents: the cover letter and the resume. When e-mailing two documents, they are guaranteed to become separated; so send the cover letter and resume as one document. It is also courteous and wise to mention that you will forward a copy of your communication through the mail. Remember to do so! Of course, your mail version will be compatible with its format: that is two repeat documents, a cover letter and a resume.

Still Confused?

If you are still confused, ask. Most people on the Web are new to it, and you'll find that nearly everyone (except some of those old-time elitist Web Neanderthals) is pleasant and helpful.

The best and first place to go is the site I have created to help you use the Internet effectively in your job hunt, *www.careerbrain.com*. At Careerbrain, I will answer your questions, teach you how to use the Internet, show you the most effective electronic tools, and provide you with a constantly changing menu of Internet chat, TV, radio, and self-awareness tests. You can also send me questions on any aspect of resume writing, job hunting, or lifetime career management. You might also use these in-print resources:

- *The Guide to Internet Job Searching* by Margaret Riley is published by VGM. This is the best book on the topic at the moment, written by a woman who has my professional respect and that of the rest of the career management community. She also has a Web site (see below).
- *Career Crossroads* by Crispin and Mehler. This self-published book reviews about five hundred employment-related sites.

Both of these books may be difficult to find in book stores. But since both organizations have Web sites, you can get purchasing information directly from them.

On the Internet, try:

- The Riley Guide   *www.jobtrak.com*

This is Margaret Riley's site. She is a very knowledgeable resource. Do her and yourself a favor by reading her FAQs carefully.

- Career Crossroads   *mmc@careerxroads.com*

Double Trouble

Now that you know how to get the computer's attention, be sure you don't get the computer's attention more than once because you've sent one too many resumes.

Suppose that, in the old days, you wanted to work for Big Boston Publishing. You might have sent one resume to the Editorial Director in application for a job as an editorial assistant; another to the Operations Manager, touting yourself as the best warehouse worker ever; and still another to the Customer Service Manager, revealing your years of intensive telemarketing experience.

So why not send three resumes to Big Boston Publishing now? Because the resume-tracking computer in the Human Resources Department is a know-it-all and a tattletale.

While the human supervisors of old might have read their copies of your resumes and never compared notes, the computer is all-knowing. With too many resumes and too many work histories in its files, the computer is likely to peg you as somebody who is at best unfocused about his or her career direction—and at worst a pathological liar.

If you do want to submit more than one resume in application for multiple jobs and you're unsure of whether or not the company is using a computerized tracking system, minimize the risks. Be sure that you don't follow up the resume that sells you as an experienced reference book editor with another that delineates your years of experience as an expert book packer.

Cover Letters

Do you ever receive junk mail? Of course you do. Who doesn't?

Junk mail. Tons of it have probably made it into your mailbox over the years. Now, what do you do with the stuff marked "Occupant"? Either junk it without reading, or junk it after a quick glance. That's why they call it junk mail! It never gets the attention a personal letter does.

The days when you could dash your resume off to "Personnel," with a clear conscience and no personal note, are long gone. It will be read by the lowest of the low, someone who probably can't even spell "professional." You will be consigning it to the mass resume graveyard that all other impersonally addressed resumes reach.

Your cover letter is the personalizing factor in the presentation of an otherwise essentially impersonal document—your resume. A good cover letter sets the stage for the reader to accept your resume as something special.

So your first effort with a cover letter is to find an individual to whom you can address it. That shows you have focus, and guarantees that a specific individual will open and read it. It also means you have someone to ask for by name when you do your follow-up—important when you are interview hunting.

Your target is someone who can either hire you or refer you to someone who can—and management rather than personnel offers you a much better chance of achieving that goal.

Your cover letter will either be sent to someone as a result of a prior conversation, or sent "cold"—with no prior conversation. You will see how to handle both these eventualities as we progress through the chapter.

When the envelope is opened, your cover letter is the first thing seen. It can make an indelible first impression. I'm not saying that it will get you the job (or even land you the interview), but it will help you along the way by getting that resume read with something akin to serious attention.

The higher up the professional ladder you climb, the more important cover letters become. For the person using written communication in the execution of daily duties (and who doesn't these days?), this letter becomes a valuable vehicle for demonstrating needed job skills.

Cover Letter Rules

Cover letters are brief, never more than a page. Write more, and you will be labeled as an unorganized windbag. You should always try to follow accepted business letter protocol, with the date, employer's name and address first. Space can be at such a premium, however, that you can dispense with the formality and begin with a normal salutation: "Dear _____." Stick with the protocol when you can, ignore it when you have to.

The following four steps will help you create the body of the letter.

Step One

Grab your reader's attention. Do this by using quality stationery. If you don't have personal stationery, use some of the sheets you have bought to have your resume printed on. That way, letter and resume will match and give an impression of balance and continuity. Basic business letters should be laid out according to the accepted standards, like this:

[YOUR ADDRESS/LETTERHEAD
AND TELEPHONE NUMBER]

                                                                [DATE]

[ADDRESSEE ADDRESS]
[SALUTATION]

Recently I have been researching the leading local companies in data communications. My search has been for companies that are respected in the field, and who provide ongoing training programs. The name of DataLink Products keeps coming up as a top company.

I am an experienced voice and data communications specialist with a substantial background in IBM environments. If you have an opening for someone in this area you will see that my resume demonstrates a person of unusual dedication, efficiency, and drive.

My experience and achievements include:

- The complete redesign of a data communications network, projected to increase efficiency companywide by some 12 percent.
- The installation and troubleshooting of a Defender II call-back security system for a dial-up network.

I enclose a copy of my resume, and look forward to examining any of the ways you feel my background and skills would benefit DataLink Products. While I prefer not to use my employer's time taking personal calls at work, with discretion you can reach me at 213/555-5555 to initiate contact. Let's talk!

Yours,

[SIGNATURE]
[TYPED NAME]

Step Two

Generate interest with the content. You do this by addressing the letter to someone by name and quickly explaining what you have to offer: The first sentence grabs attention, the rest of the paragraph gives the reader the old one-two punch. The rule is: Say it strong and say it straight; don't pussy-foot around.

A little research, for example, can get your letter off to a fast start.

I came across the enclosed article in *Newsweek* and thought it might interest you. It encouraged me to do a little research on your company. The research convinced me of two things: You are the kind of people I want to be associated with, and I have the kind of qualifications you can use.

Of course, in the real world, we don't all apply for jobs with companies that are featured in the big magazines. Here are some other examples:

I have been following the performance of your fund in *Mutual Funds Newsletter*. The record over the last three years shows strong portfolio management. Considering my experience with one of your competitors, I know I could make significant contributions.

Recently, I have been researching the local _____ industry. My search has been for companies that are respected in the field and that provide ongoing training programs. The name _____ keeps coming up as a top company.

With the scarcity of qualified and motivated *(your desired job title)* that exists today, I felt sure that it would be valuable for us to communicate.

I would like the opportunity to put my _____ years of _____ experience to work for _____.

Within the next few weeks I will be moving from New York to San Francisco. Having researched the companies in my field in my new home town, I know that you are the people I want to talk to.

The state of the art in _____ changes so rapidly that it is tough for most professionals to keep up. I am the exception. I am eager to bring my experience to bear for your company.

I am applying for a position with your company because I know you will find my background and drive interesting.

This letter and the attached resume are in application for employment with _____.

If you are looking for summer jobs.

In six weeks I shall be finishing my second year at John Carroll University. I am interested in working for your firm during the summer because…

As the summer season gets under way, I know you will be looking for extra help.

I am a high school senior looking for some real world experience during the summer break.

I am very interested in becoming one of your summer interns.

If you are writing as the result of a referral, say so and quote the person's name if appropriate:

Our mutual colleague, John Stanovich, felt my skills and abilities would be valuable to your company.

The manager of your San Francisco branch, Pamela Bronson, has suggested I contact you regarding the opening for a _____.

I received your name from Henry Charles last week. I spoke to Mr. Charles regarding career opportunities with _____ and he suggested I contact you. In case the resume he forwarded is caught up in the mail, I enclose another.

Arthur Gold, your office manager and my neighbor, thought I should contact you about the upcoming opening in your accounting department.

If you are writing as the result of an online job posting or a newspaper advertisement, you should mention both the source and the date—and remember not to abbreviate advertisement to "ad."

I read your advertisement job posting on CareerBrain.com yesterday and after researching your company, felt I had to write.

I am responding to your recent job listing on your Web site offering the opportunity to manage accounts receivable.

In re: Your advertisement in the *Columbus Dispatch* on Sunday, the eighth of November. As you will notice, my entire background matches your requirements.

Your notice regarding a _____ in the *Detroit News* caught my eye, and your company name caught my attention.

This letter and attached resume is in response to your advertisement in the *Boston Globe*.

If you are writing to an executive search firm:

(**Note:** In a cover letter to executive search firms, unlike any other circumstances, you *must* mention your salary and, if appropriate, your willingness to relocate.)

I am forwarding my resume to you because I understand you specialize in representing clients in the _____ field.

Please find the enclosed resume. As a specialist in the _____ field, I felt you might be interested in the skills of a _____.

Among your many clients may be one or two who are seeking a candidate for a position as a _____.

My salary is in the mid-20s, with appropriate benefits. I would be willing to relocate for the right opportunity.

Step Three

Now turn that interest into desire. First, make a bridge that ties you to a general job category or work area. It starts with phrases like:

I am writing because…

My reason for contacting you is…

This letter is to introduce me and to explore any need you might have in the _____ area.

…should this be the case, you may be interested to know…

If you are seeking a _____, you will be interested to know…

I would like to talk to you about your personnel needs and my ability to contribute to your department's goals.

If you have an opening for someone in this area, you will see
that my resume demonstrates a person of unusual dedication,
efficiency, and drive.

Then call attention to your merits with a short paragraph that highlights one
or two of your special contributions or achievements:

I have an economics background (Columbia) and a strong
analytical approach to market fluctuations. This combination has
enabled me to consistently pick the new technology flotations
that are the backbone of the growth-oriented mutual fund.

Similar statements applicable to your area of expertise will give your letter
more personal punch. Include any qualifications, contributions, and attributes
that qualify you as someone with talent to offer. If an advertisement (or a
conversation with a potential employer) revealed an aspect of a particular job
opening that is not addressed in your resume, it can easily be covered in the
cover letter.

I notice from your advertisement that audio and video training
experience would be a plus. In addition to the qualifications
stated in my enclosed resume, I have over five years' experience
writing and producing sales and management training materials
in both these media.

Whether you bullet or list your achievements in short, staccato sentences
will be determined in part by the amount of space available to you on the page.

Step Four

Here's where your letter turns that desire into action. You want to make the
reader dash straight to your resume, then call you in for an interview. You
achieve this with brevity.

Your one-page letter shouldn't be longer than four or five paragraphs, or
two hundred words. Leave the reader wanting more. This final step tells the
reader that you want to talk. It explains when, where, and how you can be
contacted. Then tell the reader that you intend to follow up at a certain point in
time if contact has not been established by then. This can encourage a decision
on the reader's part to initiate action, which is what you want.

Useful phrases include:

I look forward to discussing our mutual interests further.

It would be a pleasure to give you more data about my qualifications and experience.

I will be in your area around the 20th, and will call you prior to that date to arrange a meeting.

I hope to speak with you further and will call the week of the 20th to follow up.

The chance to meet with you would be a privilege and a pleasure. To this end I will call you on the 20th.

I look forward to speaking with you further and will call in the next few days to see when our schedules will permit a face-to-face meeting.

May I suggest a personal meeting where you can have the opportunity to examine the person behind the resume?

My credentials and achievements are a matter of record that I hope you will examine in depth when we meet.

I look forward to examining any of the ways you feel my background and skills would benefit your organization. I look forward to hearing from you.

Resumes help you sort out the probables from the possibles, but they are no way to judge the true caliber of an individual. I should like to meet you and demonstrate that I have the personality that makes for a successful _____.

My resume can highlight my background and accomplishments. My drive, willingness and manageability, however, can come out only during a face-to-face meeting. With this in mind, I shall call you on the 20th, if I don't hear from you before.

After reading my resume, you will know something about my background. Yet you will still need to determine whether I am the one to help with the current problems and challenges. I would like an interview to discuss my ability to contribute.

I am anxious to meet and discuss any potential opportunities further. I will make myself available for an interview at a time convenient to you.

I expect to be in your area on Tuesday and Wednesday of next week and wonder which day would be best for you. I will call to find out.

With my training and hands-on experience, I know I can contribute to your company, and want to speak with you about it in person. When may we meet?

I feel certain that I can contribute and that I can convince you I can. I look forward to a meeting at your convenience.

You can reach me at 202/555-1212 to arrange an interview. I know that your time investment in meeting with me will be amply repaid.

Thank you for your time and consideration. I hope to hear from you shortly.

May I call you for an interview in the next few days?

I am sure that our mutual interests will be served by speaking further, and am convinced a personal meeting will assure you of my ability, willingness, and manageability. I look forward to meeting with you.

A brief phone call will establish whether or not we have mutual interest. Recognizing the demands of your schedule, I will make that call within the week.

As many employed people are concerned about their resumes going astray, you may wish to add:

In the meantime, I would appreciate my application being treated as confidential, as I am currently employed.

Just as you worked to get the opening right, labor over the close. It is the reader's last remembrance of you, so make it strong, make it tight, and make it obvious that you are serious about entering into meaningful conversation.

Writing the Cover Letter

Keep your sentences short—an average of fourteen words per sentence is about right. Likewise, your paragraphs should be concise and to the point. In cover letters, paragraphs can often be a single sentence, and should never be longer than two or three sentences. This makes the page more inviting for the harried reader, by providing adequate white space to ease eye strain.

Short words work best here also. They speak more clearly than those polysyllabic behemoths that say more about your self-image problems than your abilities. A good approach is to think in terms of sending a telegram, where every word must work its hardest.

While abiding by accepted grammatical rules, you should punctuate for readability rather than strictly following E. B. White or the *Chicago Manual of Style*. Get by on commas, dashes—and periods. And in between the punctuation marks use the action verbs and phrases that breathe life into your work.

Cover Letter Examples

Notice that the italicized areas come directly from the previous examples. You too can write a dynamite cover letter with the old "cut and paste" technique. Then all you have to do is make the minor adjustments necessary to personalize your letter:

James Sharpe
9 Central Ave
Los Angeles, CA 93876

November 16, 20__

Dear Mr. Bell,

Recently I have been researching the leading local companies in data communications. My search has been for companies that are respected in the field, and who provide ongoing training programs. DataLink Products keeps coming up as a top company.

I am an experienced voice and data communications specialist with a substantial background in IBM environments. *If you have an opening for someone in this area you will see that my resume demonstrates a person of unusual dedication, efficiency, and drive.*

My experience and achievements include:

- complete redesign of a data communications network, projected to increase efficiency companywide some 12 percent;
- The installation and troubleshooting of a Defender II call-back security system for a dial-up network.

I enclose a copy of my resume, and look forward to examining any of the ways you feel my background and skills would benefit DataLink Products. While I prefer not to use my employer's time taking personal calls at work, with discretion I can be reached at 213/555-5555 to initiate contact. Let's talk!

Yours truly,

James Sharpe

James Sharpe

In response to an advertisement, here is an example using a different selection of phrases.

Jane Swift   November 16, 20__
9 Central Ave
Sunnyside, NY 11104

Dear Ms. Pena,

I have always followed the performance of your fund in *Mutual Funds Newsletter.*

Recently, your notice regarding a Market Analyst in Investors Daily *caught my eye—and your company name caught my attention—because your record over the last three years shows exceptional portfolio management. With my experience with one of your competitors, I know I could make significant contributions.*

I would like to talk to you about your personnel needs and how I would be able to contribute to your department's goals.

An experienced market analyst, I have an economics background and a strong analytical approach to market fluctuations. This combination has enabled me to consistently pick the new technology flotations that are the backbone of the growth-oriented mutual fund.

For example, I first recommended Fidelity Magellan six years ago. More recently, my clients have been strongly invested in Pacific Horizon Growth (in the high-risk category), and Fidelity Growth and Income (for the cautious investor).

Those following my advice over the last six years have owned shares in funds which consistently outperformed the market.

I know that resumes help you sort out the probables from the possibles, but they are no way to judge the personal caliber of an individual. I would like to meet with you and demonstrate that, along with the credentials, I have the personality that makes for a successful team player.

Yours faithfully,

Jane Swift

Jane Swift

The Executive Briefing

Here is a variation on the traditional cover letter. It has been developed most effectively by the recruiting fraternity for use in relation to a specific opening.

Behind the executive briefing is the belief that the initial resume screener might have little understanding of the job in question. So a format was developed that dramatically increased the odds of your resume getting through to the right people. In addition, it customizes your general-purpose resume to each specific opening you discovered. It looks like this:

EXECUTIVE BRIEFING
for a
CREDIT/LOAN SUPERVISOR
as advertised in the *Gotham Daily News*

Jane Swift   November 16, 20__
9 Central Avenue
Mesa, AZ 85201
602/555-5555

To help you evaluate the attached resume and manage your time effectively today, I have prepared this executive briefing. It itemizes your needs on the left and my skills on the right. The attached resume will give you additional details.

Job Title: CREDIT AND LOAN SUPERVISOR Required Experience:	My Current Title: CREDIT AND LOAN SUPERVISOR Relevant Experience:
• Five years in consumer banking	• Five years with a major Arizona consumer bank
• Knowledge of Teller Operations	• Four years in Teller Operations, as teller and supervisor
• Three years Consumer Loans and Mortgage Loans	• Five years Consumer & Commercial and Mortgages
• Extensive Customer Service experience	• Four years in customer service. Reviewed as "having superior communication skills."

An executive briefing sent with a resume provides a comprehensive picture of a thorough professional, plus a personalized, fast, and easy-to-read synopsis that details exactly how you can help with an employer's current batch of problems.

The Broadcast Letter

The broadcast letter is nothing but a simple variation on the cover letter. All the information you would need is available to you from the achievements section of your questionnaire. The intent is to get around sending a resume. Practically speaking, it can often get you into a telephone conversation with a potential employer, but that employer is usually likely to request a proper resume before seeing you anyway. A broadcast letter might have a place in your campaign, but do not use it as a resume substitute. Here is an example of a broadcast letter, in this instance sent in response to a blind newspaper advertisement:

Dear Employer,

For the past seven years I have pursued an increasingly successful career in the sales profession. Among my accomplishments I include:

SALES
As a regional representative, I contributed $1,500,000, or 16 percent of my company's annual sales.

MARKETING
My marketing skills (based on a B.S. in Marketing) enabled me to increase sales 25 percent in my economically stressed territory, at a time when colleagues here were striving to maintain flat sales. Repeat business reached an all-time high.

PROJECT MANAGEMENT
Following the above successes, my regional model was adopted by the company. I trained and provided project supervision to the entire sales force. The following year, company sales showed a sales increase 12 percent above projections.

The above was based and achieved on my firmly held zero price discounting philosophy. It is difficult to summarize my work in a letter.

The only way I can think of for providing you the opportunity to examine my credentials is to talk with each other. I look forward to hearing from you.

Yours sincerely,

James Sharpe

James Sharpe

As you can see, the letter is a variation on a theme, and as such might have a place in your marketing campaign.

Here is an example of a cover letter sent as a result of a conversation.

Dear Ms. _____,

I am writing in response to our telephone conversation on Friday the 10th regarding a new- and used-car sales management position.

With a successful track record in both new- and used-car sales, and as a sales manager, I believe I am ideally suited for the position we discussed. My exposure to the different levels of the sales process (I started at the bottom and worked my way up), has enabled me to effectively meet the challenges and display the leadership you require.

I am a competitive person professionally. Having exercised the talents and skills required to exceed goals and set records as a Sales Manager, I believe in measuring performance by results.

I would appreciate your consideration for a meeting where I could discuss in more detail my sales and management philosophy, and capabilities. Please call me at your earliest convenience to arrange a personal meeting.

Sincerely yours,

James Sharpe

James Sharpe

Finally, here is an example of the somewhat different cover letter you would send to a corporate headhunter:

Dear Mr. _____,

As you may be aware, the management structure at XYZ Inc. will be reorganized in the near future. While I am enthusiastic about the future of the company under its new leadership, I have elected to make this an opportunity for change and professional growth.

My many years of experience lends itself to a management position in any medium-sized service firm, but I am open to other opportunities. Although I would prefer to remain in Detroit, I would be amenable to relocation if the opportunity warrants it. I am currently earning $65,000 a year.

I have taken the liberty of enclosing my resume for your review. Should you be conducting a search for someone with my background—at the present time or in the near future—I would greatly appreciate your consideration. I would be happy to discuss my background more fully with you on the phone or in a personal interview.

Very truly yours,

James Sharpe

James Sharpe

9 | What Do You Do with It?

Creating one of the best resumes in America is a major part of your job hunt, but nevertheless, only a part. It won't get you a job by sitting on your desk like a rare manuscript. You have to do something with it.

Companies are always looking for employees. Even a company with no growth rate can still be expected (based on national averages) to experience a 14 percent turnover in staff over the course of a year. In other words, every company has openings, and any one of those openings could have your name on it.

The problem is, you won't have the chance to pick the very best opportunity unless you check them all out. The intelligent job hunter will use a six-pronged approach to cover all the bases. This process incorporates different ways to use:

- Internet Distribution
- Resume Banks
- Employer Web sites
- Newspapers
- Employment agencies
- Executive recruiters
- Vocational and college placement offices
- Business and trade publications
- Personal and professional networking

Internet Distribution

The Internet provides computer-savvy professionals in all fields. If you are not Internet savvy, I cannot urge you strongly enough to take the plunge. It will only take two days (and less if you have a friend who will lend a guiding hand) to learn the ropes and get your resume loaded for distribution. A day later you'll be ready to get your resume in front of thousands of employers and recruiters.

The ease with which you can reach potential employers is just impossible with more traditional methods of distribution.

Don't expect seamless perfection. The Internet is growing like a boomtown, and that means the buildings and infrastructure are under constant construction. Yet with all the problems you might encounter, the benefits far outweigh the drawbacks. Apart from the sheer volume of activity you can generate, your ability to use the Internet for resume distribution sets you apart from other candidates. All employers want technologically adept employees, so approaching them this way immediately makes a point in your favor.

There are two principal forms of electronic resume distribution:

- Posting your resume in resume banks, which are in turn searched by corporate recruiters and headhunters. These databases are rapidly becoming a major recruiting resource.
- Sending your resume directly to an employer's Web site.

Resume Banks

There are literally hundreds of resume banks where you can post your resume for free. Most have resume forms where you fill in the blanks. Have your resume handy; it's easier and more accurate to cut and paste an existing document than starting from ground zero every time. Your submission will look more polished (and therefore powerful) and there is less chance of spelling mistakes; with the availability of spell checking, typos are a clear sign of sloppiness.

Some of these submission forms will accept text posted from your word processing program, while others will require an ASCII text file (addressed on page 86).

Sending out 100 resumes used to be a real chore. Now, every time you post a resume it will be seen by thousands of employers . A word of caution here: In an effort to keep these resume banks fresh for the paying customers (employers pay for access to these banks) the administrators typically purge resumes over 90 days old. Every time you post to a new resume bank, make a note of its storage policies. That way you'll know when to repost your resume if you think the bank is getting you worthwhile exposure.

Employer Web Sites

While the resume banks are a godsend to people on both sides of the desk, company home pages are your very best resource, even though posting to them individually may take a little more time.

Almost every one of the millions of companies with an Internet presence uses part of their site for recruiting. By delivering your resume directly to the site you will set yourself apart from the resumes coming in from other Internet sources.

All of these sites offer information about the company (history, press clippings, even financial data in the case of public companies) so you can easily customize your cover letter and your resume to fit the company's needs.

To find e-mail addresses you can:

- Type the company name into the search engine of your choice
- Use one of the following electronic yellow pages services, each of which claims listings for over 10 million companies:

> whowhere.com   onvillage.com
> bigbook.com   superpages.gte.net

A potential employer's Web site may allow you to submit a formatted resume, an ASCII version, or you may be required to cut and paste your information into a resume template custom-designed by the company.

If you have an strong interest in a specific company, you can usually keep your resume posted there until the right opportunity comes through. Company databases are managed pretty much the same way as the commercial ones, which means they get purged on a regular basis. Sometimes the purge comes after 90 days, other times it's six months or a year. Keep a log of the e-mail addresses you've posted to and the corresponding storage policies so that you can repost when the time comes.

Your Privacy

Unfortunately, your privacy becomes more of an issue with electronic distribution. The ease with which electronic resumes are distributed means that many more people are going to see your resume. But once it's available electronically, it also becomes almost effortless to copy or forward it. If you are currently gainfully employed, you'll need to take precautions to protect your anonymity.

First, use your own e-mail, not your employer's. If this is not possible, many resume banks will provide a "blind" account to handle responses from their clients—but that only covers you for that specific bank. Many Internet service providers offer e-mail addresses. If yours doesn't, many resume writers and career counseling firms will furnish you with a numbered account that will protect your privacy in all online job hunting scenarios.

With an electronic resume, your e-mail address can replace most of your other contact information, although you may choose to provide your home telephone number. You can replace the name of your current employer with something generic, such as "A multinational bank" or "a midsized telecommunications company." Potential employers and headhunters don't take offense at these substitutions. They recognize that you are employed and are exercising discretion.

As you put together your electronic resume distribution program, you will also be laying the foundations for your next job hunt, even if it's a couple of years or more down the road.

Corporate e-mail addresses don't change as often as you might think. Even if the corporation moves from 10 Main Street to 260 Center Street, it usually keeps its "hr@bigcompany.com" (or similar) e-mail address intact. The majority of the e-mail addresses you locate now will probably still be there the next time you are looking for a new opportunity. So don't start from scratch—you may find that by keeping a careful log this time, you've saved yourself hours of time in the future.

Newspapers

A first step for many is to go to the want ads and do a mass mailing. But beware. If this is the first idea that comes to *your* mind, hitting the want ads will probably be at the front of everyone else's mind, too.

A single help-wanted advertisement can draw hundreds of responses. And that's not counting all the other unsolicited resumes that come in every day. So your approach must be more comprehensive than that of the average applicant. The following tips might be helpful.

- Newspapers tend to have an employment edition every week (usually Sunday, but sometimes mid-week), when, in addition to their regular advertising, they have a major drive for help-wanted ads. Make sure you always get this edition of the paper.

- Look for back issues. Just because a company is no longer advertising does not necessarily mean that the slot has been filled. The employer may well have become disillusioned and gone on to hire a professional recruiter to work on the position.
- Cross-check the categories. Don't rely solely on those ads seeking your specific job title. For example, let's say you are a graphic artist looking for a job in advertising. Any advertising or public relations agency with any kind of need should be flagged. On the basis that they are actively hiring at the moment, simple logic leads you to the conclusion that their employment needs are not restricted to that particular title.

Newspapers represent an important part of your marketing campaign; you should follow up all your resumes with a phone call about a week after they have been sent.

Employment Agencies

There are essentially three categories: State employment agencies, private employment agencies, and executive recruiters.

State Employment Agencies

These are funded by the state's labor department and typically carry names like State Employment Security, State Job Service, or Manpower Services. The names vary, but the services remain the same. They will make efforts to line you up with appropriate jobs and will mail resumes out on your behalf to interested employers who have jobs listed with them. It is not mandatory for employers to list jobs with state agencies, but more and more are taking advantage of these free services. Once the bastion of minimum-wage jobs, positions listed with these public agencies can reach fifty to sixty thousand dollars a year for some technical positions.

If you are moving across the state or across the country, your local employment office can plug you into a computer bank accessing major employers on a national basis (often referred to as a national "job bank"). Insiders agree, however, that it can take up to a month for a particular job from a local office to hit the national system. The most effective way to use the services is to visit your local office and ask for an introduction to the office in your destination area.

Private Employment Agencies

Here we have a definitely for-profit sector of the employment marketplace. There are some major questions that you should get answered before signing up with any particular agency. Chief among them: Are the fees to be paid by the client or by you as the job candidate? The answer distinguishes employer paid fee (or EPF) agencies from applicant paid fee (or APF) agencies. *In all but the most dire emergencies you are strongly recommended to work only with EPF companies.* Apart from the expense, you simply don't want to be known as someone who has to pay to get a job.

You are best advised to call first, verify the fee status, and then visit. Be prepared to leave a copy of your resume for their files and for possible review by interested clients.

Here are some practical ways for you to check on the professional standing of your agent. Be sure to ask:

- When was the firm established? If the company has been in town ever since you were in diapers, the chances are good that it is reputable.
- Is the agency a member of the state employment association? State associations have strict codes of behavior and ethics and provide ongoing training for their members. And as in all industries, people and companies who are actively involved in enhancing their profession invariably have an edge on the competition.
- Does your particular agent have a CPC designation? That stands for Certified Personnel Consultant, a title achieved only after considerable time and effort. Employment consultants with this designation come straight from the top drawer, so you can trust them and should listen attentively to their advice.
- Is the agency part of a franchise chain or independent network? Knowing this can be valuable to you, because both kinds of organizations provide considerable training for their associates, a feature that can enhance the level of service you receive. In addition, other members of the network may have a job suitable for you if the one you've located doesn't.

Finally—don't get intimidated. Remember, you are not obliged to sign anything. Neither are you obliged to guarantee an agency that you will remain in any employment for any specified length of time. Don't get taken advantage of by the occasional rogue in an otherwise exemplary and honored profession.

Executive Recruiters

These people rarely deal at salary levels under seventy thousand dollars a year. All the above advice regarding employment agencies applies here, although you can take it for granted that the headhunter will not charge you a fee. He or she will be more interested in your resume than in seeing you right then and there, unless you match a specific job the recruiter is trying to fill for a client. Executive recruiters are far more interested in the employed than in the unemployed. An employed person is less of a risk (headhunters often guarantee their finds to the employer for up to a year) and constitutes a more desirable commodity. Remember, these people are there to serve the client, not to find you a job. They neither want nor expect you to rely on them for employment counseling, unless they specifically request that you do—in which case you should listen to them closely.

Vocational and College Placement Offices

If you're leaving school, you should take advantage of this resource. (If you don't, you're crazy.) Many of the larger schools have alumni placement networks, so even if you graduated some time ago, you may want to check with the alma mater and tap into the old-boy and old-girl network.

Business and Trade Publications

Two uses here. The articles about interesting companies can alert you to growth opportunities, and individually can provide neat little entrees in your cover letters. Of course, there's also the welcome fact that most of these magazines carry a help-wanted section.

Networking

A fancy word from the seventies that means talking to everyone you can get hold of in your field, whether you know them or not.

The Encyclopedia of Associations (published by R.R. Bowker) tells you about associations for your profession. Networking at the meetings and using an association's directory for contacts are wise and accepted uses of membership.

At the Library

The business reference section can give you access to numerous research books that can help, including *Standard and Poor's, The Thomas Register, The National Job Bank,* and *The Directory of Directories*

Follow-Up

It is no use mailing off tens or even hundreds of resumes without following up on your efforts. If you are not getting a response with one resume format, you might want to consider redoing it another way, as discussed in chapter 5. Of course, in doing so, you should never mention your previous submission. Be satisfied with one of your baits catching a fish.

Always take five or six copies of your resume with you to interviews. Often you can attach it to those annoying application forms and then just write on the form "See attached resume." You can have one on your lap during the interview to refer to, as the interviewer does.

It is always wise to offer copies to subsequent interviewers. This is because they have very often been inadequately briefed and may have no idea about your background and skills. It's also a good idea to leave extra copies of your resume behind with managers for their personal files (which travel with them through their careers from company to company). That person may not need you today, but could come up with a dream job for you sometimes in the future. I know of people who have landed jobs years later as a result of a resume left judiciously with the right person. Who is the right person? Potentially, anyone who holds on to your resume.

The job you ultimately accept may not be your picture of perfection. Nevertheless, any job can lead to great things. You can make the opportunities for yourself in any job if you make the effort. A job becomes what you choose to make it.

In the job hunt there are only two kinds of "yes" answers: Their "yes-we-want-you-to-work-for-us," and your "yes-I-can-start-on-Monday." The joy is in the hunt, with every "no" bringing you closer to the big "yes." Never take rejections of your resume as rejections of yourself; just as every job is not for you, you aren't right for every job. Keep things in perspective.

Good luck!

10 | The Resumes

The resumes on the following pages are based on the genuine articles, the ones that really did the trick for someone who had to translate his or her fantastic skills and background into a single, compelling document.

Whether or not your background is represented in the following sample, use the resumes reproduced here as a starting point for composing your own.

Accounting Professional

Jane Swift
9 Central Avenue
Dallas, TX 75379
(214) 555-1212
Jane@careerbrain.com

Detail-oriented, organized, and efficient accounting professional with a strong background in all areas of the accounting system. Progressively responsible duties gained over the course of a career based on exceptional analytical and organizational skills. Self-motivated individual with the ability to work independently with minimal supervision and make well thought out decisions. Excellent verbal and written communications skills. Specific skills and knowledge include: accounts payable, sales and use tax, capital expenditures, accounts receivable, general ledger, check generation, payroll, asset management, invoice verification, purchasing, requisitions, budgeting.

Technical Expertise
- Infinium Fixed Assets
- Infinium Human Resources
- Windows 95/98
- AS400 programming language
- MS Office including Excel, Word, and Access
- Oracle Financials including Accounts Payable, Purchasing, and Projects
- Internet savvy
- E-mail

Professional Experience
Stewart's Shops, Dallas, Texas
Equipment Coordinator, 1998 to Present
- Managed purchasing, tracking, and delivery of $60 million in capital equipment for over 5,500 stores nationally.
- Implemented procedures to assure proper allocation of capital expenditure budget. Reviewed and analyzed project documentation. Performed financial verification to determine sufficient funding prior to purchase, delivery, and payment. Coordinated and processed all store equipment purchases and fixed asset improvements. Maintained proper documentation of all project activity. Provided consultative, liaison, and support services with vendors and management.

Napa Auto Parts, Houston, Texas, 1991 - 1998
Accounting Assistant - Financial Reporting Department   1996 - 1998
- Executed capital expenditure payments in excess of $17 million annually.
- Contributed to the development and implementation of a cost segregation program that resulted in a $75 million disbursement to stockholders.
- Performed accounts payable functions for all construction and corporate expenses for 30 new stores across 5 states as well as additional corporate projects and payables due to 250 vendors. Assisted with state sales tax returns and managed 70,000 fixed assets for 560 locations.
Accounting Assistant - Payroll Department   1992 - 1996
- Generated approximately 600 on-demand and manager fund checks monthly. Compiled total balance of employee's accounts receivable. Conducted biweekly payroll functions for 5,000 employees across 6 states.
Computer Operator   1991 - 1992
- Coordinated daily and weekly jobs for payroll, accounting, and warehouse. Received on-the-job training in AS400 computer language for use in daily tasks.

Education
University of Texas - 60+ degree hours in Computer Science, 1988 - 1991
West Texas Community College - coursework in Animal Technology, 1982 - 1983
Eastern Community College - coursework in preparatory Liberal Arts, 1978 - 1982

Administrative

James Sharpe
9 Central Avenue
South Bend, IN 46634
(219) 555-1212
James@careerbrain.com

Summary

Administrative support professional experienced working in fast-paced environments demanding strong organizational, technical, and interpersonal skills. Highly trustworthy, ethical, and discreet; committed to superior customer service. Confident and poised in interactions with individuals at all levels. Detail-oriented and resourceful in completing projects; able to multitask effectively.

Key Words   Customer Service & Relations • Word Processing • Computer Operations
Accounts Payable/Receivable • Filing & Data Archiving • Office Equipment Operation
Telephone Reception • General Accounting • Problem Solving

Experience Highlights

Administrative Support

- Performed administrative and secretarial support functions for the Vice President of a large sportswear manufacturer. Coordinated and managed multiple priorities and projects.
- Provided discreet secretarial and reception services for a busy family counseling center. Scheduled appointments and maintained accurate, up-to-date confidential client files.
- Assisted with general accounting functions; maintained journals and handled A/P and A/R. Provided telephone support; investigated and resolved billing problems for a manufacturer's buying group. Trained and supervised part-time staff and interns.

Customer Service & Reception

- Registered incoming patients in a hospital emergency room. Demonstrated ability to maintain composure and work efficiently in a fast-paced environment while preserving strict confidentiality.
- Conducted patient interviews to elicit necessary information for registration, accurate prioritization, and to assist medical professionals in the triage process.
- Orchestrated hotel special events and reservations; managed customer relations and provided exemplary service to all customers.

Management & Supervision

- Promoted rapidly from front desk clerk to assistant front office manager at an upscale hotel. Oversaw all operations including restaurant, housekeeping, and maintenance. Troubleshot and resolved problems, mediated staff disputes, and handled customer complaints.
- Participated in staff recruitment, hiring, training, and scheduling. Supervised a front-desk staff.

Employment History

ACCOUNTING ASSISTANT, Healthcare, Inc., Goshen, IN
PATIENT SERVICES REGISTRAR, University Health System Hospital, Hagerstown, MD
ASSISTANT FRONT OFFICE MANAGER, Sheraton Baltimore, Baltimore, MD
RECEPTIONIST / SECRETARY, Family Counseling & Guidance Center, Harford, MD
ADMINISTRATIVE ASSISTANT, Klein's Sportswear, Harford, CA

Education & Training

Technical College, Goshen, IN (1999 - Present)
Hagerstown Community College, Hagerstown, MD (1996) Introduction to Computers and MS Office
Harford Community College, Harford, MD (1988 - 1989) Concentration in Business Administration

Community Involvement

Committed to community service. Extensive volunteer history includes involvement in public schools, Habitat for Humanity, children's homes, community soup kitchens, work with the elderly, and quilts for children with cancer.

Applications Programmer

James Sharpe
9 Central Avenue
Arlington, MA 02174
(617) 555-1212
James@careerbrain.com

Technical Profile

A dedicated application programmer with 3 years hands-on experience using object-oriented (C++) and conventional languages with a Windows/DOS platform. Excellent design, coding, and testing skills; pays close attention to details. Clear communication abilities and strong writing capability. A team player with cross-functional awareness and above-average work/time management skills.

Object-oriented languages:	C++, Visual C++, C-Shell, Visual Basic, HTML
Conventional languages:	C, Pascal
Database packages:	Btrieve, Oracle, SQL
Operating systems:	Windows 95/98, DOS, Unix
Professional software packages:	Word, Excel, Microsoft Project, Lotus Notes

Professional Experience

A&M Data, Boston, MA   1998 - Present
Programmer/Analyst

Team development member for two banking application projects. Most recent application has been a full life cycle development project consisting of a front-end product used by bank tellers with a Btrieve database and Vermont Views GUI third-party interface. Second project was another front-end product used by banking counselors and tellers.

Team member responsibilities:
- Gather clients' requirements
- Prepare ballpark and detailed design documents
- Code I/O interfaces to peripherals
- Test and debug application; resolve clients' issues
- Track and manage changes using mainframe-based Impact tool

Selected achievements:
- Received President's Ovation Award (the highest level award given by A&M Data) in 1999 for meeting company's goal and receiving strongly positive customer feedback for application
- Selected to research and resolve Y2K compliance issues
- Implemented product to take advantage of C++ capabilities resulting in more efficient upgrades and greater flexibility to interface with different servers

Education

Bachelor of Architecture, University of Wisconsin - Madison
Certificate courses, University of Wisconsin - Madison: Oracle for Developers, C++, HTML, Pascal, System Programming in C (Unix platform), Visual C++, MFC

Banking Portfolio Manager

James Sharpe

9 Central Avenue, Kansas City, MO 64112. (816) 555-1212. James@careerbrain.com Page 1 of 2

SUMMARY

A track record of outstanding performance in the sophisticated environments of Trust and Investment Banking. Management of both personal and institutional portfolios with total values exceeding $700 million. An adept analyst of such diverse industries as energy, metals, automobile, insurance, banking, electrical, and consumer goods.

OBJECTIVE

An opportunity where a professional whose successful loss control/profit preservation approach to portfolio management can make a meaningful contribution.

CAREER HIGHLIGHTS

An Investment Banking Company: Vice President, *Institutional Portfolio Management*. 1992-Present.

Heads investment management activities of the firm's 170-account Kansas office. Reporting to Chairman. Created more effective marketing and management of large accounts, by initiating a program that resulted in:

- Upgrading and expansion of professional staff.
- Personal management of firm's 17 largest accounts.
- Effective supervision of all staff activities and performance.
- Elevation to position as member of Corporate Board of Directors and Chair of Investment Strategy and Policy Group.

Kansas Trust Company: *Vice President & Senior Portfolio Manager*. 1988-1992.

Managed a broadly diversified account base of over 395 personal and institutional accounts with total value in excess of $950 million. Improved performance of accounts supervised, shortened turn-around time of customer requests for investment reviews, cementing relations with clients. Developed effective computerized methods for rapid analysis of investment diversification.

- Program consistently outperformed the S&P index, distilled stock guidance list of 500 firms to a value-oriented 20-35 companies.
- Reduced turn-around time on investment reviews by 30%.
- Reduced time spent in review analysis by 25% while improving review quality.

Morgan Guaranty (New York): *Portfolio Manager*. 1985 -1988.

Initially recruited as a Senior Investment Analyst in the energy stock area, was promoted to Portfolio Manager within 10 months.

- Hired, trained, supervised, and directed activities of additional analysts in related research coverage.
- Dramatically reduced energy stock holdings in November 1988, a move that produced sizable realized capital gains while avoiding the sell-off that followed.
- Instituted automation and software for analytical staff. Increased the number of potential investment opportunities by 21% without additional cost.

EDUCATION AND PERSONAL

MBA, Columbia Business School	Finance and Marketing
MA, John Carroll University	Economics
BA, John Carroll University	Economics

Willing to relocate. References are available upon request.

Broadcast Sales

James Sharpe
9 Central Avenue
Tampa Bay, FL 32301
(904) 555-1212
James@careerbrain.com

Profile

Marketing/ Advertising/ Sales/ Corporate Development/ Communications/ Public Affairs/
Promotions/ Non-profit Ventures/ Events/ Sponsorships

- Creative, results-oriented professional with 12 years of experience in broadcast sales, marketing, and corporate development. Strong track record generating revenue from existing partnerships, new customers, and nontraditional sources. Oversee numerous successful promotions, projects, and special events.
- Energetic and resourceful, self-directed and innovative. Highly effective communication skills include demonstrated ability to satisfy client needs through relationship building and creative development. Career-driven, willing to relocate.

Experience

Corporate Development/Account Executive, KTTV, Tampa Bay, Florida, 1992 - present
A leading revenue producer for Fox affiliate in the nation's 34th largest television market.

- Service existing accounts and generate new business. Arrange airtime through quarterly, annual, and specific TV buys.
- Develop television media strategies through qualitative and quantitative research for clients in all categories including retail, business-to-business, and entertainment. Increased existing shares of local direct and agency business. Revenues: Average $2 million account list.
- Recruited BankSouth, MCI Wireless as third-party co-sponsors for the Theater League of Florida. Supported local productions of Broadway musicals and promoted corporate image of sponsors to community. Revenues: $240,000/year (negotiated annually).
- Directed station sponsorship of the Florida Film Festival and the Florida Summer Theater Program. Supervised contracts, promotions, production, tickets, special events, and collateral materials distributions (ads, guides, brochures, posters). Currently negotiating sponsor relationships to underwrite a documentary film on festival for distribution to schools.
- Managed creative development and revenue stream for Drive to Stay Alive, an ongoing public awareness campaign that promotes safe driving issues. Revenues: $50,000/year.
- Helped establish and promote the annual Make a Wish fundraiser and gala event. Generated incremental revenue through corporate sponsorships. Secured news talent as spokespersons and event emcees. Event attendance grew from 75 to 600+ people in 4 years.
- Coordinated station promotion and third-party sponsorship for the Florida Arts Festival, raising money for art supplies and local elementary schools.

Account Executive, KZTV, Albany, New York   1987 - 1992

- Developed new business accounts to generate advertising revenue for NBC affiliate in number 61 television market.

Professional Affiliations

- Florida Advertising Federation, Vice President 1998 - Present, Board of Directors 1995 - 1998, President-Elect 2000 - 2001: Manage public service portfolios; organize social activities; administer student services, internship program, and scholarships; oversee payroll and budgets; frequent public speaker.
- Community Advisory Board, 1999 - Present: Coordinate fundraising and corporate contributions for YMCA.
- Florida Acting Company, Board of Directors 1998 - Present

Education

B.A., Business and Communications, State University of New York at Albany

Brokerage Professional

James Sharpe
9 Central Avenue
Chicago, IL 60625
(312) 555-1212
James@careerbrain.com
Page 1 of 2

Profile

- High energy, hands-on management professional with extensive background blending operations management, high-volume brokerage information distribution, and fast-paced brokerage activities.
- Employ analysis and creativity to form productive systems and interdepartmental partnerships. Cool under pressure with an excellent on-time and on-budget record.
- Hold high personal standards and consistently lead teams to achieve departmental goals. Believe that profitability, customer service, and quality work are primary factors of success in any competitive industry.

Areas of Knowledge and Ability

●stock and brokerage service ●brokerage information distribution ●proxy processing ●
●SEC compliance ●stock inventory management ●postal rates and requirements ●ISO-9002 ●
●procedure development ●budget development ●scheduling ●training ●departmental supervision ●

Career Highlights

- Selected to participate with upper management in steering committee to plan company's ISO 9002 certification process. Project was so successful that company received certification in 6 months against 12 month industry standard.
- Achieved a consistent history of promotions and excellent performance appraisals. Started with Investor Services when division employed 5 permanent operations associates; division's operations department, at peak levels, now employs over 200 associates. Have the longest service in the operations department and have hands-on knowledge of all operational procedures.
- Wrote work instruction manual for department at general level for step-by-step process of informal to formal training. Produced written instructions for training of new associates. Designed contract review process and approval.
- Developed new spreadsheet formats for Central Investments that allowed for faster, more accurate tracking of stock inventory and over-the-counter profit and loss.
- Presented stock information to Central Investments CEO and VP level Trading Department head. Interfaced with controller on a monthly basis to reconcile profit and loss dollars.
- Supported the fast paced activities of 1,000 Central Investments brokers trading with a million plus shares of stock inventory.

Brokerage Services Experience

Investor Services, Chicago, IL	1992 to present
Manager, Data Entry and Process Control	1999 to present
Manager, Receiving	1997 to 1999
Receiving Supervisor	1995 to 1997
Data Entry Clerk	1993 to 1995

- Manage all operations of department processing over 35,000 jobs per year, peaking at more than 300 jobs per day. Mailing consists of dividend checks, monthly brokerage statements, and investor communications for 10,000 companies. Department is the hub of all other peripheral operations.
- Control the movement of sensitive, high-profile, investment-related material. Ensure compliance with SEC, client and postal regulations. Deeply involved in productivity and quality assurance issues.
- High speed operation requires exceptional on-time/on-budget performance. Develop annual budget of $600,000 and schedule staff to cover cyclical highs and lows using historical data to project volume. Determine best postal rates and discount eligibility. Come in on or below budget on a consistent basis.

Brokerage Experience

Central Investments, Chicago, IL   1992 to 1993
Assistant Manager, Trading   1993
Trading Coordinator   1992

- Tracked millions of shares of stock inventory to determine on-demand availability of company supply.
- Notified VP of levels needed for new buy. Tracked over-the-counter traders' purchases/sales and profit/loss on a daily basis.
- Followed and analyzed over-the-counter P&L and daily inventory for next days reporting and selling.

Computer Skills

Word for Windows, Excel, Windows 95/98, industry-specific software

Education

Gold Coast Community College, Chicago, IL, 30 Liberal Arts credits with concentration in math and science.
Professional Development Courses: How to Give Presentations, Fred Pryor Seminars; Business Writing

Business Development Manager/Consultant

Jane Swift
9 Central Avenue
Chicago, IL 60602
(312) 555-1212
Jane@careerbrain.com
Page 1 of 2

Expert in the Telecommunications Industry Through 20 Years Experience

Dynamic, award-winning career reflecting pioneering expertise in consultative sales and marketing of telecommunications network infrastructure equipment and services. Offer a rare combination of superior interpersonal skills coupled with in-depth technical systems understanding. Known for innovation and lateral thinking skills; consistent success in solving a diversity of demanding business problems. Outstanding record of achievement leading to accelerated sales, improved business processes, and optimized market share.

Key Words

Business Development & Marketing	Organizational & Process Improvement
Training Program Development & Management	Revenue, Profit & Market Share Growth
Strategic & Tactical Sales Planning	Staff Mentoring, Training & Coaching
Consultative & Solution Sales	Creative & Resourceful Problem Solving

Professional Experience

Patterson Technology, Rockford, IL 1996 - 2000
SENIOR SALES TRAINER

- Rejuvenated the sales training department of this $300 million manufacturer of telecommunications switching equipment. Re-engineered methodologies and processes, instituted department goals, and established training certification programs.
- Created a new training methodology that refocused emphasis to build consultative and solution sales competence. Transformed the sales process by empowering account executives with the knowledge and tools to assess customers' business needs and meet requirements through product solutions.
- Encouraged expansion into emerging telecommunications markets worldwide by introducing and familiarizing the sales team with various industry segments including ILEC, CLEC, satellite, and international carriers.
- Designed and developed a critically acclaimed multimedia web-based sales training module that taught the sales force both basic and advanced selling skills. Delivered the module to the sales team at a national sales conference.

Consulting Partners, Chicago, IL 1992 - 1996
MARKETING MANAGEMENT CONSULTANT

- Contracted as an interim marketing manager. Led interdepartmental team in the creation and roll out of a precedent-setting sales initiative that drove $9 million in sales the first year and halted the competition, protecting an additional $2 million annual revenue.
- Coordinated with stakeholders to ensure support of a streamlined methodology that cut 50% of the time required to add capacity to the 5ESS Switching system. Managed proposal and pricing development and collaborated in the winning contract negotiations; led on-time implementation.
- Designed and deployed an innovative training program for customer's engineers on the state-of-the-art telecommunications switch. Successfully transferred technical knowledge and established market positioning as a premier and adaptable solution to telecommunications needs.
- Honored with the prestigious "Technology Grows Award" for outstanding contribution. Achieved a feature story in a nationally distributed magazine that highlighted the innovative training program.

Jane Swift (312) 555-1212
page 2 of 2

Telecom Solutions, Chicago, IL   1980 - 1992
    SALES MANAGER (1992 - 1996)
    DISTRICT TECHNICAL MANAGER (1989 - 1992)
    AREA SALES MANAGER (1984 - 1989)
    ACCOUNT EXECUTIVE (1982 - 1984)

- Promoted through a series of progressive positions, selling and supporting fiber optic systems and telecommunications switching equipment. Led teams of up to 15 professionals and coordinated the activities of support personnel in a matrix management environment. Supported up to $250 million in annual sales and personally delivered on sales quotas of up to $50 million.
- Launched the SONET technology, building sales from the ground floor to $9 million within the first year of introduction. Received the "Sales Director's Award" for valuable accomplishments.
- Delivered $50 million in new annual revenue by negotiating and closing a competitive fiber cable contract that displaced a well-entrenched, existing vendor. Recognized for top sales production with the "Regional Vice President's Award."
- Created an annual $9 million revenue stream by leading a team of engineers, product managers, and marketing personnel that designed and brought to market a new fiber optic tie cable product in just 8 months. Honored for achievement with a "Sector Vice President's Award."
- Initiated and acted as a change agent to support a paradigm shift in the role of sales engineers. Transformed the position from that of a "back office" role to a customer-focused, sales support role designed to meet the unique and demanding needs of customers.
- Directed a team comprised of internal staff and customer employees in developing and implementing a new system for engineering and provisioning switching equipment that saved $1.9 million annually. Awarded special appreciation honors by the customer's top management.
- Formulated and executed a strategy that achieved 88% market share for 5ESS Switching systems in spite of a price disadvantage.
- Closed the first commercial sale statewide and managed implementation of the then cutting-edge ISDN service; earned both regional and national sales honors.
- Captured a $15 million account by developing an innovative warehousing service that met the customer's need for "just in time" product delivery.
- Increased market share 50% by closing the first multiyear contract in the company's history; led a team in improving the order realization process to optimize fulfillment times for custom orders.

Education & Training
    DePaul University - Business Administration/English
    Extensive training in:
        Telecommunications Engineering & Technology   Sales & Negotiations
        Steven Covey Leadership   Quality Management
        Process Improvement   MS Office (Word, Excel, PowerPoint, Project)

Community Affiliations
    Board of Directors, County Education Foundation
    Member, County School District Communications Team
    Coach and U.S. Soccer Certified Referee, Mustang Soccer League

Buyer

James Sharpe
9 Central Ave
Manhattan, NY 10012
(212) 555-1212
James@careerbrain.com

EXPERIENCE

3/00 - Present Ohrbach's (New York, NY), **Buyer**, Boyswear

Responsible for purchasing boyswear sold in boys departments at 45 stores chainwide, with yearly sales exceeding $5.5 million. Branch managers report to this position. Visit wholesale showrooms on a weekly basis.

- Analyze daily sales data and inventories to plan promotions and make adjustments.
- Prepare and maintain budgets. Redistribute merchandise between stores.
- Travel to branch stores to direct departmental start-ups and solve problems.
- Train and evaluate assistant buyers.

2/99-3/00 **Assistant Buyer**, Silverware/Cookware/Junior Knits

- Promoted through three different lines. Consistently exceeded quota.
- Assisted buyers in selection of merchandise.
- Prepared orders, budgets, and inventories.
- Planned and created newspaper advertisements.
- Organized and promoted annual Housewares Exposition.

8/97-2/99 **Sales Manager**

- Managed four separate departments in two stores, exceeded projections 14%.
- Trained, scheduled, and supervised salespeople; turnover dropped 20%.
- Met daily sales quotas, handled all merchandising.

EDUCATION

B.A. Merchandising: New York Fashion Institute of Technology (1996)

All education self-financed through working in Manhattan retail outlets throughout college years.

Claims Representative

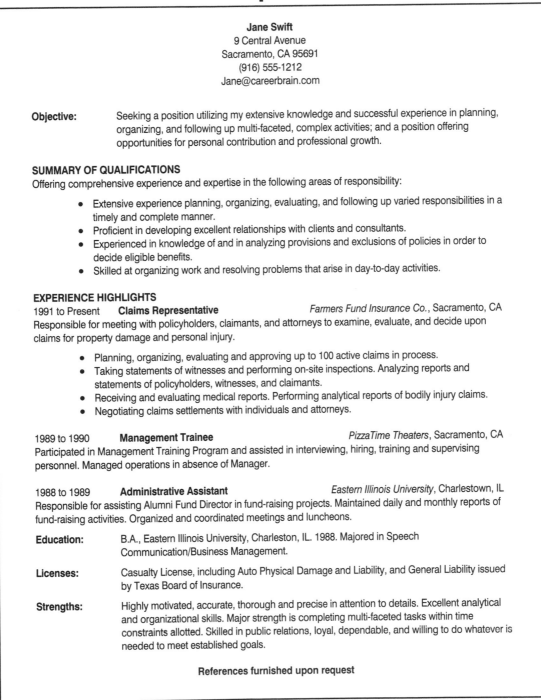

Jane Swift
9 Central Avenue
Sacramento, CA 95691
(916) 555-1212
Jane@careerbrain.com

Objective: Seeking a position utilizing my extensive knowledge and successful experience in planning, organizing, and following up multi-faceted, complex activities; and a position offering opportunities for personal contribution and professional growth.

SUMMARY OF QUALIFICATIONS

Offering comprehensive experience and expertise in the following areas of responsibility:

- Extensive experience planning, organizing, evaluating, and following up varied responsibilities in a timely and complete manner.
- Proficient in developing excellent relationships with clients and consultants.
- Experienced in knowledge of and in analyzing provisions and exclusions of policies in order to decide eligible benefits.
- Skilled at organizing work and resolving problems that arise in day-to-day activities.

EXPERIENCE HIGHLIGHTS

1991 to Present   **Claims Representative**   *Farmers Fund Insurance Co.*, Sacramento, CA
Responsible for meeting with policyholders, claimants, and attorneys to examine, evaluate, and decide upon claims for property damage and personal injury.

- Planning, organizing, evaluating and approving up to 100 active claims in process.
- Taking statements of witnesses and performing on-site inspections. Analyzing reports and statements of policyholders, witnesses, and claimants.
- Receiving and evaluating medical reports. Performing analytical reports of bodily injury claims.
- Negotiating claims settlements with individuals and attorneys.

1989 to 1990   **Management Trainee**   *PizzaTime Theaters*, Sacramento, CA
Participated in Management Training Program and assisted in interviewing, hiring, training and supervising personnel. Managed operations in absence of Manager.

1988 to 1989   **Administrative Assistant**   *Eastern Illinois University*, Charlestown, IL
Responsible for assisting Alumni Fund Director in fund-raising projects. Maintained daily and monthly reports of fund-raising activities. Organized and coordinated meetings and luncheons.

Education: B.A., Eastern Illinois University, Charleston, IL. 1988. Majored in Speech Communication/Business Management.

Licenses: Casualty License, including Auto Physical Damage and Liability, and General Liability issued by Texas Board of Insurance.

Strengths: Highly motivated, accurate, thorough and precise in attention to details. Excellent analytical and organizational skills. Major strength is completing multi-faceted tasks within time constraints allotted. Skilled in public relations, loyal, dependable, and willing to do whatever is needed to meet established goals.

References furnished upon request

Consultant

James Sharpe

9 Central Avenue • Novi, Michigan 48374 • Ph: (810) 555-1212 • Pager: (313) 555-1213
James@careerbrain.com

Executive Summary

An innovative and seasoned **Senior Executive** and **Consultant** with a successful background in **crisis resolution, turnaround and start-up situations**. More than 15 years successful, progressive experience in all phases of Strategic Planning, Operations and Financial Management. Recognized as a hands-on, pro-active **troubleshooter** who can rapidly identify business problems, formulate strategic plans, initiate change and implement new processes in challenging and diverse environments. Exceptional ability to **execute income enhancement strategies** and cost control actions.

Areas of Effectiveness

- Capital & Operational Budgeting
- Production & Inventory Management
- Financial & Operational Cost Control
- Business Valuation
- Sales/Marketing Strategies
- Corrective Action Planning
- P&L Responsibility
- Crisis Management
- Liquidation Management

Significant Accomplishments

- Recruited as a **Turnaround Consultant for ROTH,** to create spending accountability in all areas, resulting in cost reductions of $1 million annually. Facilitated successful negotiations with vendors, customers, the Internal Revenue Service, various state authorities and banks for lines of credit.
- As the **President of NoviTechnolgies**, orchestrated the start-up and growth of a subsidiary organization. Within just four years successfully established 18 retail stores, 3 warehousing/distribution locations and sales exceeding $10 million. Additionally created a wholly owned subsidiary for acquisitions and acquired 21 stores through bulk sale and transfer.
- Within 9 months, as the **Divisional Controller for The Electronics Store**, selected and implemented a fully integrated Purchase Order Management Systems enabling the centralization of national purchasing contracts and staff reductions resulting in a cost savings exceeding $2 million.
- Promoted to **Plant Comptroller**, for the **fifth largest facility in the U.S., at Warren Computers** in less than three years (the standard was seven years). Effectively negotiated with and administered 4 unions and 15 different locals. Responsibilities for this 600 employee facility included: standard cost, budgets, sales forecasting, multi-state distribution, and capital projects.
- Developed and implemented internal controls and security measures to successfully resolve an inventory shortage that exceeded $1 million per month. Additional operational improvements resulted in a 25% increase in deliveries as well as a 20% reduction in staff.
- As the **Acquisition Manager**, spearheaded the acquisition of a 95-unit, 350-employee organization. This included the creation of a new company for the bankruptcy purchase, due diligence, negotiations with creditors, inventory valuation, employee termination and selective rehiring.
- Directed the closure of a manufacturing facility: transferred assets, handled MESC, workers' compensation and union issues, dismissed staff, idled plant, absorbed production.

Education

B.B.A., *Business Management & Accounting*
Novi College

Convention Sales

Jane Swift
9 Central Avenue
Atlantic City, New Jersey 08401
(609) 555-1212
Jane@careerbrain.com

Professional Profile
Ten years experience in hotel/convention sales with demonstrated achievements in delivering winning sales presentations, new business development, account retention, and competitive marketing. Managerial background includes coordinating client services, forecasting, budgeting, personnel supervision, and training sales representatives. Consistently meet and exceed sales goals. Utilize outstanding customer relations, negotiation and conflict resolution skills to assess clients' needs and build rewarding business relationships.

Professional Experience
Atlantic City Resort and Casino, Atlantic City, New Jersey
National Convention Sales Manager, 1996 - Present
- Successfully secured and maintained trade show, corporate meeting, convention, and corporate incentive accounts; generated 30,000 to 40,000 room nights in each of the last 4 years.
- Established new key accounts including Ford Motors, Thomson Publishing, and Time Warner; coordinate with clientele regarding major convention events.
- Direct administrative staff and inter-department procedures; conduct site inspections and effectively oversee client convention/catering/hotel services and client billing.
- Attend international trade and travel shows; promote a positive public relations image and effectively develop new business leads.
- Received the Ambassador of Courtesy award in 1998 and Top Production recognition in 1999.

Director of Agency and Tour Sales, 1994 - 1996
- Cultivated series accounts, wholesale contract, and leisure group clientele.
- Generated 7,500 room nights and $600,000 in food and beverage sales by securing a large domestic wholesale account.
- Created and implemented marketing programs and promotional packages; designed marketing brochures and advertising layout.
- Developed a travel program partnership with USAirways to enhance room occupancy.
- Supervised sales and office personnel; assisted with departmental forecasting and budgeting.

Assistant Sales Manager, 1992 - 1994

Group Coordinator, 1990 - 1992

Education
Johnson & Wales University - Major: Hotel Administration

Affiliations
Hotel Sales & Marketing Association, Atlantic City Tourism Council

Corporate Communications

Jane Swift
9 Central Avenue
Los Angeles, CA 90071
(213) 555-1212
Jane@careerbrain.com
Page 1 of 2

Project Management / Media Research / Client Relations

TOP-FLIGHT MANAGEMENT CAREER building high-profile organizations that have consistently enhanced competitive market positioning, won favorable media and customer recognition, and supported substantial revenue growth. Combine strong planning, organizational leadership, and consensus building qualifications with creative design and writing skills. Proven effectiveness in successfully matching products and services with client needs to ensure consistent repeat business.

Work well under pressure. Thrive in atmosphere of challenge, creativity, and variety. Flexible work style—can adapt quickly to changing work and client needs. Assertive, hands-on leader with extensive publications, audio, video, and broadcast studio experience. Hold B.A. in Communications/Broadcasting and M.A. in Communications Research.

Key Words

Mass media communications	Public affairs	Media relations
Strategic planning	Desktop publishing	Public relations
Video and broadcast technology	Event planning and management	Trade shows
Training and development	New business development	Conference planning
Workflow planning and coordination	Performance and profit improvement	

**Creating High-Impact Images, Concepts, Services, Programs and Opportunities
to Improve Performance and Build Revenues**

OVERVIEW

- Organized, detail-oriented communications professional with demonstrated ability to successfully increase productivity and profitability.
- Versatile, with diversified experience in networking, business development, and training.
- Work well under pressure in demanding, time-sensitive environments.
- Achieved reputation for "getting the job done."
- Highly adept in developing productive internal and external business development and referral channels.

PROFESSIONAL EXPERIENCE

1999 - Present

Takeshima Electronics, Los Angeles, CA   Sales Support Representative

- Furnish product specifications in response to inquiries.
- Achieved reputation for matching product offerings to customer needs.

1994 - 1999

Professional Video, Los Angeles, CA

Fast-track promotions through a series of increasingly responsible positions.

Production & Sales Coordinator / Account Executive   1995 - 1999

- Successfully directed and coordinated high-caliber efforts to both expand and maximize company's market presence while strengthening market awareness.
- Arranged for media coverage in the trade press. Coordinated large mailings to announce acquisition of the latest state-of-the-art technology.
- Posted information to ensure mention in relevant magazine articles.
- Arranged for company presence at important trade shows. Assessed and evaluated new equipment's ability to meet upcoming needs.

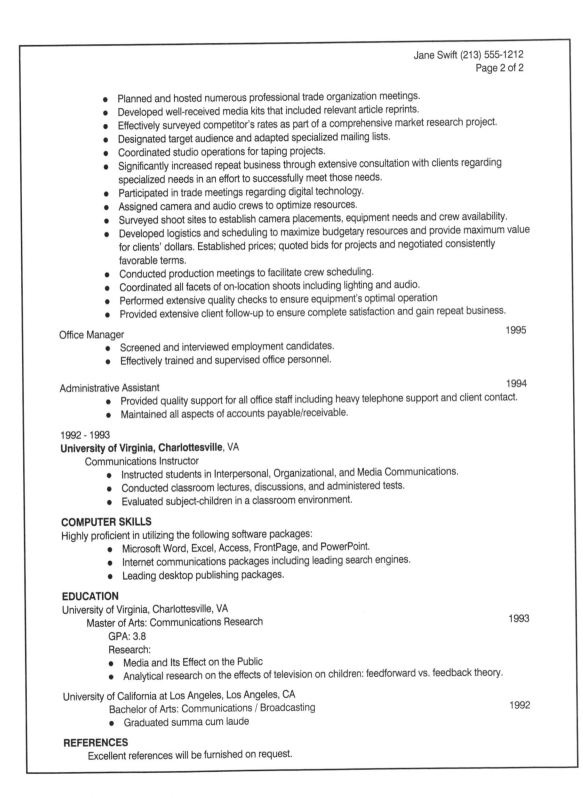

- Planned and hosted numerous professional trade organization meetings.
- Developed well-received media kits that included relevant article reprints.
- Effectively surveyed competitor's rates as part of a comprehensive market research project.
- Designated target audience and adapted specialized mailing lists.
- Coordinated studio operations for taping projects.
- Significantly increased repeat business through extensive consultation with clients regarding specialized needs in an effort to successfully meet those needs.
- Participated in trade meetings regarding digital technology.
- Assigned camera and audio crews to optimize resources.
- Surveyed shoot sites to establish camera placements, equipment needs and crew availability.
- Developed logistics and scheduling to maximize budgetary resources and provide maximum value for clients' dollars. Established prices; quoted bids for projects and negotiated consistently favorable terms.
- Conducted production meetings to facilitate crew scheduling.
- Coordinated all facets of on-location shoots including lighting and audio.
- Performed extensive quality checks to ensure equipment's optimal operation
- Provided extensive client follow-up to ensure complete satisfaction and gain repeat business.

Office Manager 1995
- Screened and interviewed employment candidates.
- Effectively trained and supervised office personnel.

Administrative Assistant 1994
- Provided quality support for all office staff including heavy telephone support and client contact.
- Maintained all aspects of accounts payable/receivable.

1992 - 1993
University of Virginia, Charlottesville, VA
Communications Instructor
- Instructed students in Interpersonal, Organizational, and Media Communications.
- Conducted classroom lectures, discussions, and administered tests.
- Evaluated subject-children in a classroom environment.

COMPUTER SKILLS
Highly proficient in utilizing the following software packages:
- Microsoft Word, Excel, Access, FrontPage, and PowerPoint.
- Internet communications packages including leading search engines.
- Leading desktop publishing packages.

EDUCATION
University of Virginia, Charlottesville, VA
Master of Arts: Communications Research 1993
GPA: 3.8
Research:
- Media and Its Effect on the Public
- Analytical research on the effects of television on children: feedforward vs. feedback theory.

University of California at Los Angeles, Los Angeles, CA
Bachelor of Arts: Communications / Broadcasting 1992
- Graduated summa cum laude

REFERENCES
Excellent references will be furnished on request.

Corporate Taxation

Jane Swift
9 Central Avenue
Ypsilanti, MI 48187
(734) 555-1212
Jane@careerbrain.com
Page 1 of 2

A highly experienced tax professional with comprehensive skills in corporate taxation. Offers 6 years of combined experience in corporate tax management, tax preparation, and budgeting. Proficient in analyzing complex tax issues, multistate income tax returns, and streamlining effectiveness and efficiency of tax management. Currently manages all state corporate tax functions of a company exceeding $250 million in sales. Reputation of a hard working and dedicated employee.

AREAS OF EXPERTISE

SBT, C-Corporation and S-Corporation State Income Tax Returns • Vehicle Use Tax Returns • State Income Tax Budgeting and Accrual • Multistate Property Tax Returns • Federal, State, and Local Exemption Certificates • State and Local Sales, Use and Excise Tax Management • Tax Audit Management • Tax License and Bonding Maintenance • Certificates of Authority and Annual Report Filing Maintenance • State Sales and Use Tax Assessment • Federal Excise Tax Collection and Deposits • Determination of Nexus • Tax Amnesty Programs

CAREER HIGHLIGHTS AND ACHIEVEMENTS

- Identified double-paid federal excise tax; resulted in federal excise tax refund of $60,000+ and 10,000+ interest
- Reversed $75,000 proposed tax assessment including penalties and interest; provided auditor appropriate documentation necessary to reverse proposed tax assessment
- Saved an estimated $10,000 in interest/penalties by filing for tax amnesty in various states
- Designed database of all applicable federal, state, and local fuel, sales, and environmental taxes—ability to price fuel with all applicable taxes at over 700 locations nationwide
- "Self-disclosed" $200,000+ fuel tax liability to taxing authority; collected 100% of tax from customer and paid tax without penalty and interest
- Manage thousands of federal, state, and local sales, use, and excise tax exemption certificates on products purchased exempt from suppliers and sold exempt to customers
- Implemented new process of filing all property tax returns for fixed assets saving the company $1,500+ in the first year
- Succeeded in creating a comprehensive database detailing multistate S-Corporation income tax filing requirements for federally elected S-Corporation, Qualified Subchapter S Subsidiary (QSSS), and nonresident shareholders

COMPUTER EFFICIENCY

In-depth knowledge of Microsoft Word, Excel, Lotus, various tax and accounting software programs, Macintosh, Internet, and e-mail

PROFESSIONAL EXPERIENCE

Finance Corporation - Ypsilanti, Michigan
Associate Tax Director (1998 - Present)
1993 - Present

- Manage filing of nearly 100 C-Corporations, S-Corporations, and composite returns including nonresident income tax returns for out of state shareholders
- File annual federal excise tax liability between $36 and $40 million
- Execute quarterly federal excise tax refund of nearly $100,000 each quarter
- Budget and accrue state income tax liability (1998: $250,000)
- Assess state sales and use tax of 500+ components of leased equipment nationwide

Tax Coordinator (1994 - 1998)
- Automated billings for parts department to bill correct amount of sales/use tax
- Instructed accounting department on scope of corporate taxation
- Managed 25,000+ client accounts and 500 vendor accounts with appropriate federal, state, and local fuel, sales, use and environmental taxes
- Assessed state sales and use tax on all labor, replacement parts, and freight related to leased equipment

Credit Card Supervisor (1993 - 1994)
- Managed operations and supervised 4 employees within department
- Handled inquiries regarding accounts and assisted clients
- Designed first comprehensive reference manual issued to clients detailing credit card process

OTHER WORK EXPERIENCE (During College)
Financed 100% of Schooling
- Chili's Restaurant - Ypsilanti, Michigan 1991 - 1993
     Waiter/Trainer
- Bill Knapps Restaurant - Ypsilanti, Michigan 1987 - 1991
     Waiter

EDUCATION
Eastern Michigan University - Ypsilanti, Michigan
Bachelor of Business Administration (Double Major) - Accounting, 1993 • Finance, 1991
Master of Business Administration Degree Program in progress

CERTIFICATION
Notary Public - Expiration 2003

Credit Analyst

Jane Swift
9 Central Avenue
Yonkers, NY 10701
(914) 555-1212
Jane@careerbrain.com

Branch Manager
Credit Analyst/Commercial Credit/Consumer Credit/Credit Administration/Credit Management/
Lending Office/Finance and Budgeting/Personnel Manager

Strong commitment to excellence. Dynamic presentation, communication, and marketing skills. Distinguished performance encompassing a steady advancement of increasing accomplishments resulting in fast-track promotion and progressively responsible banking duties. Motivated, results-oriented individual. Excellent planning, organizational, development and leadership qualifications. High-impact negotiator, spokesperson, and client service manager.

Professional Experience

ABC Financial, Regional Credit Manager: Manage 30 employees covering a tri-state region. Analyze competitor programs and develop marketing strategies for competitive market positioning to increase market share. Communicate effectively with dealers to initiate, develop, and maintain customer relationships and client satisfaction. Reporting, record keeping, and documentation of business deals, self audits, and budget control. Manage and track funding goals of credit analysts. Performance management of staff through effective training and evaluations. Conduct regular staff meeting and communicate company policy and procedures. Design, development, and implementation of effective succession plan to reduce staff turnover. (1998 - present)

Regional Branch Manager: Managed 16 employees covering the entire East Coast. Regulated and coordinated all aspects of branch operation to achieve volume and profit goals. Managed branch operation within established guidelines and budget parameters. Scope of responsibilities included lending, collections, marketing and sales, administration and personnel. Hired organized, trained, and evaluated personnel in all phases of branch operations. Motivated production while organizing marketing activities and strategies in a changing market. Facilitated monthly market, projection, and production reports for Senior and Regional Vice Presidents. Generated quality customer service and ongoing customer loyalty. (1997 - 1998)

Assistant Manager: Evaluated and reviewed credit applications submitted by auto dealerships for credit line and contract purchase in accordance with company policy. Supervised office staff to ensure company policy and procedures. Performance management, training, and evaluation of personnel. (1994 - 1997)

Northeast Bank, Loan Officer/Credit Analyst: Conducted all aspects of consumer and commercial lending. Cultivated and maintained customer relationships through quality customer service. Promoted from entry level trainee to Associate Loan Officer to Loan Officer/Credit Analyst within a 2-year period. Scope of responsibilities included cash flow, credit, financial statements, and budget spreadsheet analysis. (1992 - 1994)

Licenses and Education
Licensed Real Estate Agent (1995 - Present), Bachelor of Arts, Economics, University of Texas (1992)

Volunteer Work
Meals on Wheels, Big Sister

Credit and Collections

Jane Swift
9 Central Avenue
Charlotte, NC 28210

(704) 555-1212
Jane@careerbrain.com

Profile
- Results-oriented, hands-on financial manager with experience in accounting administration/cash management.
- Demonstrated success in analyzing business needs and providing effective financial processes to increase cash flow and reduce operating expenses.
- Tenacious, with commitment to needs analyses, timeliness, accuracy, and detail.
- Won award for creating and implementing a significant cost savings plan.
- Excellent supervisory and staff developing skills, and ability to effectively partner with management at all levels.
- Consistently strong record of performance demonstrated by promotions to increasingly responsible positions.

Areas of Expertise
- billing & auditing
- credit & collections
- financial reporting
- hiring & training
- project management
- systems development
- budgets & re-estimates
- general ledger
- bad debt reserve
- policies & procedures
- revenue & cash forecasting
- contract negotiation

Technical Skills
- MS Excel, Word, Lotus 1-2-3, WordPerfect, PowerPoint, Access, Computron, Vertex, mainframe system

Experience & Selected Accomplishments
Major Cable Company

Cash & Revenue Director	(1998 to present)
Accounting Administration Director	(1995 to 1998)
Midwestern Region Credit & Collection Manager	(1990 to 1995)

- Direct 31 employees, including 5 managers and 5 senior analysts; responsible for billing, auditing, general accounting, accounts receivable, cash forecasting, and collections totaling $1.2B of annual revenue.
- Created and implemented internal collection process that improved cash flow by $1.2M and reduced collection agency expenses by $180K in the first year.
- Provided core subscription revenue variance analyses and reports to senior management; prepared annual estimates and deviations from budget.
- Handled all banking relations; negotiated contracts; established credit card accounts.
- Formalized the review of $25M contractual liability fund; successfully reduced that liability to $11M.
- Decentralized operational controls to call centers, effecting staff reduction of 50% and cost savings of $100K.
- Created analytic process to facilitate strategic business decisions regarding profitability of market segments.
- Designed and implemented the first two automated billing systems in company's history.
- Developed and implemented accounts receivable system that improved efficiency by 50%; reduced staff by 20%.
- Devised tracking system to evaluate effectiveness and efficiency of internal audit department.
- Collaborated with CFO to establish management reports to routinely track and project subscriber trends vs. budget.

National Credit & Collection Account Manager	(1988 to 1990)
Analyst	(1986 to 1988)
Accounts Receivable Assistant	(1984 to 1986)

Education and Training
Courses taken: Effective Management, Professional Selling Skills, Dale Carnegie
University of North Carolina, Charlotte, Pursuing degree in Business Administration; anticipated completion, 2001

Customer Service Manager

JAMES SHARPE
9 CENTRAL AVENUE, MIAMI, FL 33152. (305) 555-1212, James@careerbrain.com

EXPERIENCE

CUSTOMER SERVICE MANAGER

A TELECOMMUNICATIONS SATELLITE COMPANY   5-00 to Present

Hired and developed a staff of forty people to service the customer service needs of our highest revenue commercial accounts. Maintained an account retention percentage of 99%, while keeping revenue loss through credits to less than 2%.

CUSTOMER SERVICE - TELEMARKETING MANAGER

MCI - S.E. Region Customer Service Center, Miami, FL   3-98 to 5-00

Hired and developed a staff of sixty customer service - telemarketing representatives and supervisors.

Managed a mixture of inbound and outbound call activities with job responsibilities including: sales, customer service, customer correspondence and special projects.

Responsible for a budget of close to one million dollars.

CUSTOMER SERVICE SUPERVISOR

NYNEX, New York, NY   1-97 to 3-98

Supervision of a division customer service staff. Responsibilities include: providing support for our sales force and sales management, implementing new policy and procedures for customer service, and monitoring to see that all our sales and service objectives are met.

CUSTOMER SERVICE REPRESENTATIVE

NYNEX   6-92 to 1-97

Involved in all aspects of customer service, including: answering questions, problem solving, interfacing with our sales force, and working with new customers to implement SPRINT services.

EDUCATION

B.A. 1992, Florida State University.

TRAINING

Leadership and Management of Change. Results Oriented Management. Managing Management Time.

REFERENCES AVAILABLE ON REQUEST

Electrical Design Engineer

Jane Swift
9 Central Avenue
Wilton, CT 21234
(203) 555-1212
Jane@careerbrain.com

CAREER
OBJECTIVE: Development and Design of Digital and Analog equipment.

SUMMARY: Experienced with TTL, ECL, GaAs, programmable arrays, and microprocessors. Familiar with RS-232, IEEE-488, and manchester code interfaces. Analog design included Op-Amps, D/A's, A/D's, multiplexers, and sample/holds. Secret clearance.

EXPERIENCE:
1994-Present   *ELECTRICAL ENGINEER (SIKORSKY, CT)*

Designed digital and analog equipment for Avionic Fuel Measurement and Management Systems. Prime flight hardware and support test equipment designs include:

> *Analog Signal Conditioner* - Unit to condition analog and digital signals provided to flight system computers. Design employed D/A converters, active filters, and digital logic.

> *Digital Display Indicator* - Indicator displayed fuel quantity information to ground crew. Design consisted of LCD displays, digital logic, and self-contained power supply. Dealt with small packaging requirements.

> *Analog Tester* - Designed support test equipment to perform Acceptance Tests on Analog Signal Conditioner.

> *Digital Tester* - Designed support test equipment to perform Acceptance Test on Digital Display Indicator.

1987-1993   *DESIGN ENGINEER (SIMMONDS PRECISION, VT)*

Member of circuit design group. Responsible for the design and debugging of various analog and digital circuits/systems. Responsibilities included:

> Video processing portion of a radar pulse processing system. Included work with video amplifiers, track/hold amplifiers, and the high-speed A/D convertors, as well as TTL (ALS, FAST, LS), and other high-speed logic.

> A servo-controller that used programmable array logic, TTL, Op-Amps, and D/A convertors.

> A spread spectrum radio that used high-speed TTL (FAST), programmable array logic, and a 16-bit microprocessor, with a custom interface and a RS-232 interface.

EDUCATION: Old Dominion University, Norfolk, VA
B.S.E.E., cum laude

Electrician

James Sharpe
9 Central Avenue
Metairie, LA 70002
(504) 555-1212
James@careerbrain.com

SUMMARY

Master Electrician (licensed in Louisiana A-15346). Experienced in all types of electrical work—residential, commercial, industrial, electrical construction, and estimating. Six years' management experience as a Foreman.

EXPERIENCE
1996 to present

Cajun Electric—Metairie, Master Electrician
Responsible for all sales, estimating, work scheduling, billing, ordering of parts and equipment, maintenance of inventories, and customer service. Projects have included complete wiring of a manufacturing business after relocation, new home construction, repair of equipment, building additions. Have worked as a contractor and subcontractor.

1996

Industrial Light—New Orleans. Journeyman Electrician
Foreman on medium-sized projects, with crews of 2 to 10. Scheduled the work, checked quality and productivity, provided layouts and supervision.

1994

Prudhomme & Sons—New Orleans. Journeyman Electrician
Crew member on construction of the New Orleans Sheraton.

1993

Bechte—Saudi Arabia. Journeyman Electrician
Worked on a nuclear power plant (heavy industrial project), where safety and reliability were extremely important.

1991 to 1992

Tujaques—New Orleans. Journeyman Electrician
A variety of commercial and industrial projects (hospital, high-rise condominiums, office-hotel complex).

TRAINING

Louisiana Technical College, New Orleans
Certificate in Completion of Apprenticeship program

PERSONAL

Willing to travel, relocate

References Available

Entrepreneurial

Jane Swift

9 Central Avenue   Yardley, Pennsylvania 19067   (H) (215) 555-1212   (O) (215) 555-1213
Jane@careerbrain.com

QUALIFICATIONS SUMMARY
Human Resource Management
Program Development, Recruitment, Training, Quality Process Management

EXPERIENCE

Philadelphia College of Textiles and Science, Philadelphia, Pennsylvania   1993 to Present

Director, Career Planning and Placement   1998 to Present
Liaison between college and industry, building international reputation through development of the following support and services:

- Direct professional staff of three, semi-professional staff of 10 and $175,000 operating budget in providing comprehensive placement service for 3,000 BS students, 250 MBA students, and alumni.
- Develop network of corporate and government employers within Business, High Tech, Creative, and Science areas.
- Annually achieve 90% placement of graduates, and hundreds of alumni at management level.
- Market on-campus recruiting program resulting in over 200 companies visiting each season.
- Host VIP campus visits and receptions.
- Extensive travel includes organizing and supervising trade shows, attending conferences, visiting industry.
- Provide input for academic program development through analysis of industry trends.
- Initiated seminar and workshop programs covering all aspects of career planning and search.
- Publish bi-monthly nationally circulated <u>Job Opportunities Bulletin</u>, <u>Annual Placement and Salary Survey</u>, <u>Resume Book</u>, and <u>Student Handbook on Placement</u>.
- Supervise internship and summer job programs for undergraduates.
- Directed software development and computerization of department, 1993.

Assistant Director, Placement Office   1993 to 1998

INVOLVEMENTS

- Selected for Task Force, Middle States evaluation for college accreditation, 2000.
- Visited/consulted with South African organizations on recruitment program development, 1999.
- Member, College Placement Council.
- Member, Middle Atlantic Placement Association.
- Past Chairman of Membership, Publicity and Office Training Committees.
- Published articles for trade journals, appear on media, conference speaker.
- Volunteer, Freedoms Foundation of America at Valley Forge.
- Member, Toastmasters International.
- Member, Colony Civic Organization, West Norriton, Pennsylvania.
- Accomplished Photographer, enjoy painting.

EDUCATION
PHILADELPHIA COLLEGE OF TEXTILES AND SCIENCE
Evening Division, 1993 to 1998, Marketing/Management
Numerous Technical and Business Seminars
Executive Management Program
Werner Management Consultants, 2000

Entry-Level Advertising Sales

Jane Swift
9 Central Avenue
Akron, OH 44303
(216) 555-1212
Jane@careerbrain.com

Strengths: Enthusiastic, creative, and hard working advertising major with demonstrated successful sales experience. Reputation for providing excellent customer service resulting in increased sales and improved customer retention. Eager to translate solid classroom and internship experience in advertising sales into bottom-line revenues in the radio/television industry.

Education: B.S. in Advertising, Case Western Reserve University, Cleveland, OH - May, 2000. Coursework included advertising research & strategy, design & graphics, media planning, ad sales & campaigns.

Senior Project
- *Challenge:* Create an advertising campaign for the Ohio Hospice Group.
- *Action:* As key member of a 6-person team, performed demographics survey, developed campaign strategies, created logo and slogan, authored and designed bilingual brochures, and created media kit within $250,000 budget.
- *Result:* After presenting project to 11-person panel, won first place out of 12 teams. The Ohio Hospice Group implemented the slogan and several campaign strategies.

Internships
Advertising Sales Representative, Great Lakes Advertising, Cleveland, OH, Sept. - Dec. 1999
- Sold print advertising to local businesses using cold calling techniques.

Production Assistant, TV5 (NBC affiliate), Akron, OH, Jan. - May 1999
- Assisted with production of 2 to 3 commercials a week. Accountable for delivering all technical equipment to the site and pre-production set up of lights, monitors, microphones, and cameras. Worked closely with sales department and producer, learning both the technical side of commercial production as well as sales and customer service issues.
- Handled pre-production and on-air tasks for the noon news, including studio set up, script delivery, running pre-taped segments during the news, operating on-air cameras and soundboards.

Sales/Customer Service Experience
Sales/Wait Staff, Great Lakes Brewpub, Cleveland, OH
- Consistently generate additional revenues utilizing thorough product knowledge and friendly sales technique to up sell house specials and add-on items. Contender for the "$1,000 Night" sales award.

Host/Wait Staff, Jack's Seafood, Mentor, OH
- Developed repeat business by providing excellent customer service in fast-paced environment.

Awards/Memberships
- Won Silver Addy, an annual award for college students, 1999
- Served as Co-Director of Adwerks, developing ads for nonprofit organizations, 1998
- Member and committee chairperson of the Ad Society, a college professional organization, 1998 - 2000

Equipment Sales

James Sharpe
9 Central Avenue
Lakewood, CO 80228
(303) 555-1212
James@careerbrain.com

Experience Summary

More than 15 years customer/sales experience delivering impressive results in diverse markets and industries.
Strengths include:

- Technical sales
- Banking products and services
- Contract negotiations
- Needs-specific account service
- Customer satisfactions
- Account management

Professional Experience

Customer Service/Sales Representative, Ruth's Automotive, 1998 - Present

- Secure and service field accounts. Expand customer base and increase quarterly sales 20% by winning prominent accounts. Close sales by offering unique incentives and using sales strategies to counter pricing objections. Assume control of poorly serviced accounts and rebuild relationships with customers. Prevent loss of sale by expediting turnaround time for processing product requests.
- Surpassed collections quota by 150%. Collected on difficult accounts by negotiating payment arrangements, employing refined techniques, and adhering to company policies.

Senior Technical Sales Representative, Office Electrix, 1988 - 1998

- Drove profitability of a nationally renowned retailer through consistent sales of high-dollar industrial equipment.
- Built long-term relationships and increased sales by persuading customers to purchase warranty contracts.
- Instrumental in securing multimillion dollar contracts from hotels, businesses, and property owners.
- Transformed inexperienced reps into skilled technicians through comprehensive hands-on training.
- Only technical sales rep out of 19 retail locations qualified to service industrial A/C units.

Education & Training

- Certificate, Medical Biller, Rockies Careers, Denver, Colorado
- Certificate, Computer Technology, Institute of Data Technology, Denver, Colorado; Coursework: Troubleshooting, Diagnostics, Computer Language
- Degree Program, Mechanical Engineering, Colorado University

Technical Expertise & Additional Information

- Proficient in Windows 98, MS Word, and data entry
- Designed propulsions system for motorbikes (patent pending)

Executive Assistant Legal/Medical

Jane Swift
9 Central Avenue
Wilmington, DE 19850
(302) 555-1212
Jane@careerbrain.com
Page 1 of 2

Career and Personal Profile

Assist senior management in daily operation of independent insurance adjusting firm. Provide expert and confidential executive support and office management for attorneys, physicians, and insurance companies trial preparation. Simultaneously coordinate trial prep for four or five attorneys and a half-dozen trials.
Energetic, focused, and self-directed. Excel in meeting objectives using independent action, prioritization, persistence, and leadership skills. Adapt quickly to diverse management and client styles. Use humor, positive attitude, continuous training, and high standards to motivate staff to excellence.

Areas of Knowledge

- Executive office administration
- Fast-paced calendar scheduling
- Executive-level correspondence
- Time-sensitive assignments
- Supply-inventory and purchasing
- Staff training and mentoring

- Advanced computer applications
- Confidential materials management
- Complex trial preparations
- Investigative activities
- Accounts payable/receivable
- Notary Public, 1998

Professional Highlights

- Directly contribute to company' performance by offering expertise, reliability, and continuity in office procedures, setting clear communication lines between clients and company, and managing all office activities on a day-to-day basis.
- Manage complex time constraints due to position's multitask orientation including secretarial, billing, accounts receivable/payable, and purchasing functions as well as all facets of trial preparation work.
- Use excellent communication skills to fulfill liaison nature of position, developing cordial working relationships with attorneys, physicians, insurance representatives, and expert witnesses—a crucial part of booking time-driven people who need to be "persuaded" to fit trial work into tight schedules.
- Handle all minor and major purchases, continually doing comparisons for best value. Generated thousands of dollars in savings by researching and purchasing a cost-effective alternative to a Pitney Bows mailing machine.
- Convinced management to fully computerize office. Researched other attorney's systems, spoke to their office managers, found good sources, and made decision on custom-built system.
- Initiated computerized system for processing subpoenas and for gathering investigative data from Motor Vehicle Department. Partner with Virginia office to locate trial participants through databases. Developed specific forms for many types of legal papers, and made affidavit of service.

Computer Skills

- Windows 3.1/95/98.
- MS Word, WordPerfect, Quicken, and a variety of industry-specific software.
- Dictaphone transcription.

Employment

Office Manager/Executive Assistant, Eastern Adjustment   1997 to present
Independent insurance adjusters, based in Delaware and Virginia, with gross revenues in excess of $1 million. Company currently handles trial preparation for various law firms defending physicians in malpractice, and adjusts auto claims on behalf of various insurance carriers. Eastern's previous focus was product liability and medical malpractice investigations for insurance carriers. Company acts as a liaison between attorneys and various types of clients. Report directly to senior management; work independently on a daily basis.

Administration Activities
- Manage comprehensive day-to-day office operations.
- Maintain computer systems and confidential records.
- Create and support databases, word processing, and reports.
- Exercise discretion regarding confidential records.
- Train employees for office programs and procedures.
- Field continual stream of phone calls while maintaining flow of daily activities.
- Monitor all bank accounts and investments.
- Pay all bills, do bank deposits, track all invoices and expenses.
- Trial Preparation Activities
- Often manage several cases concurrently.
- Provide meticulous follow-up through all stages.
- Interface with lawyers, physicians, insurance companies, and firm's principals.
- Prepare subpoenas.
- Arrange scheduling for expert testimonies.
- Transcribe case notes.
- Notify all parties regarding trial date and coordinate availabilities.
- Locate physicians for physicals and expert witnesses.
- Set up meetings with physicians and other participants.
- Make travel arrangements.
- Type/fax memos to all parties and law firms.
- Track case for life of situation.
- Provide continual follow-up spanning months/years until final disposition.

Education
Secretarial Science courses, Delaware State University
WordPerfect I and II, Wilmington Junior College

Executive Management

James Sharpe
9 Central Avenue
San Diego, CA 92101
(619) 555-1212
James@careerbrain.com
Page 1 of 2

Executive Management • Financial/Business Analysis • Consulting
Energy, Aviation, and High-Tech Computer/Telecom/Internet Industries

Profile

Dynamic, achievement-focused leader and manager with an established performance record and expertise in the energy and aviation industries, special interest in the high-tech industries. Couple strong analytical skills with core qualifications in accounting and administration to drive efficiency, productivity, and financial performance improvements.

Areas of Strength

Financial & Business Analysis	Organizational Re-engineering
Process Improvement	Team Building & Leadership
Energy Accounting	Project Management
Public Speaking / Presentations	Instruction / Training

Professional Highlights

Silvestri Oil and Gas, Inc., San Diego, CA   1998 - Present
   Petroleum exploration and production company operating oil and gas wells in 3 states and managing outside operated investments in a 5-state region.
   MANAGER, NEW BUSINESS VENTURES
      Senior manager with an expansive scope of responsibilities including execution of accounting, reporting, and financial functions for all operations, serving as key liaison to field operational personnel, and evaluation and coordination of prospective investments.
   Key Results
   • Streamlined administrative and reporting functions and enhanced GAAP and COPAS accounting compliance; cut costs through improvements to efficiency and increased investors' rates of return.
   • Renewed investors' faith in investment management capabilities by demonstrating improved accounting and reporting processes; elevated the company's status when proposing large projects to investors.
   • Championed the consolidation of Silvestri's 3 separate companies into a single company; dramatically improved efficiency by eliminating redundant administrative tasks.
   • Re-engineered the Production Department for optimal efficiency; introduced computerized accounting and reporting and developed automated performance monitoring systems. Saved labor costs by eliminating and reducing staff positions.
   • Led the turnaround of the Accounting Department; redesigned processes and systems for efficiency and brought all accounts current less than 90 days from inception.

United States Navy   1989 - 1998
   OFFICER and AVIATOR
      Distinguished 9-year military career, progressing rapidly through a series of performance-based advancements. Qualified as an F-16CJ Instructor Pilot, F-14A Strike Fighter Weapons and Tactics Instructor/Mission Commander, and TA-4J Advanced Jet Instructor. Total 1747 flight hours.

Representative Achievements
- Served in a variety management roles including Flight Commander, Assistant Operations Officer, Deputy Chief of Weapons, and Public Affairs Officer.
- Earned a reputation among commanding officers as one of the Navy's top fighter pilots. Hand-picked from elite teams of professionals for many demanding, critical, short notice missions.
- Recipient of more than a dozen prestigious military awards for superior service and performance, including the Meritorious Service Medal, Navy Achievement Medal, Gold Star, Air Medal, and Aerial Achievement Medal among others.
- Selected for the rare and notable honor of representing the Navy as an exchange pilot with the USAF 77th Fighter Squadron.
- Planned and managed many special projects designed to improve pilot training programs, streamline administrative tasks, and maximize squadron performance.
- Consistently selected for advanced responsibility ahead of peers based upon proven ability to deliver combined with superior leadership, management, technical, and tactical skills.

Education & Training
B.S.B.A., Economics, Cum Laude
University of Arizona, 1989
Academic Honors
- Distinguished Naval Graduate
- Business School Marshall
- Golden Key National Honor Society

Recent Additional Training
Oil and Gas Accounting, Modern Petroleum,
Microsoft Networking Essentials,
Microsoft Office, and Advanced Microsoft Excel
FAA Licensed Commercial Multi-Engine Pilot

Computer Skills
Advanced computer skills with MS Office (Word, Excel, and PowerPoint). Demonstrated ability in applying technology to improve organizational efficiency and productivity. Extensive experience developing custom Excel applications and forms and preparing PowerPoint presentations and lectures.

Executive Marketing/Sales

JAMES SHARPE

9 Central Avenue • *Venetia, Pennsylvania 15367* • *(412) 555-1212* • *James@careerbrain.com*

Executive Summary

A fast-track, highly motivated, team oriented executive with a successful background in **turnaround situations.** *More than 8 years progressive experience in all phases of* **HMO Market Development** *and* **Regional Sales Management.** *Recognized for exceptional ability to develop specialized marketing stratagems, sales methods, and training procedures. Effectively motivates others on all levels in the achievement of individual and organizational goals.*

- P & L Responsibility
- Sales Management
- Market Optimization
- Marketing/Advertising Strategy
- Training Module Development
- Benefits Program Development
- Operations Management
- Interpersonal Relations
- Provider Contracting

Selected Achievements

- *Orchestrated the turnaround of the Pittsburgh region through the creation and introduction of a prototype Medicare Risk Marketing Program which set the standard for all other* **Health Associates** *Regions.*
- *Developed and implemented sales management and advertising/marketing strategies resulting in a 260% increase in sales, from $71 million to $185 million in 1995, thus tripling profitability.*
- *Facilitated successful negotiations with Key Providers & Hospitals increasing the Primary Physician Network from 225 to 700.*
- *In just one year boosted* **Health Associates** *net membership from 40,000 to 80,000 and Medicare net membership from 2,200 to 17,000, achieving 100% and 775% increases, respectively.*
- *Developed and implemented competitive training modules ultimately utilized company-wide. Initiated the management team's supervision of all marketing and sales representatives thus assuring full compliance and a successful continuing educational process.*
- *Spearheaded new business development in Boston, a highly penetrated managed care market, and increased regional sales from $9 million to $90 million as well as net membership from 5,000 to 50,000.*

Employment History

Regional Vice President   **1998 to Present**
  Health Associates, Pittsburgh, Pennsylvania

District New Business Sales Manager   **1993 to 1998**
  Health Associates, Boston, Massachusetts

Account Executive   **1991 to 1993**
  Health Associates, New York, New York

Education

Bachelor of Science, Education/Mathematics, 1990
Cortland State College, Cortland, New York

Finance Executive

James Sharpe
9 Central Avenue
Nashville, TN 37211
(615) 555-1212
James@careerbrain.com
Page 1 of 2

Professional Profile

Corporate Finance Executive and troubleshooting specialist with a command of operations, organization, and general management. Expert competence in financial planning and analysis, cost reduction, and performance/profit improvement. Excellent qualifications in managing large-scale projects from concept through planning, design, development, and task management. Detail-oriented and analytical. Experience in the areas of:

> economic analysis • forecasting and budgeting • staffing and management • quality and finance control • sales and marketing programs • revenue management • team building and leadership • customer development • project management • strategic planning • competitive pricing analysis • diversity strategies

Performance Highlights

- Orchestrated a winning partnership between Service Parts Operations and other divisions. Supported $1.3 billion in annual sales business; reviewed all finance issues, provided profit & loss analysis, collaborated with six divisions to consummate alliance.
- Developed a $2 billion, five-year integrated business plan for partnership retention that included projected volume, sales, and business performance initiatives with the objective to establish profitable targets.
- Facilitated the business plan portion of "Troubled Products" initiative (unfavorable operating profit). Generated support to make the product lines more profitable ($57 million in favorable profits) in areas of manufacturing, distribution, pricing, and other customer-driven incentives.
- Secured approval on numerous sales and marketing proposals/programs on behalf of corporate aftermarket sales staff. Made presentations on significant programs (exceeding $500K in operating profit impact) to the Price & Policy Review Group.
- Managed a zero-based budget as Staff Assistant to the Regional Personnel Director. Project included a $30 million operating budget (400+ security personnel, doctors, nurses, and personnel benefits administration) in 11 divisions. Created budges and forecasts for the area Personnel Directors.
- Managed various functional financial departments (Budgets, Forecasts, payroll, Cost Accounting, Accounts Receivable, Audit, and Accounts Payable).
- Currently coordinating project to achieve market-based competitive prices (excess of $70 million) on aftermarket parts from suppliers.
- Experienced international traveler.
- Knowledge of conversational French; learning Swahili.

Education

Eastern Tennessee University, Masters of Science, Business Management (*Cum Laude*)
Tennessee State University, Bachelor of Science, Business Administration (*Magna Cum Laude*)

Experience

Saturn Motor Corporation, Finance Manager--Service Operation   *1999 - Present*

- Manage the Pricing and Product Programs Group; review, analyze, and report on proposals; support the sales & marketing staff; supervise and develop employees; ensure that profitability goals are met in the aftermarket channel; ensure that people development is consistent with diversity strategy; serve as financial liaison to other staffs/divisions.
- Provide financial analysis and impact on the corporation and customers; supply distribution analysis and make corporate decisions on value-added proposals.
- Currently working on introducing product lines at a national retailer/installer. Proposed package has an projected annual sales of $15 million in the first year and $80 million in the third year, with a margin of 10–15%. Process includes P&L analysis, customer/distributor partner interface, implementation using cross-functional workgroups, and 12–15 new product launches.
- Pricing/Product Programs and Market Support initiatives/objectives include:
  - Improve staff efficiency/manage head count (41 employees); implement synchronous improvements.
  - Skills enhancement/employee development; apply cross-training initiatives.
  - Strategic/action-oriented analysis; administer channel/product line/customer profitability reporting processes; utilize common processes.
  - Enhance partnership reporting; interact with divisions to establish integrated business plan and establish profitability targets for product lines.
  - Conduct competitive price analyses, family pricing, life-cycle model strategies, elasticity analyses, profitability analysis to identify opportunities.

Regional Workforce Unit, Staff Assistant   *1997 - 1999*

Developed budget and forecasts. Monitored and recorded expenses. Presented statistical data on costs, head counts, and initiatives to 11 area Personnel Directors. Coordinated billing of actual costs. Performed actual vs. forecast analysis.

Automotive Glass Plant, General Supervisor   *1995 - 1997*

Responsibilities encompassed operations analysis, payroll, receivables, and disbursement analysis; supervised 14 direct reports. Developed annual budgets and monthly plant reports; performed ad hoc analyses; reported on actual vs. budget performance. Managed all payroll, receivables and disbursement analysis liaison activities. Supervised and monitored annual $30 million inventory at glass production facility. Chief financial person who ensured accurate physical inventory count (worked with outside accounting firm of Price Waterhouse).

Manufacturing Plant, Supervisor/Accountant/Senior Clerk   *1993 - 1995*

Managed supplier disbursement payments and the audit department. Developed plant operating budget for the Maryville Engine Plant. Group leader for 40 employees in accounts payable. Generated production material cost forecasts; managed capital expenditures; recorded and audited special inventories; reconciled general ledger accounts, developed inventory forecast; journalized sales and cost of sale entries.

Finance Trust Administration

James Sharpe
9 Central Avenue
Madison, WI 53708
(608) 555-1212
James@careerbrain.com

Career Summary
A dedicated finance professional with 17 years experience in trust administration and operations. Expert analytical and technical skills. Continually monitor, update skills and maintain compliance with industry and government regulations. Highly efficient, able to read and understand complex legal documents while quickly determining most important details. Strong customer relationship management skills, driven to provide same day, high-quality service.

Experience
First National Trust, Princeton, New Jersey   1983 - Present
Assistant Vice President, Corporate Trust Bond Administration (1993 - Present)
Administer, according to governing documents, a broad portfolio of corporate trust appointments including bond trusteeships, municipal bonds, and corporate escrows. Properly invest $100 million in assets and maintain $1 billion in debt issues. Consult and work closely with bond counsels, financial advisors, and underwriters. Review and execute agreements; represent First National at closing. Develop new business and maintain strong relationships with existing clientele.

> Achievements
> - Successfully managed transfers of 4,000+ accounts when First National acquired another trust organization.
> - Headed up 3-person departmental restructure that transferred responsibility along functional rather than product lines, resulting in increased efficiencies and cost savings.
> - Developed strong industry network, allowing for timely responses to customers' inquiries.

Systems Administrator (1988 - 1993)
Oversaw all bond and stock processing for the Corporate Trust Department including administration of entire bondholders' database. Identified and solved process problems and conducted meetings to improve operational efficiency. Hired, trained, and supervised staff. Developed job standards, action plans, and goals and objectives. Fielded and researched complex investor service inquiries.

> Achievements
> - Handled conversion to Sunstar bond processing system including vendor research, vendor negotiation, and implementation.
> - Participated in nationwide user action committees to evaluate software and recommend enhancements.

Security Processing Clerk (1987 - 1988)
Accountant (1986 - 1987)
Operations Clerk (1986 - 1986)

Education
Bachelor of Business Administration in Finance, Rutgers University (1986)

Computer Skills
Sunstar, SEI, Microsoft Word, Lotus 123, Lotus Approach, Lotus WordPro

Community Service
Appointee to Community Development Authority for Princeton, New Jersey (1999)

Health Care Program Administration

Jane Swift
9 Central Avenue
Clifton, NJ 07013
(201) 555-1212
Jane@careerbrain.com

Qualifications

- Medicaid Programs Administrator offers successful experience and up-to-date, comprehensive knowledge of Medicaid services and limitations, and New Jersey Medicaid Management Information System. Broad scope of expertise in key areas such as:
  - Medicaid policies and procedures
  - Hospital, physician, and pharmacy billing
  - Claims troubleshooting and problem resolution
  - Case management and utilization review
  - Medicaid prescribed drug program
  - Centralized, electronic, and DUE claims processing
  - Social service and counseling programs
  - Coding and medical terminology
- Demonstrated ability to provide extensive technical support for pharmacies, hospitals, and physicians.
- Sound judgement across a wide spectrum of programs and applications, demonstrating an analytical approach to problem solving.
- Able to develop and deliver in-depth, hands-on training for Medicaid claims processing and billing programs.
- Exceptional interpersonal and communication skills, particularly in the areas of presentations, management reporting, people development, team building, research, negotiations, and management information systems.
- Adapts to new situations and requirements easily; quickly able to develop a productive rapport with diverse populations.
- Resourceful and creative; skilled in the planning and execution of programs and projects for optimum results.
- Recognized as a focused, practical thinker who is willing to devote the time and energy, as well as take reasonable risks, to accomplish outstanding results.

Professional Experience

State of New Jersey   *1987 - Present*
Program Specialist, Health Care Administration Agency (1994 - Present)
  Coordinate and implement policy and procedures to insure Medicaid program compliance and consistency. Provide technical support for providers and assist with written and verbal inquiries for health care and pharmacy billing and claims issues. Supervise two staff members handling provider inquiries and research requests. Maintain open communications with providers and recipients alike.
Counselor II - HCA (1993 - 1994)
  Directed the effective provision of counseling services for Medicaid clients relevant to established policies and procedures of the program, eligibility and scope of services available. Worked closely with staff and community agencies to interpret Medicaid policies and resolve problems. Served as Acting Supervisor as needed.
Counselor II - HRS (1987 - 1993)
  Maintained an active case management of 200+ clients. Extensive field work including client home visits. Provided educational and counseling to insure that children were receiving physical examinations, dental care, and eye examinations on a regular basis. Maintained up-to-date client and approved providers record. Promoted from Counselor I in 1988.

Education

Masters candidate, Social Work, Rutgers University
B.S. General Studies, Western Kentucky University

Affiliations

American Business Woman's Association (ABWA) 1999
Who's Who in the Northeast, 1993-1994

Health Care Sales

Jane Swift
9 Central Avenue
Dallas, TX 75379
(214) 555-1212
Jane@careerbrain.com

Top Performing Sales/Marketing Professional/Health Care Industry

- A natural communicator who excels in relationship building and business development. Possesses excellent presentation and public speaking abilities.
- Skilled in problem solving with an ability to learn quickly, providing a foundation for success in any organization.
- Well organized with attention to detail and accuracy in a high-pressure, fast-paced environment.
- Track record of consistently exceeding company goals.

Professional Experience

Independent Broker - Medicare Risk Sales 1998 to Present
Achieved high volume of sales, representing several major insurance companies. Optimized self-generated business by developing and maintaining strategic alliances with MDs and key decision-makers at medical groups.

Individual Specialist, Texas Medical 1996 to 1998
Consistent top producer for leading Medicare contracting organization. Successfully built and nurtured relationships with IPAs and their office staffs. Maximized exposure through skill in community-based marketing. Performed extensive follow-up and public relations to encourage member retention. Diligently monitored competition and industry trends.
- Special achievements included:
    Outstanding Sales Achievement Award in 1997 for top production in area;
    Top Sales Production Award 9 out of 12 months, 1997 - 1998;
    Leadership Award, Nov. 1996; Rookie of the Month, Jan. 1997.
- Consistently exceeded all goals with average monthly closing rate in excess of 90%.
- Selected to train new representatives.

Assistant Manager, Lone Star Drug Stores, 1990 to 1994
Promoted to Assistant Manager after 2.5 months employment—company average is 9 to 12 months.
- Assisted in overseeing all day-to-day operations of second highest grossing store in chain with weekly sales of $325,000. Supervised and managed support staff of up to 65 employees.
- Identified sales trends; implemented innovative marketing strategies, maximizing sales results. Developed monthly, quarterly, and annual budget projections.

Education
Bachelor of Arts in Psychology, Texas A&M University, 1989

Human Resources Generalist

Jane Swift
9 Central Avenue
Cleveland, OH 44113

(216) 555-1212
Jane@careerbrain.com
Page 1 of 2

MS and BS Degrees ~ Extensive Continuing Education
10 Years Success in Corporate HR ~ Promoted Ahead of Peers, Delivered Results in Special Assignments

---

Key Words
HR and Benefits Administration ~ Healthcare Product Development ~ Open Enrollment
Labor Relations ~ Grievances ~ Arbitration ~ Job Bidding ~ Team Building ~ Hiring ~ Discipline
Sexual Harassment ~ Unemployment Compensation ~ Safety Training
HCFA, HIPAA, COBRA ~ EEOC/PHR Compliance

RESULTS - HR, BENEFITS and TRAINING

- LAUNCHED MULTI-TIER HEALTHCARE PRODUCT: 1 of 4 who negotiated with and hired vendor; achieved higher benefit value with minimal investment; implemented immediately for management, negotiated union contract specifications.
- OVER / ABOVE: Due to HR background and reputation, emerged as #1 contact for 5 entrepreneurial affiliate companies; while coordinating medical, life, 401(k) and optional coverage for 3,500 in-house employees, traveled 3+ years to inform and enroll acquisitioned staff in corporate benefits packages; extended interim HR support to entrepreneurial companies; counseled affiliate decision-makers in staffing problems, disciplinary procedures, and policy interpretation.
- POLICY / PROCEDURES: Track record opened opportunity for 2-year directorship; simultaneously provided HR support for Finance Division while writing corporate policy for 3,500 employees.
- IMPROVED QUALITY: While managing employee service awards and retirement programs, identified need to update offerings; not only enhanced quality of awards, but also cut turnaround from 6 months to 30 days via personal negotiation with vendor.
- BARGAINING: 4 years as primary contact for bargaining unit leadership; involved with grievance, discipline, and arbitration hearings since 1987.
- PEOPLE: Managed up to 27-member staffs; analyzed positions and successfully redirected work flow of an office without contradicting union contract stipulations; screened, hired, trained, disciplined, dismissed employees since 1991.
- TRAINING: Annual / semi-annual training—delivered required benefits, safety training, special HR programs since 1985; 1 of 8 individuals who facilitated "out of the box thinking" training for senior managers that greatly improved their finesse in daily interaction.
- ENROLLMENT / MARKETING: Created theme for pre-enrollment flyer, "Our Way to the Future," and coordinated graphic designer's efforts—booklet took second place, international competition.

MAJOR UTILITY COMPANY, Cleveland, OH   Present
$1B Public Utility ~ Integrated Benefits During Mergers ~ Emerged as #1 Contact for 5 Entities ~
Promoted 7 Times

SENIOR COMPENSATION ANALYST   *Present*
DIRECTOR, HEALTH AND INSURANCE PLAN SERVICES   *1994 to 2000*
Administered $20MM Health / Welfare Benefits ~ 3,500 Employees ~ Parent Company, 5 Subsidiaries ~
Launched Multi-Tier Healthcare ~ Selected to Troubleshoot Affiliates' HR Issues ~ Improved Service Awards
DIRECTOR, POLICY AND HR ADMINISTRATION   *1991 to 1994*
Policy Development ~ Interpretation for Senior Management ~ Sexual Harassment, Performance Leadership and
Benefits Update Programs ~ Transitioned Finance and Power Generation Divisions During Restructuring ~ Front
Line, Bargaining Unit Leaders ~ 3 Years Working with Corporate Kickoffs for United Way Campaigns

Jane Swift (216) 555-1212
page 2 of 2

RECORDS SUPERVISOR   *1989 to 1991*
$500K Annual Budget ~ Staff of 7 ~ Corporate-Wide Document Management / Storage ~ Liaison for PUC Audit
~ 1 of 30 Selected as ECAC Member, Improving Company's Public Image through Community Involvement
SUPERVISOR, SUPPORT SERVICES   *1987 to 1989*
100 Percent Accuracy in Assigning and Monitoring 27-Person Clerical Staff at 3 Sites ~ Analyzed Union Positions
and Laid Groundwork Restructuring Workflow for 10-Employee Department
TRAINING INSTRUCTOR   *1985 to 1987*
Recruited to 8-Member Training Team Targeting Senior Management ~ Ongoing Safety Training and Orientation
~ Company Representative for Pittsburgh Area in 1986 PA United Way Campaign
PERSONNEL ASSISTANT and STENOGRAPHER POSITIONS prior to HR / Training / Management

EDUCATION
Case Western Reserve University, Cleveland, OH
    Master of Science, Human Resource Management
Lycoming College, Williamsport, PA
    Bachelor of Science, Business Administration

RECENT CONTINUING EDUCATION
CORPORATE-SPONSORED - Customer Focused Training
TOM PETERS TRAINING - Circle of Innovation
TOWERS PERRIN: In-Depth Study of Health and Welfare Plans, Breathing New Life into Flex Plans, International
    Flex, Financial Planning, Navigating the Changing Health Care System, Reorganizing the
    Human Resources Function, Recognition and Reward in Periods of Changes, Driving
    Business-Strategy through Learning and Development, Employer Smart, Employee Friendly,
    Competency Based Pay, Computing Based Pay, Getting the Stars and Keeping Them,
    Compensation—Challenges and Changes, Mergers and Acquisitions, To Outsource or Not to
    Outsource
SKILLPATH - Thinking Out of the Box
MICROGRAPHICS CONFERENCES - 2-Time Attendee

PROFESSIONAL COMMITMENT
Member, Human Resource Association, 1991 to 1998 - coordinated 1994 Annual Conference.

Human Resources Professional

James Sharpe
9 Central Avenue
Chapel Hill, NC 27516
(919) 555-1212
James@careerbrain.com
Page 1 of 2

HUMAN RESOURCE PROFILE

Self-motivated human resource professional, successful in leading cross-functional project teams by cultivating and promoting effective working relationships. Goal-driven manager with proven track record of establishing strategic plans, priorities, work assignments, and solutions within allotted time and resources. Collaborator with human resource manager, sharing restructuring and rewriting of job descriptions, performing applicant screenings and initial interviews.

KEY STRENGTHS

Career Pathing	Adult Learning Strategies
New Hire Orientation	Human Resource Partnerships
Performance Reengineering	Change Management
Corporate Technology Trainer	Curriculum Design
Train-the-Trainer	Software Applications, SAP R/3

CAREER HIGHLIGHTS

Smart Manufacturing , Inc., Chapel Hill, North Carolina   *1/91 to Present*
Technology Education Manager, Human Resources (9/97 to present)

Launch, implement and coordinate companywide training programs and curriculum for 2,400 employees. Support Information Technology Department with focus on high commitment work systems and ongoing improvement. Assess worker competencies through consultations with department and project managers to devise learning strategies and delivery methodologies.

- Joined forces with human resource management team to reorganize department.
- Oversaw design and growth of innovative curriculum with over 300 various module addressing all aspects of new company global business processes.
- Instituted company's first online learning system for desktop applications with skills assessment and self-paced tutorial resource tools.
- Created and executed training with support efforts for new worldwide e-mail and calendar system to meet company Y2K objectives.
- Set up and led change management process from centralized computer training to decentralized environment.

Team Leader (1/91 to 9/97)

Hired and supervised desktop computing team, responsible for performance appraisals and advising workers on career advancement. Planned and administered special activities related to vendor negotiations on renewal agreements.

- Introduced college intern program that reduced workload of full-time staff without paying high cost of consultants. Benefit: Some interns retained as permanent staff after graduation.
- Spearheaded development of Power Users in "Train-the-Trainer" program resulting in major training cost savings and well-informed workforce.

James Sharpe (919) 555-1212
page 2 of 2

PROFESSIONAL SYSTEMS, INC., Chapel Hill, North Carolina   *1/84 to 12/90*
        Reseller of personal computing products to medium to large U.S. companies
Area Training Manager (5/86 to 12/90)
        Coordinated sales activities related to computer training for major and national accounts. Hired and coached instructors and administrative personnel, conducted performance reviews, and assisted workers with career development issues. Managed eight training facilities while steering activities related to class scheduling and curriculum development for each location. Constructed long-range sales quotas and plans for mid-central area, preparing and maintaining budgets and related financial reports.
- Received National Achievement Award for exceeding sales quotas by 158%, 1988-1989.
- Opened company's first satellite training facility in a secondary market, generating 1/3 of North Carolina's profits by end of first year of operation.
- Invented and installed volume purchase coupon program, giving customers method to purchase training at volume discounted rate, redeemable at any of 126 company training facilities. Benefit: Moved company to top slot as national training vendor.
- Coordinated production of national training tool that furnished company with centralized consistent tracking and reporting system.

Sales Training Manager (1/84 to 5/86)
        Inaugurated and promoted sales and technical training program activities in central region. Initiated ongoing sales development program, cross-training store managers in delivery process.

EDUCATION
Master degree program   University of North Carolina, Chapel Hill, North Carolina
Business Management   4.0/4.0
Bachelor of Arts   University of North Carolina, Chapel Hill, North Carolina
Business Management/Human Relations   3.6/4.0

PROFESSIONAL CERTIFICATIONS AND AFFILIATIONS
- Certified Instructor, Dale Carnegie Human Relations and Effective Speaking
- Training and Development Certification, University of Kansas
- Leadership Certificate, Dale Carnegie Leadership Management Course
- Certificate, Situational Interviewing Techniques, Computer Systems, Inc.
- Member, American Society of Training and Development
- Member, Masie Center Organization

COMMUNITY INVOLVEMENT
- Consultant, Junior Achievement Program, 2000
- Participant, Everybody Wins, literacy program for children, 1996 to 2000
- Fund raiser, American Diabetes Association, 1998 to 1999
- Fund raiser, Multiple Sclerosis Association, 1998

Human Resources Recruiter

Jane Swift
9 Central Avenue
Salt Lake City, UT 84106
(801) 555-1212
Jane@careerbrain.com

Dynamic Human Resources Professional with a proven record of top performance in recruiting, screening, and placing professional, managerial, and technical candidates. Committed to exceeding performance expectation. Excellent communication and problem resolution skills; energetic motivator. Computer proficient. Expertise in:

- recruitment/hiring
- benefits administration
- employee relations
- training and assessment
- compensation package negotiations
- policies and procedures

Selected Highlights

- Recognized as a Top Producer in 1998 and 1999 by filling an average of 37 positions monthly
- Appointed to serve on the task force charged with developing and implementing regional recruiting and transfer policies and procedures; selected as chairperson for the non-nursing task force
- Spearheaded use of Internet recruiting methods, significantly reducing print advertising costs and increasing candidate pool

Relevant Career Experience

Summit Health System, Salt Lake City, Utah
Recruiter/Employment Coordinator (since 1997), *Benefits Specialist* (1996 - 1997)

Promoted to employment coordinator and charged with recruiting non-nursing personnel for a 9-hospital health system alliance. Create advertising copy, attend trade shows, develop recruiting campaigns, screen and evaluate prospects, conduct interviews, and negotiate compensation packages. Worked with cross-functional teams to administer flexible benefits plans including COBRA and HIPPA. Background in HRIS/DBS. Knowledgeable in FSA, DCA, FMLA, disability, medical, dental, 403(B), and life insurance plans.

Smith Communications, Salt Lake City, Utah
Marketing Coordinator (1995 - 1996)

Recruited to launch training and employee learning division; reported to COO of division. Scheduled training with top executives of companies; managed lead processing/tracking database; recruited and trained new hires.

Utah Outdoors Corporation, Orem, Utah
Sales and Marketing Manager (1991 - 1994)

Professional Memberships

Society for Human Resource Management & HR Salt Lake City, Utah Health Recruiters Assoc.

Education

B.A., Business Administration, Brigham Young University

Information Technology Consultant

James Sharpe
9 Central Avenue
Dayton, OH 45401
(513) 555-1212
James@careerbrain.com
Page 1 of 2

Summary

Talented, profit-driven professional qualified by nearly 10 years of visible achievements in leading-edge information technologies. Expertise in high-volume territory sales management, demonstrating skills in maintenance of revenue-generating accounts in highly competitive markets. Areas of strength include: key account management, staff recruiting/development, strategic business planning, product presentation, technical staff management, relationship building, client consulting, value-added selling, contract negotiation, project management. Technically proficient in Win95, Win98, Windows NT Workstation, Windows NT server, Novell 3.x and 4.x, SMS, SQL, TCP/IP, cc:Mail, Microsoft Exchange and most Microsoft applications; trained in CISCO and Synoptics Design and Diagnostics.

Recent Consulting Projects

Lloyd Corporation. Orchestrated marketing and configuration of Compaq servers and all peripherals valued at $5 million annually; successfully sold and managed company-wide roll-out of new computer and software encompassing over 7,000 desktops, valued at $1 million in four states. Accountability for placement and management of 10 technical service professionals generating $624,000 annually.

Royal Uniforms of America. Cooperatively secured $2.5+ million nationwide contract for full inventory of desktops, servers, laptops, and peripherals with services including setup/configurations, depot repair, and on-site support at 500 locations.

Dayton School Board. Provided expertise in $1.2 million sale consisting of 550 computers with complete setup and configuration to desktop; successfully negotiated service agreements valued at $325,000 annually.

United States Department of Defense. Participated in sale of over 600 machines valued at $1.5 million with four technical professionals generating $625,000 annually.

Western Hospital. Key player in successful marketing complete Intranet and online policy manual ($60,000), total help desk solutions ($89,000), various service agreements ($50,000 annually), and technical personnel ($120,000 annually).

Navy Technology Center. Successfully directed installation and configuration of all LAN/WAN equipment (3Com) purchased for two-story building and valued at $250,000.

Garcia Industries, LTD. Placement and management of four technical professionals generating $350,000 annually.

Professional Experience

United Technologies, 1996 - Present
Director of Technical Service & Sales

- Manage $3.2 million full-service profit center supporting business development and technical service efforts for computer reseller/integrator generating $12 million in annual revenues.
- Direct workflow of 12 in-house and 30 on-site technical associates involved in repair and service of hardware from all major manufacturers in addition to LAN/WAN network design, support, and maintenance.
- Key member of sales function focused on new business development, client needs analysis, product/service presentation, suggestive/strategic selling, and extensive ongoing value-added selling, customer service, and problem resolution.

- Oversee special projects, workflow management, quality assurance, and technical troubleshooting; significant achievements managing priorities under pressure while maintaining positive client relations.
- Credited with increasing number of technicians from 17 to 42, doubling service department revenues within two years while increasing response time to fewer than eight business hours and maintaining less than 15 percent employee turnover.

Southeastern Capital, 1992 - 1996
Senior Engineer

- Orchestrated on-site technical services at corporate headquarters for four years; instrumental in placement and management of 11 on-site technicians; spearheaded numerous special projects to assure quality and efficient information management for all accounts.
- Supported 1,200 PCs, 300 printers, 14 NT file servers, and 12 Novell servers and provided support on Windows 3.x, Win95, Windows NT Workstation, Windows NT server, Novell 3.x SMS 1.1, SQL, TCP/IP, cc:Mail, and all Microsoft applications.
- Managed entire quick response team for headquarters and several remote sites including all desktop and server-related hardware or software problems.
- Project manager of NT roll-out team, responsible for converting over 1,200 PCs to Windows NT 3.51 workstation and 12 NT servers with back-office products.

Helwett-Packard, 1990 - 1992
Technical Services Manager/Sales Representative

- Directed daily shop operations, sales, inventory control, call dispatching and weekly reporting for small organization offering full line of information technology solutions; instrumental in increasing annual revenues from $500,000 to $1.5 million.
- Gained valuable background in troubleshooting, maintenance and repair of all types of computer systems, printers, monitors; setup, supported, and administered several Netware servers and supported Windows and DOS applications.

Education/Certification
Dayton University, Dayton, OH, BS in Computer Information Technology
Certified in MCP, NT Workstation, NT Server

Information Technology Instructor

Jane Swift
9 Central Avenue
Sterling Heights, Michigan 48310
(810) 555-1212
Jane@careerbrain.com

Qualified computer training specialist and information technology instructor. Trained and instructed numerous accounts for Fortune 500 companies. Known for compliance and clarity; regarded for competence and creativity. Areas of expertise include:

computer training and coaching	technical writing	presentations/demonstrations
syllabus composition	resource documentation	technology instruction
Internet/e-mail	Microsoft certified	

Career Summary

Computer Trainer - certified in Microsoft products; competent in numerous Windows applications.

Technical Writer - developed user manuals, technical documentation, classroom syllabus design, presentations, and demonstrations.

Freelance Employment Columnist - for the *Business News.*

Employment Specialist - trained, evaluated, and interviewed prospective employees; effectively matched qualified candidates with positions.

Guest Speaker/Facilitator - speak for various groups and organizations; facilitate job search and career enhancement workshops.

Memberships - American Society for Training and Development (ASTD), National Association for Job Search Training (NAJST).

Computer Expertise

Word Processing: Microsoft Word, AmiPro
Operating Systems: Windows 3.1/95/98, OS/2
Graphics: PowerPoint, Harvard Graphics
Spreadsheets: Microsoft Excel, Lotus 1-2-3
Database Management: Microsoft Access
Other: E-mail/Internet, PROFS

Experience

Chicago Medical Center, Information Analyst	1999 - Present
Remote Solutions, Information Technology Trainer/Consultant	1997 - 1999
Offsite Resources and Services, Trainer/Staffing Specialist	1995 - 1997
Career Counseling Services, Owner	1995 - Present
Chicago Business Center, Word Processing Specialist	1993 - 1995

Education and Professional Development

University of Michigan, BA
Oakland Tech, AAS

Information Technology Professional

James Sharpe
9 Central Avenue
Salt Lake City, UT 84101
(801) 555-1212
James@careerbrain.com
Page 1 of 2

SUMMARY

- Information Technology professional with extensive knowledge of Windows NT Server 4.0 and Novell Net Ware operating systems.
- Practical, hands-on experience with assembly, troubleshooting, and repair of personal computers.
- Excellent customer relations skills, including delivering training and providing "Help Desk" support for end users on a variety of Microsoft applications.
- Demonstrated ability to function effectively as a team player, as well as work independently to achieve organizational objectives.

TECHNICAL EXPERIENCE

DATA SYSTEMS; Center City, Utah   *1998 - Present*
Senior Technical Business Analyst

> Provide systems technical support for Fortune 100 Corporation's sales force throughout the continental United States, Puerto Rico, and Guam. Configure x86 platforms, which include Windows NT Server, Windows NT Workstation, Windows 95, and Windows 98, to operate with proprietary software package written for Xerox. Support Microsoft Access database used for sales contact management.

- Provide end user/Help Desk support for PC-based systems utilized by Fortune 100's employees.
- Train users on applications through teleconferencing, one-on-one training, and on-site classes.
- Set up PC systems and configure software/hardware to meet individual users' needs.
- Diagnose software/hardware problems and address compatibility issues across Windows 3.x and Windows 95/98 platforms.
- Utilize Ghost application to clone PCs for use by other team members. Update and maintain hardware/software systems for 23 users.
- Administer one Novell 3.1 Server, one NT Stand-Alone Server, update all installed software, configure all software on local PCs, and maintain inventory of software and licenses.
- Serve as "Subject Matter Expert" for LAN, NT, and virus issues.

> Major Project
>
>> Served as member of "Travel Team" that performed remote installations and conducted on-site training for Fortune 100 facilities throughout the United States. Troubleshot system problems and addressed user concerns.

COMPUTING SOLUTIONS; Orem, Utah   *1998*
Contract Consultant

- Installed and configured NT Server Network for 25 users in an office setting. Updated software applications, wrote log scripts, and installed Transaction and Index Servers.
- Adapted 386 DX platform for use with thermal camera in healthcare applications.

ADDITIONAL EXPERIENCE

Sales Associate - Superior Cellular - Outback, Utah   1997 - 1998
Manager - Gepetto's Shoe Shoppe - Outback, Utah   1993 - 1995

EDUCATION

Microsoft Certified Systems Engineer   (Anticipated) Spring 2000
Microsoft Certified Professional   1999

- Server Administration
- Windows NT Core Technician

Utah Technical College; Provo, Utah, Associate of Science, Computer Science   1997

James Sharpe (801) 555-1212
page 2 of 2

TECHNICAL PROFICIENCIES

Operating Systems

- Windows 3.1x; Windows 98/95
- Windows NT Server: PDC, BDC and Stand-Alone Servers
- Windows NT Workstation
- Windows 2000 Beta3
- Configured systems to run Dual boot with Windows NT and Windows 98/95.
- Linux
- Solaris
- Novell 3.12

Networks

- Windows NT Networks with both PDC and Stand-Alone Servers
- Windows 98/95 peer-to-peer networks
- User and Queue Administration on Novell 3.x and NDS 4.x
- Installation and configuration of all types of network hardware including: Hubs, Cat 5 Cable, Ether Cards, and Network Drops
- Configuration of TCP/IP, WINS, DNS, IPX/SPX, NetBEUI, NetBios, Gateways

Hardware

- X86 based machines from 286 to Pentium III, including Celeron and AMD CPU's
- Sparc IPX, Sparc 2 and Sparc 5
- Installation and configuration of PDC running on Compaq Proliant 1600 Dual Pentium II 450, Ultra Wide SCSI
- Installation and configuration of various hubs/Ethercards including: 3Com, Lynksys, Intel, SMC, Compaq NetFlex, Novell NE2000 compatible
- Installation and configuration of various ISA/PCI/AGP cards
- Cat5 Cabling
- APC uninterruptible power supplies
- Andataco Drive Arrays--both 27gig and 16gig
- Various CD-ROM burners including Mitsumi, Hewlett Packard, and Hi-Val.

Software

Ghost	Microsoft Outlook 98/2000
Netscape	CDRWin
McAfee 4.x	Sygate
Visual C++	Rumba
PC Anywhere	Ghost Explorer
Microsoft Office 97/2000	Internet Explorer
Adaptec CD Creator	Microsoft Proxy
Microsoft Masm	Borland C++
Host Explorer	

Insurance Claims

Jane Swift
9 Central Avenue
Yonkers, NY 10701

(914) 555-1212
Jane@careerbrain.com

Career Profile

High-energy, cross-functional background as resourceful fast-track insurance claims specialist with an outstanding record of success in winning settlements and reducing claims payouts to acceptable and just amounts. Investigate, negotiate, and settle complex claims, from beginning stages up to trial, for Hartford and Aetna.

Areas of Expertise

Administration

- organized and effective performance in high-pressure environments
- presentation development and delivery
- claims investigation with meticulous documentation
- heavy phones/switchboard
- skilled customer care
- word processing and spreadsheet development (type 60 words per minute)
- Microsoft Office, Internet, and Intranet proficiency

Insurance Claims

- commercial and personal lines liability
- general liability, auto, homeowners, and products liability
- property damage and bodily injury claims
- injury exposure values
- claimant, attorney, and litigation representation
- complex arbitration and mediation negotiation
- settlement and target value range setting
- medical and liability evaluation

Highlights

- Handle case load of up to 230 pending commercial and personal lines claims. Establish contact within 24 hours, maintain impeccable documentation, and determine value of case based on liability/injury. Decide claim values up to $50,000. Negotiate/settle cases in mediation, arbitration, or litigation. Productive in judge's chambers, courtroom, or at mediation table.
- Delivered a $15,000 saving to Hartford by obtaining a defense verdict on a case that a judge suggested Hartford "buy out" for $15,000. Communicated with attorneys, evaluated liability/facts and determined feasibility for trial. Case went to trial and Hartford paid nothing but legal costs.
- Saved Aetna $40,000 on complex $100,000 second-degree burn claim by determining case's suitability for mediation, and meeting with judge and plaintiff's attorneys. Case was settled for a fair $60,000 without incurring major legal costs for Aetna.
- Promoted onto Aetna fast-track after only one year; became the youngest adjuster in company history. Track record of positive mediation, arbitration, and litigation outcomes is equal to or better than that of more senior professionals.
- Possess outstanding administrative/organizational skills, superior presentation and negotiation abilities, a passion for excellence, and a contagious enthusiasm. Work well in independent or team environments. Tenacious, with the stamina needed to function in high-pressure environments.

Employment

Hartford Insurance Corp., Claims Representative	1998 to Present
Aetna Claims Services	
Claims Specialist	1997 to 1998
Fast-track Representative	1995 to 1997
Claims Assistant	1994 to 1995

Education and Professional Development

A.A.S. in Business, Insurance, and Real Estate, Bronxville Community College
Pepperdine Law University: Two-day Negotiation Seminar
Industry Courses: Commercial General Liability, Claims Statements, Property Casualty Principles, Litigation Guidelines, Medical Terminology and Treatment, How to Handle Cases to Avoid Litigation, Accurate Reserving

Insurance Executive

James Sharpe
9 Central Avenue
Memphis, TN 38137
(901) 555-1212
James@careerbrain.com
Page 1 of 2

Career Profile

- Over ten years background in casualty insurance.
- Key player in the building of the one of the nation's top ten insurers.
- Senior Vice President and Core Management Team member of Casualty Insurance. Recognized as an astute visionary, delivering fresh perspectives and keen assessments using intellect, judgement, and character. Known for making and upholding tough decisions.

Areas of Expertise

Management Skills:

- program creation/strategic planning
- resource development
- multimillion-dollar budget creation
- budget management/cost controls
- corporate restructuring
- relationship and team building
- boardroom-level presentations

Insurance Experience:

- loss development and analysis
- high-level claims analysis and resolution
- high exposure claims
- severe injury and multiple policy management
- complex litigation management
- medical profession liability policies
- reserving and settlement authority

Executive Highlights

- *Accelerated Growth*
  During senior management tenure, helped to grow company from 3,000 to 7,500 policyholders, adding a wide range of clients. Growth exploded business and caused expansion of department from 15 to 50 employees.
- *Financial Analysis and Cost Improvement*
  Handled complex financial analysis and legal cost containment. Reduced litigation costs by 15% to 20%. Streamlined claims handling process by enabling claims examiners to handle larger caseloads through realignment of custodial tasks to clerical staff. Collaborated with company actuaries to interpret and act upon loss trends and developments.
- *Profit and Loss*
  Developed highly accurate, multimillion dollar budgets. In addition, effective personal handling of reserving and settlement authority, legal cost containment, favorable trial results, and efficiency measures directly affected corporate bottom line.
- *New Systems and Technology*
  Significantly reduced legal costs through research, development, and implementation of innovative automated legal processing and auditing program.
- *Business Reorganization*
  Following CI's recent acquisition, collaborated as key member of transition team to develop and implement efficient reorganization plan to achieve efficiency gains.
- *Career Advancement*
  Fast-tracked from claims representative to vice president in four years. Was handpicked, recruited, and mentored by CEO during CI's initial period of accelerated growth.

Employment
Casualty Insurance (CI), Memphis, TN

• Senior Vice President	1999 to present
• Vice President	1993 to 1998
• Claims Manager	1992 to 1993
• Claims Supervisor	1991 to 1992
• Claims Representative	1990 to 1991

- *Management Summary*

  Report directly to the CEO and Board of Directors. Oversee two direct reports administering activities over 60 headquarters and branch staff members. Direct and manage claims reserved in excess of $900 million, handling reserving and settlement of individual claims of up to $1 million. Daily functions include $4 million budget development and management, staffing, cost control, appointment of legal counsel, policy creation, determination of complex coverage issues, high-exposure claims monitoring, and interface with re-insurers/excess insurers.

- *Significant Achievements*

  Track record of wide ranging contributions in systems development, cost containment, and claims management. Maintained severity at flat levels for the past five years, reduced litigation costs, and improved beneficial trial results. Fast-tracked from claims representative to VP in four years.

Professional Development
American Management Association continuing professional development courses include annual seminars on insurance issues, Accounting for Non-Financial Executives, Managing Conflict, Interpersonal Skills, Management of Reciprocals and Mutuals.

Education
Bachelor of Science in Biology, Memphis State University, Pre-Med Program

Investment Banking Executive

James Sharpe
9 Central Avenue
Fox Hills, CA 90230

(310) 555-1212
James@careerbrain.com

Investment Banking/Telecommunications/Media

- Fast-track and comprehensive career path to Vice President in Investment Banking for Wells Fargo Securities. Wide experience in media and telecommunications industries.
- Originate, execute, and close deals representing a career total of $5.6 billion. Author and deliver dynamic Board of Director-level presentations, achieving bottom-line results through a blending of financial acuity, industry knowledge, and humor. Proactively originated and managed 18 months of VP-level projects as an associate. Accomplished in M&A cost analysis, valuation, and due diligence.

Areas of Knowledge and Expertise

•Telecommunications	•Media/entertainment	•Equity
•Equity-linked	•Fixed income	•IPOs and secondaries
•Mergers/acquisitions	•Private placements	•Debt financing
•Corporate finance	•Origination	•Fairness opinions
•M&A cost analysis	•Valuation	•Due diligence
•Client presentations	•Team building	•Research
•Internet	•MS Office Suite	

Career Highlights

- Originated and closed a $15 million convertible mandate for MANEX (revenue: $4 million). Managed origination effort, wrote and led all presentations, partnered with team to execute transaction, and coordinated with CEO of investment banking. Created road slide shows, wrote valuation, and performed due diligence.
- Originated and currently executing a $10 million private placement mandate for an Internet retailer of collectibles (anticipated revenue: $700,000). Created and co-led all presentations. Currently working with team to execute transaction. Presently writing valuation and projections.
- Originated research relationship with the Houston Group (revenue: $50,000). Persistently contacted client to originate relationship. Authored and led all presentations. Officially commended for presentation's hard facts, energy, and humor.
- Originated $100 million IPO mandate for XTR Pacific. Managed origination effort with head of global equity underwriting. Wrote and delivered all presentations, valuation, and performed due diligence. Effort established quality of presentation skills and precipitated fast-track career path.
- Assisted origination and closing of $100 million sell-side M&A mandate for NuevoTel (revenue: $1 million). Participated in strategic buyer solicitation and closing while an associate. Performed all valuation work, conducted due diligence in Latin America, and co-authored selling memorandum.
- Assisted origination of $350 million IPO mandate for TTI International. Performed all valuation work. Cowrote and attended presentations.

Career Development

Wells Fargo Investment Banking

Vice President   1998 to present
Senior Associate   1996 to 1998

> Developed relationship and led team effort that won and closed a lead-managed, $15 million convertible issue for small cap MANEX. Currently executing a personally originated $10 million private placement mandate for Internet retailer of collectibles. Originated co-managed mandate for $100 million IPO of Pacific Rim communications company (XTR Pacific). Originated research relationship with satellite communications operator (Houston Group). Advised privately held Latin American communications company (NuevoTel) on $100 million strategic sale.

Conglomerate Media
Corporate Consultant   1996
> Assisted in evaluation of offering memoranda and investment banking proposals. Advised Conglomerate Media on entry options into textbook publishing, focusing on strategic fit, cross licensing opportunities, and return on invested capital.

Price Waterhouse
Senior Investment Banking Associate   1994 to 1996
> Won $350 million IPO mandate for global communications firm (TTI International). Delivered fairness opinions for sale of publishing companies.

First Houston Corp.
Associate in Investment Banking   1990 to 1994
> Assisted in start-to-finish origination and closing of buy-side mandate for Casualty Underwriters Insurance Corp. Co-wrote fairness opinion. Co-authored valuation models and performed due diligence. Involved in capital markets transactions for large cap clients. Total capital raised: $500 million.

Education, Certification, and Registrations
M.B.A. Northwestern University
B.A. University of Houston
Certificate: Investment Banking, University of California, Berkeley
> Series 63, 7

Jewelry Sales

Jane Swift
9 Central Avenue
Wilton, CT 21234
(203) 555-1212
Jane@careerbrain.com

Professional Sales
A position to use proven sales and relationship building skills to develop new business, retain existing clients, and positively affect the bottom line.

An expert professional with a passion for sales and an ability to develop rapport and trust with new clients. Cultivate existing relationships using a strong follow-up technique and gain significant add-on and repeat business. Persuade "on the fence" clientele to make a purchase; oftentimes upselling the client as well. Participate in team selling and train new employees in consultative approach, needs identification, closing, and follow through.

- Consistently surpass monthly sales quotas by at least 50%.
- Ranked as top producer among a sales team.
- Awarded Platinum Club (or equivalent) status 3 years in a row for outstanding sales figures.
- Developed a strong following of international and out-of-state clientele.

Endorsements
Physician
"I have found her to be intelligent, friendly, and well spoken. She has had a remarkable grasp of understanding the medical issues we've encountered and her questions and comments showed insight. I would recommend her as an employee based on her communication skills, intellect, and motivation."

Sales Manager
"I would highly recommend you look at her for employment with your company. She has qualities that would be an asset to you...self-motivated, self-starter, quick learner, and most important, she was my top salesperson. I could always count on her to get the job done with little supervision."

Professional Experience
Sales Representative - Smith and Jones Jewelers, Wilton, CT   1998 to Present
- Highlights: Recruited to expand retail sales at the top selling location in area. Produce new and repeat business and train sales representatives on techniques.

Sales Representative - Zachary's Jewelers, Danbury, CT   1995 to 1998
- Highlights: Led the store in sales volume. Trained new staff and shared helpful sales and marketing hints. Assumed additional responsibilities for ordering, vendor contact, and office work.

Sales Representative - Bryan's Jewelers, Hartford, CT   1994 to 1995
- Highlights: Used consultative approach to sell high-end jewelry and gems. Completed training in sales methods, gemology, and winning attitude.

Education
Bachelor of Arts in Language, University of Cairo, Egypt
English as a Second Language Program, City University of New York
Certified Travel Consultant, Travel Academy, Wilton, CT

Law Firm Internship

Jane Swift
9 Central Avenue
Columbus, OH 43215

(614) 555-1212
Jane@careerbrain.com

OBJECTIVE

A LAW FIRM INTERNSHIP which will utilize strong organizational skills, effective research skills, and the proven ability to get the job done.

OVERVIEW

- Organized, highly-trained individual with exceptional follow-through abilities and excellent management skills, able to plan and oversee projects from concept to successful conclusion.
- Strong interpersonal skills; proven ability to work well with individuals on all levels.
- Possess strong problem resolution skills.
- Dedicated individual; achieved reputation for consistently going beyond what is required.
- Proven ability to gather, extract, identify, and effectively utilize data.
- Computer literate; proficient in using current business software; exposure to legal packages: West Law and Lexus Nexus.

EDUCATION

OHIO STATE UNIVERSITY SCHOOL OF LAW, Columbus, OH

- Juris Doctor candidate, May 2001
- Current course work: Contracts, Property, Administrative Law, Torts, Constitutional Law, American Legal History, Civil Procedure, Criminal Law

OHIO UNIVERSITY, Athens, OH
Bachelor of Science in Language: German   May 1998

- Concentration: International Business
- GPA: 3.67   • Honors: *cum laude*
- Volunteer Tutor: tutored disadvantaged children, three times per week as part of the Athens Schools project. Taught English, Reading, and Math one-to-one. Also taught foreign-born students with limited English proficiency.

UNIVERSITY OF TUEBINGEN, Tuebingen, Germany
Semester Abroad: Full Matriculation into a German speaking university.   January - July 1997

ACHIEVEMENTS

- Achieved superior score on the PWD business German test developed by the Goethe Institute and the Association of German Chambers of Industry and Commerce, signifying an advanced level of German language proficiency in a business environment.
- Recognized for outstanding achievement by the German Department; First Honors once; Second Honors twice; Dean's List twice.

EMPLOYMENT

Summer 1998, CAMP NITTANY, Mohawk, PA   Head Counselor

- Supervised two assistant counselors in servicing 20 eight-year-old campers.
- Recognized for achieving excellent rapport with both campers and parents.

1996 - 1998, ACCESS SERVICES; OHIO UNIVERSITY LIBRARY, Athens, OH   Security Manager

- Supervised staff of three in maintaining security and order during late hours.
- Controlled access to the Library.

Summers 1996 & 1997, CERTIFIED TAX CONSULTANTS, New York, NY   Accounting Assistant

- Interviewed clients to gather information for tax returns.
- Maintained organized flow.
- Utilized computer software to produce final documents.

Lawyer (Entry-Level)

JAMES SHARPE
9 Central Avenue, Chicago, IL 60606 (312) 555-1212, James@careerbrain.com
Page 1 of 2

OBJECTIVE
A position as an Associate in a Law Firm where I can expand my knowledge and gain experience and expertise in the area of Corporate and Transitional Law.

SELECTED REFERENCES
- "…professional in manner, dress and approach…well-educated, articulate and well prepared…passionate, committed and focused on a goal-or goals…ethical and honest…will make a difference wherever (he) goes…," John Bryant, Chairman, Founder and CEO, OPERATION HOPE.
- "…outstanding young man, intelligent, capable and hard-working…well respected by his peers, a team member, a natural leader that I recommend for scholarship…," Marc Massout, Accounting Professor, Claremont McKenna College.

EDUCATION
UNIVERSITY OF CHICAGO LAW SCHOOL, Chicago, IL.
<u>**J.D. Degree**</u>, to be awarded June, 2000
- <u>**Student Lawyer**</u>, University of Chicago Mandel Legal Aid Clinic Member, Employment Discrimination Project, 1999 to Present
- <u>**Member & Prospective Student Host Coordinator**</u>, Student Admissions Committee, 1997 to 1998
- <u>**Treasurer**</u>, Black Law Students Association, 1998 to 1999

CLAREMONT McKENNA COLLEGE, Claremont, CA
- <u>**B.A. Degree, Dual Major, Government & Economics/Accounting**</u>
- <u>**Graduated with Honors**</u>, May 1997
- <u>**Awarded "Claremont McKenna College Scholar"**</u>
- <u>**Appointed Member of Student Board.**</u> Academic & Student Affairs Committee
- <u>**Awarded 4-Year Merit Scholarship**</u>
- <u>**Senior Thesis:**</u> "The Nature and Extent of Police Power in the United States" (Tracing Evolution from Plato, Socrates, Machiavelli to Current Community-Based Policing)

PROFESSIONAL EXPERIENCE
<u>**Legal Experience**</u>

1998 to present   **UNIVERSITY OF CHICAGO MANDEL LEGAL AID CLINIC**, Chicago, IL
<u>**Student Lawyer**</u>. Member of Employment Discrimination Project. Appeared in Federal Court and State Administrative Court; co-authored a brief submitted to Illinois State Appellate Court. Certified to practice as a Senior Law Student under Illinois Supreme Court Rule 711. Research issues regarding handicapped discrimination, racial discrimination, and procedural issues. Develop legal theories; interview prospective clients; negotiate and opposing counsel; prepare briefs and argumentative memoranda.

1998   **KIRKLAND & ELLIS**, Law Firm, Los Angeles, CA
<u>**Summer Associate**</u>. Participated in Kirkland & Ellis Institute of Trial Advocacy. Researched and produced memos, gave oral presentations regarding a wide range of legal issues, i.e., real property, trade libel, procedural issues, employment law, environmental matters, white-collar crime.

Page 2 of Sharpe (312) 555-1212

PROFESSIONAL EXPERIENCE (Continued)

<u>Business Experience</u>

1997   **OPERATION HOPE**, Los Angeles, CA
<u>Summer Intern</u>. Selected to intern directly for the CEO of Organization. Created and reviewed proposals to the Department of Commerce.

Drafted a general framework of proposal and created a condensed synopsis of a specific proposal to operate a Minority Business Development Center in Los Angeles. Contributed promotional ideas and support to launch of Operation Hope Banking Center.

1992 to present   **"REAL MEN COOK" FOUNDATION**, Fund raising Organization, Marina Del Ray, CA
<u>Board Member,</u> 1995 to present, <u>Executive Administrative Assistant</u>, Summers, 1990 to 1993 in conjunction with major pharmaceutical company, key member of team to plan, promote, and implement annual fund-raisers for 600 to 800 guests. Funds raised have supported 4 minority medical schools and increased awareness and prevention measures for prostate cancer. Additionally, prepare in-house financial reports for the Program Director.

<u>Government Experience</u>

1996   **U.S. DEPARTMENT OF COMMERCE** (California Task Force), Washington, DC
<u>Summer Intern</u>, researched to assure acquisition of funds and grants allocated for California. Worked directly with Office of Management of Budget as well as HUD. Prepared and delivered oral reports directly to Task Force Director. Helped to evaluate the potential of grants to foster recovery and economic growth in California cities formerly engaged in the defense industry.

1995   **OFFICE OF CONGRESSMAN CRAIG WASHINGTON**, Washington, DC
<u>Summer Intern</u>. Attended committee hearings, researched issues and bills, and corresponded with constituents regarding legislation.

ADDITIONAL REFERENCES AND RELATED DATA AVAILABLE UPON REQUEST

Management Consultant

James Sharpe

9 Central Avenue • Centreville, Virginia 20121 • Phone: (703) 555-1212 • James@careerbrain.com

Professional Profile

A seasoned, highly motivated senior executive with a successful track record in international operations and project management. Recognized for exceptional problem solving and motivational skills as well as the ability to **negotiate, deal, and close successfully across cultural barriers**. Extensive experience in management consulting in diverse industries, ranging from unit construction and mining/drilling operations to industrial equipment procurement, sales and distribution. **Bilingual with extensive international experience**, including Africa, the Middle East, South Asia, and Western Europe.

Areas of Impact

- International Conflict Resolution
- Operation and Project Management
- Global Emergency Planning
- Worldwide Corporate Security
- New Business Development
- International Public Relations
- Risk Assessment
- International Law
- Recruitment/Training

Career Highlights

- Successfully provided diplomatic, risk management, and crisis resolution services to a broad range of Fortune 100 companies, Ambassadors, Heads of State, cabinet ministers, and senior government officials, U.S. and foreign.
- Successfully negotiated, on behalf of Pete's Oil, with an east African government to resolve a cross-cultural crisis and avoid closure of a $1 billion distribution facility.
- Developed and implemented logistics and training programs involving several thousand U.S. and foreign personnel and a $40 million annual budget. Effectively achieved all objectives with a budget savings of 12%.
- Directed Jones & Jones, Big Truck Co., and Movers International in the successful negotiation of more than $15 million of capital equipment sales to a west African government.
- Conducted numerous feasibility studies and risk assessments, both political and economic forecasts, for a variety of projects including gold, platinum and diamond mining, nuclear energy development, port, railroad and packaging facilities.

Employment History

International Affairs Consultant
> Professional Services Provided to: Whitman International, Virginia Properties International, Pete's Oil, Tall Trees, Inc., Rothstein's Petroleum, Movers International, Jones & Jones, Big Truck Company, Top Flight Airlines, Technology USA, PTR International, Ltd., National Telecommunications Foundation, Master Technologies.

National Security Agency
> Near East and Africa Referent…Chief of Station…Chief of Operations…Chief of Branch, Counterterrorism…Deputy/Chief of Station.

Education

Juris Doctorate, *International Law,* University of Denver, Denver, CO
Master of Arts, *History,* University of Denver, Denver, CO
Bachelor of Arts, *History,* New College, Sarasota, FL

Marketing Analyst

JANE SWIFT
9 Central Avenue
DEARBORN, MI 48126
(313) 555-1212
Jane@careerbrain.com

EXPERIENCE:

Daytons, Inc. (Detroit, MI)   July 1998 to Present
MARKETING ANALYST - Provide a broad-based flow of data for merchandisers, buyers, Catalog Distribution Center associates, and management to assure continuing high-level profitability of the company's catalog sales. Access all databases by CRT terminal using CRIMS, an on-line system interfacing with ISA, IDB, and MIDB. Computer Analyses focus on:

- Historical applications, such as impact of season, media ads, space, price, and color changes
- Reliable pre-season forecasts of catalog demand patterns and in-season revisions where necessary to maintain inventory control
- Study of inventory turnover in relation to buying estimates, commitments, and quality of merchandise
- Choice of models and development of new ones for item estimating
- Identification of systems problems in estimates above or below plan
- Establishment of recommendations for inventory surplus solutions
- Decision-marketing, planning, scheduling to meet data deadlines

Zachary & Front Advertising, Inc.   New York, NY Summer 1997
OFFICE MANAGER - Arranged for in-house weekly newsletter and biweekly policy memos for new agency. Developed billing system, dealt with clients, and managed clerical staffing.

Tisch Properties   New York, NY Winter 1997
ASSISTANT BOOKKEEPER - Worked with accounts receivable/payable, bank reconciliations

EDUCATION:

State University of Ohio
B.S., Business Administration, 1998
Concentration: Marketing and Management Information Systems

COMPUTER SKILLS:

Visual Basic, C++, FCS-EPS, and SPSS software package

References Available Upon Request

Marketing Management

Jane Swift
9 Central Avenue
Lexington, KY 40579

(606) 555-1212
Jane@careerbrain.com

Profile

Marketing Management ● Promotions Management ● Sales Management

A goal-oriented, decisive manager with 10+ years experience in a corporate sales and marketing environment. Exceptionally creative with effective organizational abilities and interpersonal skills. Powerful leadership and management expertise with especially strong planning, coordinating, and delegating capacities. Solid problem solving abilities. Demonstrated capacity to successfully manage multiple projects and deadlines, coming in on time and within budget.

Demonstrated Strengths

- key account development and relations
- new product introduction
- sales and trend analysis
- target market development
- software proficiency with PowerPoint, Excel, Word, and FM Pro
- presentation development and delivery

- creative purchase incentives and promotions
- sales management
- distributor management
- project management

Selected Achievements

- Received Achievement Award 2 years in a row for double-digit increases in sales and development of promotional strategies and programs.
- Selected as one of 19 managers nationwide to participate in pilot program to restore positive sales growth in Southwest market areas.
- Developed numerous creative merchandising pieces throughout career that increased visibility and sales.
- Key player in several marketing initiatives such as a marketing partnership that brought several major companies together in a massive merchandising program. Effectively managed essential initiatives that positioned Pepsi very competitively.
- Guided distributors to improve sales and marketing figures.
- Increased sales figures 50% in one year in a targeted segment. Increased sales in key accounts an average of 5% and improved feature activity and display performance from 50% to 80%.
- Counseled sales representatives and helped one improve performance from marginal to outstanding in one year.
- Met project deadlines (average lead time 4 - 6 weeks) 98% of the time.

Professional Experience

Pepsi Cola Bottling Company
Promotions Manager, Lexington, KY   1998 to Present
Assist National Sales Manager and key accounts by developing customized, value-added promotions that drive volume and gain ad and display activity. Manager over 150 programs annually. Purchase incentives include cross-merchandising programs with other vendors, coupons, rebates, liquidators, and sweepstakes. Coordinate promotional ideas and programs with creative agencies, sports marketing, and legal departments. Manage project costs and a budget of over $4 million.

Sales and Merchandising Manager, Boston, MA   1997 to 1998
Supervise a team of sales and marketing specialists to increase sales in the Boston/New England markets. Develop distributor incentives. Work alongside distributors and corporate personnel to cultivate key retail accounts, sell product and displays, increase cooler space, and improve merchandising.

Marketing Manager, Chicago, IL   1995 to 1997
Manage territory that generates sales of 40+ million cases of Pepsi products annually--the region's largest in terms of volume and budget. Work closely with media partners to foster awareness and develop promotional lineup. Integrate regional marketing efforts with national brand strategies. Directly accountable for $600,000 budget.

Sales Manager, Phoenix, AZ   1994 to 1995
Aggressively lead targeted incentive programs and promotions. Improve distributor sales by conducting surveys and developing action plans to capitalize on sales opportunities. Make frequent calls on buyers. Increase company awareness through development of a monthly newsletter.

Sales and Marketing Planner, Lexington, KY   1992 to 1994
Assist Regional Manager in managing sales/marketing activities. Develop "how to" promotional manual for field personnel. Improve media support of promotions in 3 states. Administer a $200,000 budget.

Education
BS in Business Administration, Major: Marketing, University of Kentucky, Lexington, KY

Medical Technology Sales

James Sharpe

Page 1 of 2

9 Central Avenue
Beaverton, OR 97005
(503) 555-1212
James@careerbrain.com

Summary of Qualifications

Medical Technology/Software Sales and Marketing Executive specializing in opening new markets and introducing new products. Combining strategic sales expertise, marketing creativity, and clinical knowledge to successfully communicate product benefits to end users. Reputation for envisioning future client needs and translating those needs into products that provide solutions. Team player who recognizes strengths in people and corporations and brings them together to form strategic alliances to reach common objectives. Major strengths include:

- Market forecasting and new business development
- Product development (inventor of two medical products)
- Solid blend of people, sales, and business skills
- Sales and distribution channels
- Strategic alliances and acquisitions
- Technically competent with many different software applications
- Communication and formal presentation skills

Employment History

Medical Technology Systems, Beaverton Oregon   1997 - Present
  Health care information systems company with a customer base of 480 hospitals throughout the U.S. Develops point-of-care software systems/databases for clinicians in various specialties.
  Vice President of Sales
  - Recruited to develop sales organization and build customer base for emerging technology.
  - Instrumental in increasing annual sales from $1.5M to $6.5M over two years.
  - Built sales channel operation based on nationwide reputation with distributors, enabling company to grow rapidly with minimal investment.
  - Direct product managers in developing specifications and requirements for new products.

XYZ Technology, Portland Oregon   1980 - 1997
  Distributor specializing in introduction of new medical technology products. Recruited early on by president of company and promoted through several increasingly responsible positions. Instrumental in increasing annual sales from $4M to $20M with a 40% gross profit margin.
  General Manager of Information Systems
  - Recognized significance of emerging market for information systems within health care. Charged with creating and launching this brand new division.
  - Drove sales from $0 to $2.5M within two years.
  - Developed hospital client base of 100 installations.
  - Helped guide product development by interpreting market trends to product managers.

  Sales Manager of the Hospital Division selling 30+ different types of medical devices such as IV pumps, infusion supplies, hypo- and hyperthermia equipment. Covered six states and managed 12 sales reps.

<u>Pain Management Specialist</u>. Developed consulting service to help hospitals establish acute pain management services. Working with pharmacies, physicians, and nurses, assisted hospitals with organizing pain management committees, developing policies and procedures, and defining reimbursement protocol.

- Established 30 hospital programs along West Coast.
- Recruited by C.R. BARD's Med-Systems Division to consult with their clients on a national level.
- Developed Excel spreadsheet for sales force to demonstrate potential revenue stream from this new service to physicians.
- Attended BARD's national sales meetings and trained their sales reps.

<u>Field Manager for Oregon</u>. Produced $1.4M/year in personal sales while also supervising sales reps.

<u>Product Manager</u>. XYZ developed and manufactured the first IV filter designed to withstand the pressure of an IV pump.

<u>Field Sales Representative</u>. Promoted after 9 months to Product Manager.

Dale Carnegie, 1975 - 1980

<u>Sales Manager/Instructor</u>. Recruited by Dale Carnegie at the age of 20 to conduct seminars after completing their Sales and Management course. Youngest Dale Carnegie instructor in history of company.

Education
University of Michigan, Business Management courses
Dale Carnegie Sales & Management course

Music Teacher

James Sharpe
9 Central Avenue
Miami, FL 33161
(305) 555-1212
James@careerbrain.com

● Music Educator ● Adjunct Professor ● Master Class Teacher ● Professional Performer ●
● Arranger Composer ● Conductor ● Arts Council Consultant ● Who's Who in American Teachers ●

Mission Statement

To inspire students and audiences to achieve a deep appreciation for the many aspects of music. To devote my personal passion for music performance and theory to impact students at the college level. To instill a respectful dedication for the beauty and discipline of music that will enhance all aspects of academic and personal achievement.

Credentials

- Director of Broward County Community College Guitar Ensemble.
- Awarded inclusion in 1998 Who's Who Among America's Teachers
- Professional Guitarist: Classical, Jazz, and Improvisational music.
- College-level Applied Music Instructor: Classical Guitar Technique.
- Author of over 70 arrangements for guitar ensemble.
- Composer of four original works for guitar ensemble.
- Studio musician: recorded at the Power Station in Manhattan.
- Consultant to local arts councils: Miami Beach Arts, Port Davis
- Developer of original music theory program for Miami Beach Arts Council
- Expert in Encore, Finale, and IBIS music notation/dictation software.

Education

Master of Arts in Music Theory, University of Miami, 1997
Master of Music: Classical Guitar Performance, University of Miami, 1993
Bachelor of Arts in Music, University of Miami, 1989

Professional Development

Member of Guitar Foundation of America
Music Teachers' National Association
Master Classes and Workshops:
 Classical: Eduardo Fernandez, David Starobin, Jerry Willard.
 Jazz: Howard Morgen, Howard Roberts, Barney Kessel.
 Progressive: Robert Fripp.
 Locations: Florida State University, University of Florida, The American Institute of Guitar, Miami University

Nurse

JANE SWIFT, R.N., C.

9 Central Avenue • Phoenix, AZ 85016 • (602) 555-1212 • Jane@careerbrain.com
Page 1 of 2

CAREER PROFILE

Dedicated medical professional with nine years practical experience in a fast-paced hospital setting. Resourceful problem-solver capable of initiating formative solutions to complex problems. Possess special sensitivity to meeting diverse needs in varied situations. *Key strengths include:*

- Remain calm and professional during times of critical need.
- Strong analytical skills, easily assess conditions and implement appropriate intervention.
- Ability to motivate, produce and coordinate instructions, organize assignments, and evaluate staffing requirements.
- Relate well to people from a variety of cultures and socioeconomic conditions.
- Readily develop rapport with patients, families, staff, physicians, and other health care professionals.
- Proven record of reliability and responsibility.

PROFESSIONAL EXPERIENCE AND ACCOMPLISHMENTS

1992 to Present   ARIZONA MEMORIAL HOSPITAL, Phoenix, AZ

Staff Nurse—Respiratory Care
Responsible for respiratory patient care in a highly technical and complex hospital environment.
Participate in unit Quality Assurance program and work cooperatively with physicians, medical professionals, patients, their family members, and other hospitals to provide quality patient care.

Specific responsibilities:

- Alternating charge nurse accountability as assigned by nurse manager.
  - Supervise 8 to 12 staff nurses.
  - Evaluate staffing requirements, floor assignments and organize unit activities.
  - Communicate physician orders to appropriate departments utilizing computerized data system.
- Implement total patient care (physical, psychological and cognitive aspects) for 7 to 9 patient assignment.
- Supervise Licensed Practical Nurses, non-licensed support staff and orient new staff members.
- Perform clinical skills according to hospital policies and standards of practice.
- Interact with applicable departments regarding patient care.
- Act as patient advocate; assess patient status and notify physicians of clinical changes.
- Educate patient/family members to health care needs, conditions, processes, agendas and options.
- Collaborate with case management regarding discharge needs.
- Served on Hospital Quality Assurance Committee and Task Force to develop a new care system.

1997 to 2000   **Instructor**
Developed lesson plans and curriculum for the Nurse Refresher Program and Adult Respiratory Education for group of up to 35.

1991 to 1993   ARIZONA HEALTH CENTER, Phoenix, AZ
Nursing Assistant

EDUCATION

ARIZONA GRADUATE CENTER, Scottsdale, AZ
Master of Science in *Health Care Management,* 1998

UNIVERSITY OF ARIZONA, Scottsdale, AZ
Bachelor of Science in *Nursing,* 1990

LICENSURE/CERTIFICATIONS

- **R.N. License,** Arizona
- **R.N. License,** New Mexico
- **Nurse Preceptor**
- **Medical/Surgical Nursing Certification**

Operations and Executive Project Management

James Sharpe

9 Central Avenue • White Sulphur Springs MT 59645 • Ph. (406) 555-1212 • Fax (406) 555-1213
James@careerbrain.com

Executive Summary

*A seasoned, team-oriented business executive with a highly successful track record with start-up and turnaround situations. More than 15 years progressive experience in all phases of **Operations and Project Management** with particular strength in feasibility analysis. Recognized for exceptional organization building skills as well as the ability to motivate others on all levels in the achievement of individual and organizational goals.*

- *Business Process Re-engineering*
- *Feasibility Analysis/Projections*
- *Negotiation and Arbitration*
- *Project Management*
- *Crisis Resolution*
- *Start-up Management*
- *Business Valuation*
- *Liquidation Management*
- *P&L Responsibility*

Selected Achievements

- Successfully administered a portfolio of contracts with a value exceeding $10 million. The average income of each client **increased by 15%, a gain of more than $1.5 million.**
- Provided consulting services to more than 1,090 clients from numerous parts of the U.S. and Latin America as well as conducted numerous feasibility studies for projects valued at up to **$100,000,000.**
- Orchestrated a successful start-up company with responsibilities including site selection and acquisition through P&L accountability; **annual sales exceeded $50 million within ten years.**
- Aggressively negotiated, supervised, or advised in the negotiation of several contracts totaling in excess of $68 million, **savings clients at least $6.5 million.** Recent negotiations resulted in a verifiable return of **40% over current market value, a total gain of $520,000.**
- Pioneered state-of-the-art plant expansion that involved a capital investment of $500,000 and realized a **50% increase in plant capacity.**
- Successfully restarted an organization that had been shut down due to severe labor-management and production problems. Through various management techniques and styles that motivated the employees, **production increased by nearly 50% while operating costs stayed constant.**

Consulting Highlights

Wright and Holmes, Inc., *White Sulphur Springs, MT*   ***Since 1992***
President

Representative List of Clients

Dodson & Mark	*The Life Insurance Co.*	*Ambrose Technologies*
Montana Trust	*Sulphur Springs Real Estate*	*Pacific Northwest Financial*
Horn Communications	*Jervais Investments*	*UpStart USA*
Jones Timber	*Mountain Hydraulics*	*National Research Foundation*

Education

Bachelor of Science, Business Administration
University of Montana, Missoula MT

Interim assignments and consulting projects preferred. Available for extensive travel in U.S. and abroad. Undeterred by the most arduous conditions.

Operations Management Investment / Securities Industry

Jane Swift
9 Central Avenue
Nyack, NY 10960
(914) 555-1212
Jane@careerbrain.com
Page 1 of 2

Expert in Process Redesign, Performance Reengineering & Productivity/Performance Improvement

RESULTS-DRIVEN PROFESSIONAL with 13+ years experience in leading-edge investment industry research production systems. Excellent analytical and problem-solving skills. Able to work under pressure in fast-paced, time-sensitive environments. Experienced in analyzing and streamlining systems and operations to increase productivity, quality, and efficiency. Proven ability to manage projects from planning through execution. Strong contributions in driving organizational change and improvement. Highly experienced in using spreadsheet, database, and word processing applications. Additional expertise includes:

- Strategic Planning
- Team Building and Leadership
- Financial Models
- Financial Analysis
- Operational Benchmarking
- Systems Administration

PROFILE

- Organized, enthusiastic management professional; willing to hear new ideas and go the extra mile to improve performance.
- Possess strong interpersonal skills; able to work effectively with individuals on all levels.
- Demonstrated ability to develop and maintain sound business relationships with clients, anticipating their needs.
- Strong problem resolution skills; able to efficiently and effectively prioritize a broad range of responsibilities to consistently meet deadlines.
- Hold both Series 7 and 63 licenses.
- Catalyst for change, transformation, and performance improvement.
- Achieved reputation as a resource person, problem solver, troubleshooter, and creative turnaround manager.

PROFESSIONAL EXPERIENCE

Dulce & True, New York, NY   October 1989 - Present
Senior Business Analyst - Fixed Income Pricing Group   May 1998 - Present
- Currently developing the tactical capability to reprice over 3,000 issues in the Salomon Corporate Bond Index on a daily basis and package these prices for sale to buy-side investment companies.
- Designed and implemented Web-based data verification process, improving the quality of Salomon's corporate bond pricing data to the point where customers want to purchase the data to compute daily NAVs.
- Innovated pricing system on the High Yield trading desk, providing sales staff access to valuable pricing data used to generate increased trading with customers.
- Recognized for the ability to work with many areas of the firm, bridging the gap between competing and sometimes adversarial departments to create business opportunities.

Manager - Fixed Income Index Production Group   May 1994 - May 1998
- Streamlined the index production process, responding to customer requests for earlier publication and also allowing index production personnel more time to get involved in more challenging, productive, and profitable projects.
- Effectively implemented several new systems versions and processes without any disruption to our business, our customers, or the business of other areas of the firm.
- Built and maintained strong relationships with customers, ensuring their continued business with the firm.

- Implemented verification processes to prevent the publication of inaccurate data, thereby avoiding strained relationships with customers.
- Improved accuracy of index products, generating greater market share, and confirming our position as market leaders in the fixed income index business.
- Assumed responsibility for the Index Production Group at a very crucial time in the development of indexing as a primary portfolio management strategy. Managed staff of eight responsible for the timely and accurate production of the Aggregate, Global, and Eurobond Indices.
- Improvised in the event of system failures or other problems and made quick firm decisions directing subordinates to focus on the solution or their part of the plan of action.
- Successfully introduced Eurobond Index providing the foundation for subsequent European Fixed Income Indices.
- Directed the conversion to SUN based pricing system for over 5,000 corporate and high-yield bonds from a clumsy and inefficient paper based system eliminating the need for data to be handled twice.
- Researched accuracy problems, reorganized and restructured verification procedures surrounding the Salomon Indices, significantly enhancing the accuracy and reliability of published numbers.
- Reduced production time by more than 60% while increasing quality standards.
- Never had to republish or restate monthly index results.

Portfolio Strategist - Fixed Income Strategy Group   July 1992 - May 1994
- Formed constructive ongoing relationships with several clients around structuring their fixed income portfolios, which generated increased trading with the firm and an additional communication link to the customer.
- Trained customers with respect to the workings of the index and our analytics, increasing their comfort level and willingness to do business with Salomon.

Analyst - Fixed Income Index Production Group   October 1989 - July 1992
- Organized and streamlined the production of the Daily Treasury Index leading to daily publication in the *Wall Street Journal*.
- Designed and implemented all data verification and distribution procedures.
- Published hourly U.S. Treasury market commentary on Telerate News Service.

Hartford Life - Hartford, CT   February 1987 - October 1989
Regional Accounting and Coordinating Divisions

COMMUNITY INVOLVEMENT
CENTRE COLLEGE ALUMNI CLUB, Danville, KY
  President (1997 - 1999), Executive Committee Member (1992 - 1999) for College Alumni Organization committed to supporting college athletic programs.
LACROSSE CLUB, Hartford County, CT
  Member (1987 - 1994) and Coach (1993 - 1994)
SPORTS FITNESS CLUB, Greenwich, CT
  Yoga Instructor (1995 - 1998)

EDUCATION
CENTRE COLLEGE, Danville, KY
  Bachelor of Arts: Economics   May 1987

REFERENCES
Will be furnished on request.

Organizational Management

Jane Swift
9 Central Avenue
Arlington, MA 02174
(617) 555-1212
Jane@careerbrain.com

Organizational Manager/Program Coordinator/Turnaround Strategist

Career Profile

Accomplished administrator with over ten years of experience in cost-effective program development and revitalization. Work with large not-for-profit entities providing therapeutic and preventive services focusing on restoration of families to productive employment and societal relationships. Run programs with a social worker's compassion blended with a corporate manager's productivity, fiscal responsibility, and results.

Areas of Expertise

- Total program administration
- Cost-effective management
- Long-term strategic planning
- Team building and leadership
- Staff training and mentoring
- Fundraising and grant writing

- Multimillion dollar budget oversight
- Program start-ups and turnarounds
- Program development/enhancement
- Crisis intervention
- Public speaking and education
- Windows 98, Microsoft Word, Internet

Career Highlights

- **Instrumental in start-up of association formed to assist former inmates with re-establishment of family units, drug-free living, and employment.** Hired to aid in the From Prison to Paycheck start-up. Created "preventive" element of program, hired professional staff, constructed organizational structure, planned services, trained staff, and authored treatment plans. Ensured retention of funding by meticulous following of state mandates.

- **Revitalized and dramatically expanded youth program slated for closure.** The Dorchester Foster Home for very troubled children was running at less than half capacity. Immediately strengthened referring relationships and implemented new policies and procedures. Increased to 24-resident capacity within first year. Now, after five consecutive successful years, have a $6 million budget, over 80 children in program, and substantial government funding. Program is community-based and more cost effective than treating children in a facility.

- **Received Best Site award for successful revamping of poorly run teen group home.** Created general structure, daily living schedule, and boundaries; revised mental attitudes; established consequences; and instituted a reward system. Retrained staff and reduced turnover. Changes precipitated a stronger sense of self esteem, instilled a sense of home in the residents, reduced AWOL rate, decreased school absenteeism, and raised residents' grades.

- **Restored program suffering from lack of proper casework processing.** Recruited as Supervisor to resolve near-crisis situation. Mandated monitoring and tracking was not being performed to standard. Department was overwhelmed with new daily cases and over 100 ongoing cases requiring (by mandate) 24 hours to investigate, 7 days to recommend, and 30 days to refer. Took over, cleaned up unit, saved funding, and prevented closure of vital program.

- **Addressed Fortune 500 CEOs as keynote speaker at the Athenaeum.** Presented an informative presentation about the day-to-day operations of a successful therapeutic foster care program, an overview of its management, and a perspective on its bottom-line value.

Education and Certification

M.S.W. Harvard University; B.S.W. Boston University; C.S.W. University of Massachusetts

Professional Development

Dorchester Foster Home: Program Director, Program Coordinator   1998 to present

> Recruited to revive ailing program and prevent closure. Have tripled enrollment, expanded to multiple locations, and obtained needed government funding. Manage overall administration and $5 million budget. supervise 32 staff members in 3 offices. Coordinate referral intake process and recruitment/training of therapeutic foster parents. Liaison with all relevant government and community agencies. Provide 24/7 crisis intervention coverage.

From Prison to Paycheck: Start-up Consultant, Case Work Supervisor   1997 to 1998

> Oversaw 70 preventive cases of people involved with the criminal justice system. Supervised staff. Monitored all mandated paperwork. Coordinated workshops. Obtained linkages with community organizations. Provided emergency beeper coverage.

Family Crisis Foundation: Site Supervisor, Case Manager   1990 to 1997

> Revitalized ailing group home for troubled youth, creating a model that received Best Site of the Year award. Managed total operation of home including hiring, budgetary, physical site, casework, staff oversight, and intensive casework. Oversaw 100 active crisis and long-term cases. Supervised child protective workers and case workers. Consulted with agency attorney's. Provided 24/7 emergency coverage. Developed goals for a caseload of 33 families, utilizing direct services, advocacy, and referrals. Supervised visitation. Responded to crisis situations.

Awards and Service

- Mayor's Award for Outstanding Service
- Distinguished Service Award
- Best Site of Year Award

Outside Sales/Account Manger/Customer Service

Jane Swift
9 Central Avenue
Wilmington, DE 19801
(302) 555-1212
Jane@careerbrain.com

Energetic and goal-focused sales professional with solid qualifications in large account management and customer relationship building/maintenance. Proven ability to develop new business and increase sales within established accounts and mature territories. Self confident and poised in interactions across all business hierarchies; a persuasive communicator and assertive negotiator with strong deal closing abilities. Excellent time management skills; computer literate. Areas of demonstrated value include:

- Sales Growth / Account Development
- Commercial Account Management
- Prospecting & Business Development
- Customer Liaison & Service
- Consultative Sales / Needs Assessment
- Territory Management & Growth

PROFESSIONAL EXPERIENCE

Morris Mtr. Co., Wilmington, DE   1995 - Present
    SALES EXECUTIVE (1997 - Present)
    Promoted and challenged to revitalize a large metropolitan territory plagued by poor performance. Manage, service, and build existing accounts; develop new business, establishing both regional and national accounts. Serve as key liaison for all customers and work as the only outside sales representative in the company. Produce monthly reports for major national accounts.
    Selected Results
- Reversed a history of stagnant sales; delivered consistent growth and built territory sales 22%, to $4.75 million annually, in less than 2 years.
- Surpassed quota by a minimum of 20% for 14 consecutive months.
- Personally deliver 95% of all sales generated for the company's main site.
- Prospected aggressively and presented products to key decision-makers during cold calls; opened more than 60 new commercial accounts.
- Improved account service and applied consultative sales techniques; grew sales in every established account a minimum of 15%.

    MANAGER, Harrisburg Store (1995 - 1997)
    MANAGER TRAINEE, Wilmington Store (1995)
    Initially recruited as a management trainee and rapidly advanced to management of a retail location generating $1 million annually. Supervised and scheduled 12 employees. Budgeted and produced advertising, oversaw bookkeeping, and set/managed sales projections and growth objectives.

EDUCATION AND CREDENTIALS
B.S., BUSINESS MANAGEMENT, 1995
Wilmington College, New Castle, DE

Additional Training
- Building Sales Relationships, 1998
- Problem Solving Skills, 1998

Professional & Community Associations
- Member, Chamber of Commerce, 1996 - Present
- Member, Country Club and Women's Golf Association, 1996 - Present
- Youth Soccer Coach and FIFA Certified Referee, 1999 - Present

Paralegal

JAMES SHARPE, 9 Central Avenue, Cleveland, OH 44115 (216) 555-1212, James@careerbrain.com

EXPERIENCE:

Robert Schoenberg P.C. Cleveland, OH
Paralegal
Responsibility for various financial aspects of the partnership; organized the office work schedule. Answered the calendar calls in motion part, argued the motions and adjourned cases when necessary; conferenced cases in pre-trial procedure.

Drafted summons and complaints, subpoena duces tecum and judicial subpoena, answers to interrogatories, and all notices of discovery.

Reviewed experts' reports and evaluated their relevance in the case.

Prepared clients for examinations before trial and city hearings.

1994 - Present

Appellate Division Municipal Court of Hong Kong
Judicial Assistant
Participated in civil and criminal trials; took depositions. Drafted the court decisions.

1986 - 1992

EDUCATION:

Brooklyn Law School, Brooklyn, New York
Graduated with diploma in Foreign Trained Lawyers Program
February, 1994

Ohio State Bar Examination taken in July, 1997

Bernard Baruch College of the City University of New York
Paralegal Studies
Certified as a Paralegal in August, 1994

University of Hong Kong
Faculty of Law
Master of Arts - Specialty: Law, February, 1991

SKILLS:

Fluent in Japanese and several Chinese dialects
Freelance writer for Asian newspapers published in the United States
Translator from above languages into English and vice versa

Pharmaceutical Sales, LPN

Jane Swift
9 Central Avenue
Sacramento, CA 95691
(916) 555-1212
Jane@careerbrain.com

Professional Objective
- Position as sales representative, health care liaison, or account relationship manager in the field of pharmaceutical or medical sales.
- Will utilize comprehensive health care training, proven high-ticket sales support expertise, excellent communications skills, and self-directed prioritization abilities to produce an immediate, bottom line impact.

Career Profile
- Six years of experience as LPN caring for patients in intensively active, fourteen doctor/nurse practitioner practice with daily patient load of approximately 450 (infants to age 21).
- Three concurrent years of high-ticket sales support background with busy construction firm.
- Exceptionally flexible, diplomatic, organized, dedicated, patient, calm, and reliable. Eager and willing to learn new skills and transition knowledge to produce profitable corporate achievements.

Employment
Licensed Practical Nurse, 1994 to Present
Mid-California Pediatric, Sacramento, California
- Balance a nonstop schedule, assisting 50 to 60 patients each day, performing accurate assessments, a full range of nursing functions, and limited lab work.
- Partner with doctors to competently and compassionately serve patients, and to establish a genuine patient and family rapport.
- Act as doctor/patient liaison for phone and office consults. Conduct patient education sessions. Deliver doctors' follow-up instructions.

Sales Representative and Office Manager, 1995 to Present
Farrell Construction, Sacramento, California
- Perform work in sales, relationship management, and office support for this residential construction firm specializing in basic to luxury renovations.
- Work closely with potential customers to assist firm's closing of deals in a highly competitive field. Typical sales range from $3,000 to $20,000.

Education, Licensure, and Certification
- Graduate Practical Nurse, Mid-California School of Nursing
- Associates degree in progress, University of California at Davis
- Infection Control Certification, Napa Community College

Probation Officer

James Sharpe
9 Central Avenue
Phoenix, AZ 85016

(602) 555-1212
James@careerbrain.com
Page 1 of 2

Profile

- Over fifteen years Human Services experience as Probation Officer, Peace Officer, and Officer of the Court. Academic and professional background in Social Services and Business. Currently enrolled in university-level Human Resource Management certificate program. Hold Bachelor of Science in Criminal Justice.
- Use personal initiative to review operations and develop programs that improve client services, build communication between agencies, and promote efficient functioning with reduced resources.
- Recipient of two service awards for distinction in police work. Enthusiastic and self-driven "go-to" person with proven ability to master whatever is needed to meet goals and achieve excellence.

Areas of Expertise

• program creation and development • departmental restructuring • comprehensive investigative and psycho-social reporting • counseling and supervision • agency relations • court appearances •

Employment

Maricopa County Probation Department (Human Services)

Overview

- Work in one of the nation's largest suburban counties, with a probationer population of 16,500. Currently manage a caseload of screened clients in an innovative prison alternative "day-reporting" program. Previously managed a 150-probationer caseload in an economically depressed, drug involved neighborhood with limited resources. Area included large percentage of individuals with drug and alcohol involvement, educational deficits, and limited job skills.
- Use social service skills and expert fieldwork as well as meticulous record keeping and timely follow-up on a daily basis. Always work with limited staff and unrelenting deadline pressure. Put in long days and do paperwork into the early hours of the morning.

Highlights

- Integral member of an award-winning probation team that was requested to become a key component of "Weed and Seed," a federally sponsored task force. In 1998, received an Arizona State Assembly Citation for team's groundbreaking work with Weed and Seed program. Original pilot program has been so effective that it is currently in use by six additional probation teams.
- Developed innovative approach that combined caseloads with two remaining team members, in crisis response to loss of two additional members. New approach allowed processing of a greater number of clients, supported an effective network of resources, and better aided high-maintenance and high-risk clients. Extensive resource network enabled team to obtain preferential client treatment as organizations became dependent on team's referrals and became more effective in developing client treatment plans.
- Currently working in prison-alternative day treatment program that serves screened mentally ill and/or chemical dependent abusers through medication administration, counseling, and education programs. Center had difficulty in maintaining schedule of medications necessary for clients' stability, as hostile and uncooperative individuals needed to be escorted to health clinics for their medication and medical needs. These patients were also unreceptive to rehabilitative programs.
- Convinced clinics to provide an on-site registered nurse to perform home-based visits so that clients' medications could be administered, dramatically reducing client hospitalization times, keeping clients stable, and making families receptive to team's efforts. Client stability now allows effective use of rehabilitative GED and counseling programs.

Other Experience
- Worked as part-time Veterans Benefits Counselor for the U.S. Office of Veterans Affairs.
- Functioned as part-time Security for various companies
- Provided supervision as part-time Direct Care Counselor for mentally retarded and disabled individuals living in group homes.
- Served in United States Army, Corporal, Personnel Administration Clerk/Instructor

Education
Arizona State University, School of Management and Division for Professional Development
- Certificate program: Human Resources Management, Summer 2000
- Certificate in Business Use of Computers, 1998
- 12 Management credits

State University of New York at Albany
- BS in Criminal Justice, Sociology minor, 1993

Technology Skills
Fluent in Windows 95/98, Knowledge of Microsoft Office Suite, WordPerfect, Internet, E-mail

Affiliations
Police Association of Maricopa County, Arizona Fraternal Order of Police, Marine Corps League

Project Manager/Programmer Analyst

James Sharpe
9 Central Avenue
Minneapolis, MN 55402
(612) 555-1212
James@careerbrain.com

Senior project manager with nearly 20 years experience in technical project management, systems hardware, and software applications. Skilled in day-to-day management operations of large systems support center. Successful in developing and integrating technologies to support operational, financial, and organizational needs. Recognized for excellent problem-solving skills and developing/managing various programs and projects successfully.

TECHNICAL PROFICIENCIES

- VSE/ESA • VM • MVS • VSAM • CICS • VOLLIE • Librarian • DYNAM •
- BAL • COBOL • COBOL II • Easytrieve Plus • ORACLE • PL/SQL •
- SQL • C++ • Borland C++ Builder • MS Windows 95/98 •
- Windows NT • Internet • E-mail •

QUALIFICATION HIGHLIGHTS

- Well-versed and highly skilled in system programming
- Exhibits excellent problem-solving and analytical skills
- In-depth knowledge of programming languages and hands-on experience
- Learns and applies new skills quickly—takes advantage of resources and tools available
- Demonstrates team leadership and promotes positive management style
- Strong ability to guide and mentor junior programmers

PROFESSIONAL EXPERIENCE

Bank Services Provider, Minneapolis, Minnesota   1995 - Present
Data Center Support Manager - Provide management support of retail banking system through designing and coding new programs, resolve production issues and oversee program maintenance.

- Developed SQL and PL/SQL programs for client server programming groups
- Produced written procedures automating job scheduling enabling company to complete 4 conversions within a 2 day period
- Streamlined client acquisition process during increased acquisitions/mergers within banking industry by successfully designing, coding, and implementing "internal acquisition conversion" system
- Improved data mapping process by automating manual tasks by designing program to read COBOL copy book, creating Doner File Data Directory
- Reduced CPU utilization by 50% through major code revisions in conversion software

Financial Management Corporation, Minneapolis, Minnesota   1993 - 1995
Systems and Programming Manager - Administered project life cycle from initial systems planning and technology acquisition through installation, training, and operations.

- Managed and coded major system modifications to deposit application systems to support Tax Equity and Fiscal Responsibility Act (TEFRA)
- Revitalized programming code, eliminating errors and improving IRS Reporting System
- Designed and coded data conversion algorithms, eliminating processing errors and improving reliability of Certificate of Deposit System

Prior Professional Experience

Jones Consultant, Inc. - Minneapolis, Minnesota
   Specializing in Program and Project Management Systems
Quick Data Processing - Minneapolis, Minnesota
   Retail Banking Systems Development Director
Computer Group, Inc. - Minneapolis, Minnesota
   Senior Systems Consultant

Education

Minnesota Technical College
- Network Essentials (Courses Completed), 1999
- Beginning/Advanced C++ (Courses Completed), 1998/1999
- Associate in Applied Science - General Studies, 1991

Property Management

Jane Swift
9 Central Avenue
Omaha, NE 68106
(402) 555-1212
Jane@careerbrain.com

OBJECTIVE
Position in Property Management.

QUALIFICATION HIGHLIGHTS
- More than six years of experience assisting in the management of multiple rental properties.
- Thoroughly familiar with both tenant and landlord laws and guidelines; experienced in collections and municipal court procedures.
- Extensive business background in general management, customer service and support, and subcontractor supervision.
- Advanced computer skills and demonstrated proficiency in streamlining administrative tasks through the application of technology.
- Resourceful and innovative in problem solving; adapt quickly to a challenge. Strong prioritization, delegation, and planning skills.
- Relate warmly to diverse individuals at all levels; respectful yet assertive communication style.

KEY SKILLS & ABILITIES
- Perform background, reference, and credit checks; select quality tenants and maintain high occupancy rates.
- Show available properties to prospective tenants; negotiate lease and rental agreements.
- Handle tenant communications; respond to requests for maintenance and answer questions.
- Troubleshoot and resolve disputes, including evictions and cleaning/damage deposits.
- Research legal issues utilizing Nolo Press publications, file court documents, and represent property owner in court.
- Schedule and supervise subcontractors; oversee upgrades, maintenance, and renovations.
- Plan and manage budgets; execute general accounting functions.
- Set up and maintain computerized property management systems.
- Coordinate and track rent collection, maintenance, and repairs. Proactively address security issues.

CAREER HISTORY
Assistant Property Manager (1998 - Present)
> Smith's Realty, Omaha, NE
>> Assist in the management and oversight of multiple residential rental properties. Set up efficient administrative systems, coordinate rent collection, handle tenant disputes, and resolve legal issues.

Owner-Manager (1986 - 1998)
> Computer Works, Omaha, NE
>> Founded and managed this micro/mini-computer sales and systems integration company. Achieved status as a Southwestern Bell Master Vendor.

EDUCATION
Metropolitan Technical Community College (1985 - 1986)
Emphasis in Business Administration

Public Relations/Media Spokesperson

JANE SWIFT
9 Central Avenue
Phoenix, AZ 85016
(602) 555-1212
Jane@careerbrain.com

OBJECTIVE:

 A position in Public Relations where I can utilize my skills as a media spokesperson and my ability to execute a variety of projects simultaneously.

EXPERIENCE:

Public Relations Associate/Media
ADRIENNE ARPEL. Phoenix, AZ. 1992 to Present

- Media spokesperson for 12 western states: Interviewed and trained personnel for TV, radio and print
- Established contacts with producers and editors
- Wrote press releases
- Developed media and promotional packages
- Booked interviews with press

District Sales Manager
ADRIENNE ARPEL. Phoenix, AZ. 1989 - 1992

- Supervised 169 representatives with a $500,000 sales volume

Account Executive/Radio Reporter
KTUV RADIO. Phoenix, AZ. 1986 - 1989

- Designed and sold advertising for KTUV Radio
- Developed a $9,000 account list in the Phoenix metro market
- Sports and news announcer (included in-studio as well as location)
- Traffic reporter

Assistant Editor
Daily Argus Observer, Ontario, OR, Summers 1984/1985

- Feature writer, reporter, photographer, layouts and design

EDUCATION:

B.S., Speech Communications, University of Arizona, 1986

AWARDS:

1994 Arizona Business and Professional Women's "Young Careerist" Annual Award

OTHER FACTS:

Experience as a Public Relations Seminar Leader

References/Portfolio/Video and Cassette Tapes available upon request

Publishing/Marketing Professional

Jane Swift
9 Central Avenue
Seacliff, NY 11579
(516) 555-1212
Jane@careerbrain.com

PROFESSIONAL EXPERIENCE:	*A New York Publisher of trade and scholarly books*

DIRECTOR OF ADVERTISING AND PROMOTION (March 1998-Present)

Key responsibilities include: managing advertising/promotion department with staff of four; overseeing and actively engaging in all aspects of promotion, advertising, and publicity. I have established and am maintaining a 22-person national sales force and make seasonal visits to the nation's two largest bookstore chains.

Active in negotiating special sales and acquiring new titles, and as liaison with domestic and foreign rights agents. In 1998 I traveled to England, visited several publishers, bought and sold rights.

Frequently arrange author appearances on television and radio talk shows. As a company spokesperson, I have been interviewed numerous times by newspapers, magazines, syndicates, and radio stations.

ADVERTISING AND PROMOTION MANAGER (1996-1998)

Advertising and Direct Mail: Created, designed, and wrote copy for brochures, flyers, and display ads; created direct-mail campaigns; represented company at publisher's book exhibits.

Publicity: Wrote news releases, selected media, made follow-up calls, arranged author media appearances.

ASSISTANT EDITOR (1994-1996)

Responsibilities included reading authors' manuscripts, copyediting, proofreading; writing jacket copy, coordinating and writing copy for catalog. Some editing and proofreading was done on a freelance basis.

Compton Burnett (New York, NY) ADVERTISING COPYWRITER (1992-1994)

Responsible for designing and writing copy for bimonthly catalog and supplementary flyers. Created ads and brochures; wrote sales letters and edited and rewrote direct-mail pieces.

EDUCATION:	State University of New York at Buffalo Degree: B.A. in English, 1992 Minor: Social Sciences
SKILLS:	Word processing, working knowledge of typography, research proficiency.
REFERENCES:	Will be provided on request.

Real Estate Development

James Sharpe
9 Central Avenue
Overland Park, KS 66210

(913) 555-1212
James@careerbrain.com
Page 1 of 2

OBJECTIVE
A position in REAL ESTATE DEVELOPMENT that will utilize strong analytical skills, knowledge of marketplace trends and practices, and benefit from my legal background.

OVERVIEW
- Organized, take-charge professional with exceptional follow-through abilities and detail orientation; able to plan and oversee a full range of events from concept to successful conclusion.
- Demonstrated ability to efficiently prioritize a broad range of responsibilities in order to consistently meet deadlines.
- Dynamic negotiator; effective in achieving positive results. Licensed Mediator in NJ.
- Demonstrated capability to anticipate and resolve problems swiftly and independently.
- Possess strong interpersonal skills; proven ability to develop and maintain sound business relationships with clients, anticipating their needs.
- Highly articulate, effective communicator, experienced presenter: possess excellent platform skills.
- Highly adept in utilizing state-of-the-art software packages for industry-related functions, from data and finance management to CADD. Hands-on experience with Argus and Project.
- Currently completing Master's Degree in Real Estate Development at NYU.
- Demonstrated skills in:

• Research	• Mediation	• Mergers & Acquisitions
• Urban Development	• Legal Writing	• Real Estate Tax Issues
• Accounting	• Analytical Writing	• Corporate Finance
• Bankruptcy	• Financial Analysis	• Administrative System Design
• Small Business Planning	• Small Business Development	• Foreclosure

PROFESSIONAL EXPERIENCE
May 1999 - Present
SMITH & ASSOCIATES, Overland Park, KS
Special Projects Consultant for well-respected communications consulting firm. Firm's principal authored two critically acclaimed standards in the marketing/business field: *The New Positioning* and *The Power of Simplicity.*
- Perform directed Internet and other research in preparation for an upcoming book.
- Analyze research and draft description for inclusion in articles and future book.
- Specifically recruited for special projects on basis of past performance.

September 1998 - Present
RIVERVIEW ARTISANS INC., Overland Park, KS
Assistant Manager for firm affiliated with the Mapleridge Design Center.
- Collaborate with decorative artist on projects in the $75K range, custom building business furniture, conference rooms, mahogany libraries, etc.
- Perform multitude of skilled operations from rough milling to fine detail finishing and veneer application.
- Assist in project estimates and sales proposals.

June 1997 - December 1997
WALTERS, JUSTA & MILLSTEIN, Kansas City, KS
    Law Clerk
- Gained valuable experience in bankruptcy proceedings.

January 1997 - May 1997
HONORABLE HENRY MARGOLIS, Kansas City, KS
    Judicial Internship
- Legal research and writing on legalities relating to general equity matters.

September 1996 - December 1996
HONORABLE ROSE GIARDELA, Kansas City, KS
    Judicial Internship

Summer 1996
STRATTON, BRIGGS & ROTHMAN, Overland Park, KS
    Law Clerk

January 1994 - June 1994
UNITED STATES DEPARTMENT OF JUSTICE, Washington, DC
    Intern

EDUCATION
UNIVERSITY OF MISSOURI, KANSAS CITY, Kansas City, MO
Master of Science: Real Estate Development   May 2000

UNIVERSITY OF KANSAS SCHOOL OF LAW, Lawrence, KS
Juris Doctor   June 1998
Admitted to Kansas Bar 1998
Honors and Activities:
- Seton Hall Constitutional Law Journal - NOTES & COMMENTS EDITOR (1997-98)
- Who's Who: American Law Students - 16th Edition (1997)
- Tax Law Society

KANSAS WESLYAN UNIVERSITY, Salinas, KS
Bachelor of Arts, Political Science   August 1995
Honors and Activities:
- Dean's List
- Pi Sigma Alpha Honor Society (for outstanding Political Science Majors)

REFERENCES
Excellent references will be furnished on request.

Retail District Manager

James Sharpe
9 Central Avenue
Metairie, LA 70002
(504) 555-1212
James@careerbrain.com

Profile

Highly focused, enthusiastic and goal-driven professional with solid experience in marketing, management, sales, operations, and training. Demonstrated success in implementing test marketing programs and promoting products that consistently increase sales. Reputation for innovative problem solving, organization, and professionalism.

Employment History

Stop & Go Convenience   1996 - Present
District Manager - Louisiana

Recruited to provide leadership and management for stores with high employee turnover and lagging sales. Supervise day-to-day operations of 6 retail stores with full responsibility for P&L. Hire, train, and manage 60 to 70 employees. Develop and maintain vendor relations. Introduce new products and plan marketing strategies for all stores. Plan and conduct area training meetings.

Selected Accomplishments:

- Increased inside sales 15–20% over a year, and total sales by 10%, through improved management techniques, attention to detail, inventory control, and developing good relationships with vendors.
- Reduced employee turnover 50% by fostering a team atmosphere through improved training, communication, and motivation.
- Received five merit-based salary increases.
- The second most senior (and youngest) supervisor in Texas.
- Won sales award for increased profits per store.
- Selected out of 80 people by the VP of Operations to attend National Association of Convenience Stores (NACS) to lobby congressmen in Washington D.C. along with the CEO and president.

District Manager - Texas

Promoted from Manager. Recruited from Alabama to work with 3 stores to improve management, decrease turnover, and increase sales. Ran several successful pilot/test programs that were implemented throughout the company.

Manager - Birmingham, Alabama:

Promoted from Management Trainee.

Computer Skills

PowerPoint, MS Word, Excel, Lotus, Internet (PC and Mac)

Education

Auburn University, B.A. in Communications. Courses included marketing, publicity, media, group dynamics, speech writing. Paid for 100% of college through employment.

Retail Management

Jane Swift
9 Central Avenue
New York, NY 10017
(212) 555-1212
Jane@careerbrain.com

Profile

Accomplished manager with more than 15 years experience managing high-profile, upscale operations, leading teams, and consistently delivering sales, profit, and organizational improvements. Recognized for ability to achieve results through leadership, teamwork, and exceptional customer service.

~Operations Management~Business Analysis & Planning~Expense Control~
~Inventory Management~Human Resources (interviewing, evaluating, scheduling, counseling, coaching, and developing)~Buying and Merchandising (maximizing sales volume and profitability)~

Selected Achievements

Management/Leadership

- Currently managing the largest branch store with 40 executive reports and 600 staff associates.
- Brought in to turn around an underperforming back-of-house operation that was impacting negatively on profitability of entire operation. Reorganization showed immediate improvement and brought store back on plan.
- Drove sales and profits at Galleria store despite mall renovations and store's own 30,000 square foot expansion and renovation.
- Opened three new multilevel stores in major malls from the ground up. All stores exceeded plan.
- General Manager of the Year (1997) for the entire company.

Merchandising/Customer Service

- Won CEO's Cup for sales/profitability and excellence in customer service. Shared award with 4 others out of 70 general managers.
- Took Miami Beach store to Top Ten status in customer service throughout chain.
- Led Scarsdale store to Top Ten in customer service
- Drove Albany store to Number One in customer service
- Selected to pioneer a pilot project for a Selling Skills Training Program for all stores nationwide. Resulted in target stores all ranking highest in chain.
- Instrumental in company's customer service program. Consistent top ten producer.
- Worked with Hub Merchandising Organization to restructure merchandise mix to better serve South Florida market.
- As buyer, increased department 14% in first year and by 23% in second. Expanded private label program in Orient, increasing gross margins and upgrading fashion image.

Career History

Saks Fifth Avenue, New York, NY (1990 - Present)
    Vice President and General Manager (1999 - Present)
        General Manager Divisional Vice President (1994 - 1998)
        General Manager (1992 - 1994)
        Buyer (1990 - 1992)
Lord & Taylor, New York, NY
        Assistant Buyer (1985 - 1990)

Education

AAS in Fashion Buying and Merchandising, Fashion Institute of San Francisco

References upon request.

Sales and Marketing Executive

Jane Swift
9 Central Avenue
Seattle, WA 98101

(206) 555-1212
Jane@careerbrain.com
Page 1 of 2

Business Development ● National Accounts ● Government Contracts ● Sales Management

Entrepreneurial executive offers accomplishments in sales/marketing of high-tech, industrial, and financial products. Strong technical background with substantial knowledge of marketing using the Internet and telecommunication technologies.

SELECTED ACCOMPLISHMENTS

- Spearheaded two start-up companies into competitive enterprises. Raised capital, launched product line, and built successful sales force.
- Negotiated major contracts with government agencies and large defense contractors. Secured vendor status in record time.
- Expanded sales presence in both national and international markets. Developed niche areas based on demand.
- Consistently maintained production record within top ten percent in highly competitive financial services industry.

Technical/Industrial

XYZ RECYCLED ENTERPRISES INC., Seattle, WA   1996 - 2000
Director of Sales

    Directed sales and marketing for this start-up company using a first-of-its-kind technology to manufacture recycled polypropylene products for cleaning oil spills. Raised $1.8 million to purchase predecessor company from bankruptcy. Negotiated 100% credit for all money due stockholders of RFI.

- Developed and launched product line. Worked closely with EPA to ensure new standards. Generated sales of up to $300,000 by year three.
- Negotiated contract and stocking program with Government Services Agency (GSA), which proactively advertised product. Achieved feat in year two due to intensive marketing efforts.
- Recruited and trained national sales force. Successfully penetrated government market.
- Created all marketing materials including Web site and Thomas Register advertising. Gained orders before product became available.

BEST TECHNOLOGY, Seattle, WA   1990 - 1996
Partner/Director of Sales

    Founded new firm distributing and converting high temperature alloys, titanium, and exotic alloys. Established three domestic offices and three international representatives covering Europe, Israel, and South America.

- Developed business with defense contractors and commercial aircraft/engine manufacturers including Boeing, General Electric, and Aerospatiale/British Aero Space. Products used in production of Titan missile and Airbus.
- Grew sales by expanding sales force to 15 and securing additional distributorships from domestic and foreign mills. Generated sales of up to $4 million annually.
- Reduced turnaround delivery time by 40% as compared to industry average through use of specialized conversion technologies.
- Implemented QC program that qualified quickly for government/corporate vendor status.

ADVANCED TECHNOLOGY, Seattle, WA   1986 - 1990
Vice President

Directed sales and marketing for this distributor and converter of high temperature, titanium, and exotic alloys with major accounts in aerospace industry.

- Developed a professional national/international sales force of 25 reps. Grew sales from $7 million to over $22 million during tenure.
- Structured sales commissions to reflect true cost of goods sold. Reduced commissions paid by over 20%.
- Increased mill representation enabling company to compete more aggressively for larger, more lucrative orders.
- Initiated computer system to control material production, inventory, and sales monitoring.
- Arranged U.S. government approval for military use of foreign titanium for secret projects. First company to buy titanium from China.

Financial Services

NATIONAL CAPITAL, San Francisco, CA   1981 - 1986
INVESTOR'S SOURCE, San Francisco, CA
National Sales Manager/Branch Manger

Directed sales for two retail brokerage firms dealing in high-risk/ high-reward investments to an affluent clientele.

- Doubled monthly sales revenue ($500,000–$1 million) by expanding sales staff and upgrading training methods.
- Initiated a computerized commission system (Broker Portfolio) that tracked individual production and served as a managerial tool for monitoring sales of retail products.
- Set up training programs, incentives, and lead systems that significantly improved production as well as staff morale. Emphasized one-on-one marketing.

PREVIOUS EXPERIENCE includes sales positions in dental supplies and catalog sales of rare coins. Among many accomplishments, negotiated a Japanese contract for equipment manufacturing.

EDUCATION

Stanford University, Palo Alto, CA - BS in Economics/Finance

TECHNICAL

MS-Office 97	Maximizer	QuattroPro
Quicken	MYOB	Day Timer
Pstudio	MGI Photo Suite	WinFax Pro
Netscape Communicator	MS-Internet Explorer	Corel Print & Photo House
Power Point		

References available on request.

School Psychologist

Jane Swift
9 Central Avenue
Beaumont, TX 77705
(409) 555-1212
Jane@careerbrain.com

Summary of Qualifications

- Experience includes 33 years within the educational system: Past 21 years as School Psychologist, 7 years as a Guidance Counselor, 5 years as an elementary school teacher.
- Assessment of student weaknesses and strengths; preparation of written psychological reports; interpretation of psychological testing; professional presentations and workshops; curriculum development; provide recommendations to improve student's overall learning/adjustment; collaboration with teachers and parents; small group and individual counseling.
- Have the ability to work well with people; possess excellent communication skills; am considered to be energetic, results-oriented individual.

Education

Doctoral Program: Educational Leadership, Baylor University
Certification in School Psychology, Baylor University
M.Ed.: Guidance and Counseling, Baylor University
B.A.: Elementary Education, Baylor University, Summa Cum Laude

Certifications/Licenses

School Psychologist, Guidance Counselor (K-Jr. College level),
Elementary Education Teacher,
Nationally Certified School Psychologist,
State Licensed School Psychologist

Experience

School Psychologist, Brown County School Board, 1981 - Present
Responsibilities: Assessment of student strengths and weaknesses. Collaboration and interpretation of psychological test results and recommendations with teachers and parents. Assist in educational planning, programming, and development of individual educational plans for special educational students and develop interventions for students who do not qualify for placement in an educational program. Assessment of ADHD/ADD and appropriate interventive strategies. Assist in the development of behavior and functional behavior assessment plans, consultation (i.e. academic, social, and behavioral interventive strategies). Work directly with students and families to assist in solving conflicts and problems related to learning and adjustment. Professional presentations and workshops.

School Psychologist, Grant County School Board, 1978 - 1981
Served as a school psychologist in the Head Start and Migrant Education programs, in addition to serving two elementary schools. Assisted in educational program development, utilizing specialized knowledge of child growth and development, learning theory, personality dynamics and motivation. Presented workshops and in-service training for school personnel and parents.

Guidance Counselor, Pauls Elementary, 1971 - 1978
Started as guidance counselor and eventually combined duties as school-based psychologist. Was responsible for over 750 students K-5. Counseled with students and parents; coordinated services with various community agencies. Was a facilitator in career education, early identification program, model school programs, and drug abuse education. Taught parent workshops in the areas of learning disabilities and effective parenting.

Security/Operations Management

James Sharpe
9 Central Avenue
San Francisco, CA 94124
(415) 555-1212
James@careerbrain.com

Career Profile

- Over 14 years of management and leadership experience in security operations and related functions with prominent hotels, retailers, and security providers.
- Currently functions as Director of Security for a prestigious four star/four diamond hotel, earning the highest performance ranking in the company in 1998. Have directed up to 200 officers and developed/managed $500,000+ budgets. Possess an extensive knowledge of security industry standards.
- Develop and lead effective and united teams, transforming fragmented factions into a cohesive alliance of professionals producing exceptional results and adhering to strict codes of conduct. Employ a dedicated hands-on management style that has dramatically increased effectiveness and reduced turnover,
- Certified in Lodging Security Directorship, Hospitality Law, Hotel Security Management, Disaster Preparedness and Emergency Response, Threat Management, Workplace Violence, and OSHA Regulations. Member of the American Society for Industrial Security and the Northern California Security Chiefs Association.

Areas of Expertise

- Security industry standards
- Budget creation and management
- Human Resources management functions
- Recruiting, training, and development
- Coaching, counseling, and motivation
- Departmental turnarounds
- Program and procedures development
- Motivational team leadership
- Interviewing, selection, performance evaluations

Career Development

Director of Security Operations, Four Star Hotel, San Francisco, California   1994 to Present

- Manage all aspects of the security operation of this prestigious, top rated, 600,00 square foot luxury hotel with 300 rooms, a daily roster of 1,000 employees/guests, and 14 full-time security officers.
- Dramatically reversed poor performance history of key hotel departments, achieving ranking of first in the company in 1998
  - Decreased number of security-related incidents by 30%, the lowest in hotel's history.
  - Lowered workers' compensation injuries to 7 cases (of 300 workers), the smallest in the company's history.
  - Raised quality/efficiency while reducing overtime by 65%, the lowest rate in the department's history.
  - Instituted standards that did not allow a single successful safety or security litigation in five years.
  - Earned top ranking as company's best managed department.
  - Achieved lowest employee turnover rate in the entire company.

Produced these results by creating and implementing leading-edge programs including... Innovative training, evaluation, and TQM programs that produced employee motivation, attention, interest, cooperation, and desired response... Standard operating procedures for crisis management, disaster prevention and recovery, risk management, emergency response, incident investigation, and report writing... Detailed investigation standards for all security and safety incidents, including policy violations, and guest or employee injuries.

Chief of Security, DeLuxe Hotel, San Francisco, California   1993 to 1995

Directed security operations of this three star/ four diamond national chain hotel with 200 guest rooms, 200 employees, and 6 security officers, devising effective security policies and procedures, and budgeting and monitoring department's expenditures.

- Produced a 20% decrease in security-related incidents.
- Reduced employee turnover by 50%.

Established new standard operating procedures. Developed and implemented emergency action plans. Contributed to creation of multiple departments' security and safety requirement training programs. Cooperated closely with the Human Resources department on OSHA, workers' compensation, and other industrial safety matters to ensure state and federal compliance.

Operations Manager, Redwood Security, San Francisco, California   1990 to 1992
Managed over 200 plainclothes and uniform contract security officers in multiple facilities, including defense contractors and film studios. Developed and promoted a proactive culture of risk management and prevention. Promoted through the ranks from Field Officer to Operations Manager, the highest rank within the division.
- Implemented new rewards and recognition programs that raised morale and provided continuous feedback.
- Frequently volunteered extended hours to meet clients' needs and critical project deadlines.
Acted as client liaison to develop partnerships and strategic loss prevention and asset protection programs. Oversaw Human Resources operations including officer selection, field deployment, training, scheduling, inspections, evaluations, and disciplinary actions. Established professional ties with local police authorities.

Loss Prevention Manager, Nordstrom's, Thousand Oaks, California   1987 to 1990
Oversaw security staff and operations at this upscale retailer.
- Protected assets and reduced legal liability by creating ongoing prioritized loss prevention initiatives.
- Developed effective loss countermeasure strategies and prevention awareness training programs.
- Conducted comprehensive internal audits and investigations for external/internal sources of loss and employee misconduct.
- Minimized accidents and injuries by managing effective safety programs.

Technology Skills
- Proficient in Microsoft Word, Excel, IRIMS, and PPM2000.
- PC proficient in Windows 98/95/3.1
- Extensive knowledge of computer-based, audio/visual, and access control systems.

Education and Certification
Bachelor of Science in Political Science, University of Southern California
Certifications:
- Lodging Security Director (CLSD), American Hotel & Motel Association
- Hospitality Law, AH&MA Educational Institute
- Hotel Security Management, AH&MA
- Disaster Preparedness and Emergency Response, City of San Francisco Fire Department
- Threat Management and Workplace Violence, City of San Francisco Fire Department
- OSHA Regulations and Workplace Violence, California Hotel & Motel Association
- Food Handler, San Jose County Department of Health

Security Services Sales

Jane Swift
9 Central Avenue
Raleigh, NC 27612
(919) 555-1212
Jane@careerbrain.com

Professional Profile

Sales • Account Management • New Business Development Professional

Sales and Account Management Development professional with expert qualifications in identifying and capturing market opportunities to accelerate expansion, increase revenues, and improve profit contributions in highly competitive industries. Outstanding record of achievement in complex account and contract negotiations.

Key Strengths:

- Account development/management
- Customer service/satisfaction
- Bilingual English/Spanish
- Customer needs assessment
- PC proficient
- Consultative/solutions sales
- New market development
- Account retention
- Presentation and negotiations skills

Professional Experience

Key Account Executive, 1996 - Present

American Security Services, Largest privately held security company in the nation with annual sales over $400 million.

Recruited to start up and oversee the market development of contract security services in North Carolina. Conduct in-depth client need assessments and develop technology-based security strategies to ensure maximum efficiency.

- Achieve consistent annual sales production in excess of $2.5 million
- Built territory from ground zero capturing 55% of market share in region
- Expanded annual billable hours from 300 to more than 5,000, fostering a rapid growth in staffing from 30 to more than 300 employees in Raleigh branch
- Successfully negotiated and secured sales ranging from $300K to $1.2 million
- Earned several national and local awards for top sales performance, including the prestigious "Rookie of the Year" award

Account Executive/Loan Officer, 1995 - 1996

Equity Finance, Inc., Nation's oldest finance company, a division of a Fortune 500 company.

Generated and sold bill consolidation loans through telemarketing.

- Consistently exceeded monthly sales objectives
- Received national recognition as one of the Top 10 salespeople in the nation, and Number 1 salesperson in Raleigh branch.

Education

Bachelor of Arts, Business Administration/Finance (GPA 3.8) 1994
University of North Carolina, Chapel Hill

Senior Account Executive

Jane Swift

9 Central Avenue
New York, NY 10012
(212) 555-1212
Jane@careerbrain.com

- 15+ years' experience building partnerships with leading corporations to develop consumer packaging, sales promotions, and collateral to strengthen brand identity and awareness. In-depth understanding of technology, household products, personal care, liquor, and food categories.
- Account management capabilities enhanced by professional design, production, printing, and technical background. Formal design education and commitment to ongoing professional development.
- Adept in Macintosh and Windows applications for graphic design, desktop publishing, word processing, spreadsheets, email, database management, Web site development, and multimedia presentations.

Key Words

Consultative Sales	High-Impact Presentations
Customer Service	Problem Solving & Decision Making
Project Management	Sales Closing & Negotiating
Design Process	Team Building & Leadership

Achievements

- Generated nearly a million dollars in annual sales for packaging design firm by winning key accounts and cultivating relationships.
- Won four Package Design Council (PDC) Gold Awards for package design in personal care and household appliances categories.
- Won account with major multinational corporation and developed packaging, promotional displays, trade, and consumer collateral material. Facilitated the national redesign (60 SKU's) in order to establish products as the technologically superior brand within the category.
- Collaborated on the national implementation of a "company first" branding strategy. Key objective: to reinforce the brand name, weakened by a four-year trend of sub-branding. Brainstormed with marketing and creative executives to create a set of graphic standards to communicate the essence of the brand. Applied this branding system to the entire product line.
- Increased sales and distribution through development of innovative club-store packaging and promotions for a leading liquor supplier.
- Guided design and production of packaging and product launch materials for a 30 SKU line of household products. Product was picked up nationally by Wal-Mart and sales jumped 19% in an introductory period.
- Worked with a leading cereal maker to develop promotional back panel games, sweepstakes, and in-pack offers.
- Directed development of displays, brochures, and merchandising materials for Certs Candy and Ocean Spray Fruit Waves (created through licensing agreement).
- Introduced multimedia capability to firm's new business presentations. Created Web site content including a company tour, an interactive portfolio, and a creative access section—allowing clients online, confidential access to view work.

Career Chronology

Senior Account Executive—1998 - Present
Leading Package Design Firm, Fort Lee, NJ

- Hired as a junior account executive to assist in all aspects of client services. Within seven months, promoted to account executive to develop new business in the consumer electronics category. Established key contacts with industry leaders through cold calling, direct marketing and client presentations. Consulted with clients to determine marketing objectives, packaging requirements and budgetary limitations. Directed numerous packaging, promotion, trade and consumer collateral material projects. Managed staff of five to implement the electronic design and production process.

Computer Graphics Artist—1995 - 1998
Big Design Firm, New York, NY

- Worked with designers and art directors to take concepts through to highly refined computer based production. Trained members of the design and production department in the use of Adobe Illustrator. Setup a high-speed remote viewing network enabling select clients to simultaneously view design concepts.

Account Executive—1991 - 1995
Freelance Placement Agency, New York, NY

- Instrumental in establishing a lucrative desktop publishing placement division. Identified and cultivated profitable markets. Managed and art directed freelancers and worked with clients through all project stages.

Graphic Designer—1985 - 1990
ABC Marketing & Communications, New York, NY

- Accountable for all stages of the design and production of consumer packaging. Participated in beta testing of proprietary graphics software and various high-end peripherals, giving product reviews to manufacturers.

Education

BFA: Graphic Design, Industrial Design, Computer Graphics and Marketing - 1985
New York University

Ongoing Professional Development

- Earned Certificate in Sales Promotion - St. John's University
- Intensive seminars in Web site design, multimedia, and advertising - Brown University

Senior International Marketing and Business Development Executive

Jane Swift   Page 1 of 2
9 Zentral Strasse
Dusseldorf, Germany
Jane@careerbrain.com

Expertise in Product Development • Commercialization & Global Market Expansion
Telecoms • Consumer Electronics • Sports & Leisure Industries

Dynamic management career leading turnaround and high-growth organizations through unprecedented profitability and explosive market growth worldwide. Combine extensive strategic planning, competitive positioning, life cycle management, channel management and product development/management qualifications with strong general management, P&L management, organizational development, workforce management, and multicultural communication skills. MBA; multilingual - fluent German, English, Italian, intermediate Japanese.

PROFESSIONAL EXPERIENCE

MAJOR ELECTRONICS COMPANY, Dusseldorf, Germany   1992 to 2000
        The second largest electronics company worldwide ranking #15 in the Global Fortune 500 ratings.
Senior Vice President Marketing
        Executive Board Member recruited to design marketing strategies and implement systems/processes to lead a worldwide marketing function as part of the business group's aggressive turnaround program.
        Accountable for a $250 million marketing budget. Oversee worldwide marketing operations including business strategy and benchmarking, technology strategy, market research, consumer marketing, regional marketing (EMEA, Asia, U.S.), marketing communications, new media including Internet, intranet, and extranet, and business-to-consumer e-commerce. Manage a staff of 77 through 10 direct reports.

- Led the marketing initiatives for the successful launch of two mobile phone product lines transitioning losses of $200 million in 97/98 to profits of $30 million in 98/99 and doubling world market share to approximately 8%.
- Delivered a 5-point improvement in brand awareness, and 50% relevant set improvement for mobile and cordless phones throughout China and Europe.
- Introduced a worldwide marketing communications spending performance initiative slashing communication costs by $10 million.
- Identified and initiated business development strategies and technology vehicles instrumental in developing international marketing partnerships and equity investments.
- Established a price/value-based market analysis instrument together with the market research and consumer marketing groups to develop pricing accuracy generating revenue increases exceeding $20 million.
- Directed e-commerce marketing initiatives leading to the development of 7 operational online stores in 5 European countries generating 4 million contacts with CAGR of 20% per week, followed by development of a virtual Customer Care Center.
- Conceived and initiated PR strategies for a new product launch generating over 130 million contracts within a few months.
- Led improvements in competitive market intelligence through enhancements to statistical reports and customer satisfaction surveys.

ELECTRONICS COMPANY, Bonn, Germany   1987 to 1992
A leading European high-end TV, audio and consumer electronics company.
Marketing Director
Joined this privately held company to improve product life cycle management and channel marketing initiatives. Oversaw budget administration, strategic planning and market research, international communications, training and product management. Directed a staff of 21.
- Instituted a series of channel management and segmentation improvements to correct market planning and positioning initiatives and reduce price erosion throughout retail distribution channels.
- Led development of product definition, life cycle management, and market launch strategies positioning company as the value-based market leader of high-end TV sets in Germany with market share exceeding 14%.

ABC BICYCLE COMPANY, Berlin, Germany   1983 to 1987
A global leading automotive, motorcycle and bicycle component equipment manufacturer.
Director of Marketing International
Led transition from an engineering-driven traditional gear hub manufacturer to a market-oriented competitor in the sport and leisure industry. Reported to Division President.
- Established a marketing department, devised strategies for over 1,000 SKUs within 6 product lines, delivered a profit for the first time in 8 years, and boosted new product sales ratios from 10% to 40%.
- Headed up a special internal R&D audit and restructuring project leading to the creation of marketing-driven product development teams. Replaced 15% of R&D personnel, established R&D controls, reduced R&D costs by $500,000, and earned a $30,000 project completion bonus.

ABC AUTOMOTIVE, Wolfsburg, Germany   1980 to 1983
Leading automotive and home appliance manufacturer.
Product Group Manager
Oversaw European product management and marketing initiatives for the $500 million Electronic Division. Successfully introduced brands in France, Italy, and England.

EDUCATION
M.B.A., University of California, Berkeley
Diplome d'enseignement Supérieur Europeen de Management, Centre d'Etudes Européennes Supérieures de Management (CESEM), France
Diplom-Betriebswirt (FH), Business Administration, Europäisches Studienprogramm für Betriebswirtschaft (ESB)

INTERNSHIPS
Country Chamber of Commerce, Osaka, Japan, Oskar Duisberg Society Scholarship
Counseled German and Japanese firms in all aspects of business for their respective countries.
Kornwestheim Club Vertrieb GmbH, Kornwestheim, Germany, Marketing concepts in direct sales.

Senior Management Executive

Jane Swift
9 Central Avenue
San Diego, CA 92109
(619) 555-1212
Jane@careerbrain.com

New Business Development ● *Strategic Partnerships* ● *Product Marketing*

Accomplished Senior Executive with a strong affinity for technology and a keen business sense for the application of emerging products to add value and expand markets. Proven talent for identifying core business needs and translating into technical deliverables. Launched and managed cutting-edge Internet programs and services to win new customers, generate revenue gains, and increase brand value.

Unique combination of technical and business/sales experience. Articulate and persuasive in explaining the benefits of e-commerce technologies and how they add value, differentiate offerings, and increase customer retention. Highly self-motivated, enthusiastic, and profit oriented.

Expertise in Internet services, emerging payment products,
secure electronic commerce, smart card technology, and Java.

AREAS OF QUALIFICATION

Business

●Sales & Marketing	●Business Development	●Strategic Initiatives
●Business Planning	●Project Management	●Strategic Partnerships
●Business & Technical Requirements		●Revenue Generation
●Contract Negotiations		●Relationship Management

Technical

●Electronic Commerce	●Encryption Technology	●Key Management
●Public Key Infrastructure	●Firewalls	●Smart Cards
●Stored Value	●Digital Certificates	●Internet & Network Security
●Complex Financial Systems	●Authorization, Clearing, Settlement	●Dual and Single Message

PROFESSIONAL EXPERIENCE

ABC Credit Card Corp., San Diego, CA 1999 to Present
E-COMMERCE AND SMART CARD CONSULTANT

- Developed strategic e-commerce marketing plans for large and small merchants involving Web purchases and retail transactions using a multifunctional, microcontroller smart card for both secure Internet online commerce and point-of-sale offline commerce.
- Combined multiple software products for Internet and non-Internet applications: home banking, stored value, digital certificates, key management, rewards & loyalty program, PCS/GSM cell phone, and contactless microcontroller with RF communications without direct POS contact.
- Consulted on business and technical requirements to define new e-commerce products and essential deliverables for ABC Credit Card, valued at $2.5 MM, supporting and enhancing Internet transactions.
- Analyzed systems relating to the point of sale environment in the physical world and at the merchant server via the Internet for real-time authorization, clearing, and settlement.
- Managed projects including the requirements management system for electronic commerce products affecting core systems: authorization, clearing, and settlement. Provided expertise about business and technical issues regarding SET and the Credit Card Payment Gateway Service.

Communications Technology Corporation, Miami, FL   *1994 to 1999*
MANAGER OF WESTERN REGION CHANNEL PARTNER PROGRAM
- Developed and maintained business relationships with large Fortune 500 customers and partners that use or resell client-server software for applications and contracts involving e-commerce and smart card technology for a variety of Internet/Intranet products: home banking, EDI, stored value, digital certificates, key management, perimeter defense with proxy firewalls, secure remote access.
- Negotiated an exclusive contract with one of the largest government and commercial contractors in the industry, projected to generate $2–4 million over a 24–36 month period. Contract includes secure remote access, telecommuting, secure health care applications.

Avanta Corp., Miami, FL   *1990 to 1994*
SENIOR SOFTWARE ENGINEER / SOFTWARE INSTRUCTOR
- Designed new programs and trained software engineers in object oriented analysis and design using UML. Solutions that were implemented in C++ in a UNIX environment.
- Managed a software engineering group of 53 individuals. Developed in-house program that saved over $150,000 in training costs for state-of-the-art communications system software development.
- Received Peer Award for outstanding performance; earned a performance evaluation rating of 4.2/5.0.
- Developed and maintained C and C++ communication software in a UNIX environment.
- Created curriculum and course materials that reduced overall training costs by more than $150,000. Coordinated and presented software training programs.

EDUCATION AND CREDENTIALS
- B.S., Electrical Engineering, University of Miami, Emphasis: software engineering, Minor: Psychology, President of the Sigma Sigma Fraternity
- Top Secret Security Clearance with Polygraph

Senior Sales and Marketing Manager

JAMES SHARPE
9 Central Avenue
Atlantic City, NJ 08404
(609) 555-1212
James@careerbrain.com
Page 1 of 2

Top-producing sales and marketing professional with nine years of management experience in world-class organizations. Consistently successful in developing new markets, penetrating new territories, identifying and capturing new business, and managing large-scale events for Fortune 500 companies worldwide. Goal-driven manager committed to developing outcomes mutually benefiting the company and the client. Excellent qualifications in building corporate relationships with industry leaders.

Areas of expertise include:

- New Account Development
- Key Account Management
- Client Needs Assessment
- Contract Negotiations
- Competitive / Strategic Planning

- Large-Scale Meeting / Event Planning
- Catering Planning / Management
- Co-Marketing Partnerships
- Relationship Management
- Customer Service / Satisfaction

PROFESSIONAL EXPERIENCE

EXQUISITE RESORT SUITES, Atlantic City, NJ   1996 to 2000
Senior Sales Manager

Joined company to lead market entry/penetration initiatives throughout the Northeast Region of the U.S. for this privately-held exclusive resort with 800 suites, a 60,000 sq. ft. conference center, and a full range of guest amenities. Managed business growth among Fortune 500 corporate accounts and national association accounts.

- Developed and maintained relationships with corporate meeting planners of major accounts including IBM, AT&T, Ralston Purina, Bell South, AT&T, Siemens, Medtronic, and others to develop custom-tailored business meeting packages.
- Worked closely with corporate planners throughout all phases of strategic and tactical planning, coordination, and execution of major events to insure superior service and guest relations.
- Captured national association accounts including American Cancer Society, American Heart Association, New York Bar Association, and New Jersey Institute of CPAs.
- Sold and orchestrated multiyear bookings to numerous associations and corporate accounts.
  Achievements
  - Built territory and increased revenues from $1 million to over $7 million within first year.
  - Achieved 157% of annual booking goals (2500 room nights per month).

BUSCH GARDENS, Tampa, Florida   1993 to 1996
Catering Sales Manager

Challenged to develop new markets and products for multicultural groups visiting Walt Disney World.

- Identified target market, initiated contact with prospects, developed proposals, and forged major account relationships.
- Worked closely with corporate planners at Exxon, Compaq, IBM, Frito Lay, McDonald's, and others to create unique and extravagant parties and events ranging up to $2 million per event.
- Sold, planned, and coordinated catered group events for corporate accounts and private parties ranging from 2 to 19,000 guests.
- Developed comprehensive strategic and tactical plans for every phase of event including logistics, transportation, food and beverage, entertainment, and gifts to create a memorable occasion.

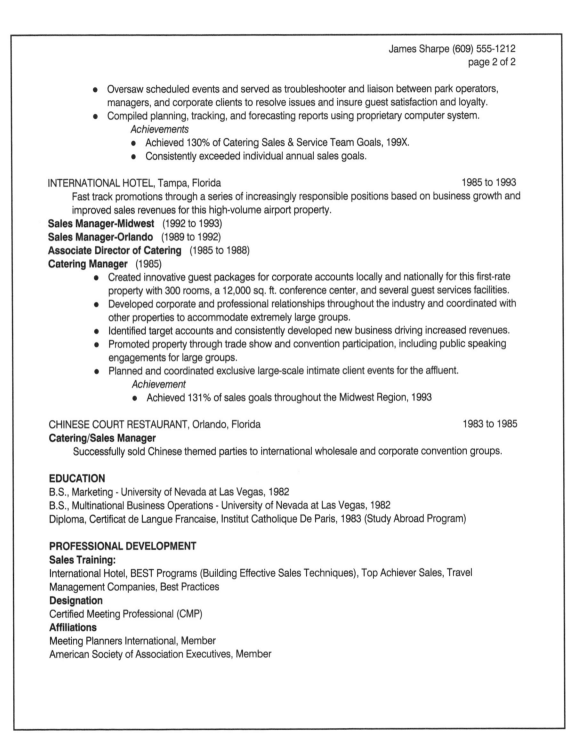

- Oversaw scheduled events and served as troubleshooter and liaison between park operators, managers, and corporate clients to resolve issues and insure guest satisfaction and loyalty.
- Compiled planning, tracking, and forecasting reports using proprietary computer system.
  - *Achievements*
    - Achieved 130% of Catering Sales & Service Team Goals, 199X.
    - Consistently exceeded individual annual sales goals.

INTERNATIONAL HOTEL, Tampa, Florida   1985 to 1993

Fast track promotions through a series of increasingly responsible positions based on business growth and improved sales revenues for this high-volume airport property.

Sales Manager-Midwest (1992 to 1993)
Sales Manager-Orlando (1989 to 1992)
Associate Director of Catering (1985 to 1988)
Catering Manager (1985)

- Created innovative guest packages for corporate accounts locally and nationally for this first-rate property with 300 rooms, a 12,000 sq. ft. conference center, and several guest services facilities.
- Developed corporate and professional relationships throughout the industry and coordinated with other properties to accommodate extremely large groups.
- Identified target accounts and consistently developed new business driving increased revenues.
- Promoted property through trade show and convention participation, including public speaking engagements for large groups.
- Planned and coordinated exclusive large-scale intimate client events for the affluent.
  - *Achievement*
    - Achieved 131% of sales goals throughout the Midwest Region, 1993

CHINESE COURT RESTAURANT, Orlando, Florida   1983 to 1985
Catering/Sales Manager

Successfully sold Chinese themed parties to international wholesale and corporate convention groups.

EDUCATION
B.S., Marketing - University of Nevada at Las Vegas, 1982
B.S., Multinational Business Operations - University of Nevada at Las Vegas, 1982
Diploma, Certificat de Langue Francaise, Institut Catholique De Paris, 1983 (Study Abroad Program)

PROFESSIONAL DEVELOPMENT
Sales Training:
International Hotel, BEST Programs (Building Effective Sales Techniques), Top Achiever Sales, Travel Management Companies, Best Practices
Designation
Certified Meeting Professional (CMP)
Affiliations
Meeting Planners International, Member
American Society of Association Executives, Member

Senior Technology Executive

James Sharpe
9 Central Avenue
Charleston, WV 25301
(304) 555-1212
James@careerbrain.com

Accomplished Management Executive with 15+ years of experience and a verifiable record of delivering enhanced productivity, streamlined operations, and improved financial performance. Natural leader with strong entrepreneurial spirit and a special talent for transitioning strategy into action and achievement. Highly effective team building and motivational skills.

Multifunctional expertise includes:

- Corporate Information Technology
- Staffing & Management Development
- Quality & Productivity Improvement
- Marketing Strategy & Management
- Strategic & Business Planning
- Customer Service & Satisfaction
- Operations Management
- Team Building & Leadership

PROFESSIONAL EXPERIENCE

Roberts Company   1992 - Present
CHIEF INFORMATION OFFICER, Roberts Co., Charleston, WV (1997 - Present)
PRESIDENT, Martins Systems (Roberts Co. subsidiary), Elmview, WV (1997 - Present)

Appointed to these dual senior-level positions and challenged to create and execute technology strategy for Roberts Co. and subsidiaries of the $700 million Roberts Information Services Corporation. Concurrently provide executive oversight for the development and deployment of software products/services and MIS solutions for Martins Systems, affiliate offices, and 3,900 independent agents.

Provide leadership for a team of 200 management and support personnel. Administer a $16 million annual budget. Scope of accountabilities is expansive and includes planning and strategy, operations management, human resource affairs, customer service, marketing, management reporting, and communications.

Key Management Achievements

- Built the complete corporate technology infrastructure from the ground up. Developed technology strategies and tactical plans mapped to align with corporate goals.
- Serve as a member of the corporate Leadership Council. Define corporate vision; develop business plans, create strategies, and establish tactical goals for all business units.
- Established a high-performance management staff and created a team-based work atmosphere that promotes cooperation to achieve common corporate objectives. Instituted a series of initiatives that substantially improved communications between staff and management.
- Developed and integrated programs to maximize productive and efficient use of technology throughout the corporation. Instituted "user champions" to serve as technical experts within each business unit, launched executive "boot camps" to train management in aggressive computer use, and built responsive help centers for technical support.
- Spearheaded creation and implementation of a customer information and marketing team responsible for developing an award-winning marketing program, promotions, direct-mail campaigns, and demonstrations and tours.
- Created innovative processes utilizing product specialists for management of sales leads and distributor networks, resolution of customer escalated issues, and provision of work-flow and engineering consulting for company offices and agents.

Key Technical Achievements

- Led implementation of client/server software suite that won the industry's 1996 and 1998 Title Tech Discovery Award for best and most innovative title industry software.
- Spearheaded development of numerous technical infrastructure projects including the corporate Internet presence, corporate intranet, Web hosting solutions for independent agents, and electronic commerce solutions for offices, agents, and service providers in the real estate industry.
- Orchestrated development of an award-winning marketing program, Power Tools for the Modern World, that won the local and district GOLD ADDY awards for best overall marketing program.
- Guided development and implementation of a title industry software suite installed in 400 systems throughout the distributor network. Designed and deployed training programs to insure high quality service levels.
- Managed creation of an Electronic Underwriting Manual that was selected as best policies and procedures implementation in the National Folio Awards competition, 1996.
- Led design and implementation of a 1,200-user corporate WAN, a centralized help desk, a 2000-user corporate e-mail system, and a comprehensive training center for desktop applications.

PRESIDENT, Roberts Gilday, Gilday, FL (1988 - 1992)

Promoted to manage all operations for this Roberts Company subsidiary. Took over leadership for a staff of 25 and recruited/built to 90+ personnel. Oversaw all management reporting, finances, marketing, product delivery, and closing services.

Key Management Achievements

- Delivered profits throughout a severe recession that crashed the local real estate market.
- Maintained a consistent 15% market share despite a tripling in the local competition.
- Achieved standing in the top 15% in profitability and revenues across all company offices nationwide.
- Created and deployed a realtor marketing program including a series of 20 seminars; built strong industry relationships and established a reputation as the area's premier experts.
- Pioneered innovative marketing strategies to reach new markets and build a network of industry professionals.

COMMERCIAL CLOSER, Roberts Gilday, Gilday, FL (1985 - 1988)

Hired to develop and manage a commercial closing division. Achieved the highest market share of commercial closings in the local market.

EDUCATION
Juris Doctor, West Virginia University (1985)
Bachelor of Arts, Business, West Virginia University (1982)

PROFESSIONAL ACTIVITIES
Frequent Lecturer, Title Tech Technology Conferences, 1995 - Present
Member, Systems Committee, American Land Title Association, 1994 - Present
Member, "Technology 2000" Planning Committee, American Land Title Association, 1994 - Present

Senior Technology Executive

Jane Swift   Page 1 of 2
9 Central Avenue
Los Angeles, CA 90071
(213) 555-1212
Jane@careerbrain.com

SENIOR TECHNOLOGY EXECUTIVE
Project Management ● *Multimedia Communications & Production* ● *MIS Management*

Exceptionally creative management executive uniquely qualified for a digital media technical production position by a distinctive blend of hands-on technical, project management, and advertising/communications experience. Offer a background that spans broadcast, radio, and print media; fully fluent and proficient in interactive and Internet technologies and tools.

Proven leader with a strength for identifying talent, building and motivating creative teams that work cooperatively to achieve goals. Highly articulate with excellent interpersonal skills and a sincere passion for blending communications with technology. Capabilities include:

- Project Planning & Management
- Account Management & Client Relations
- Multimedia Communications & Production
- Information Systems & Networking
- Conceptual & Creative Design
- Work Plans, Budgets & Resource Planning
- Department Management
- Interactive / Internet Technologies
- Technology Needs Assessment & Solutions
- Team Building & Leadership

PROFESSIONAL EXPERIENCE
LaRoche Investments, Inc., Los Angeles, CA   *1986 - Present*
VICE PRESIDENT OF MIS (1997 - Present)
ASSISTANT VICE PRESIDENT OF IT/CORPORATE COMMUNICATIONS (1992 - 1997)
CORPORATE COMMUNICATIONS OFFICER (1988 - 1992)
ASSOCIATE (1986 - 1988)

Advanced rapidly through a series of increasingly responsible positions with this U.S. based, European investment group. Initially hired to manage market research projects, advanced to plan and execute corporate communications projects, and in 1992, assumed responsibility for spearheading the introduction of emerging technologies to automate the entire company.

Current scope of responsibility is expansive and focuses on strategic planning, implementation, and administration of all information systems and technology. Lead technical staff members, manage budgets, select and oversee vendors, define business requirements, and produce deliverables through formal project plans. Manage systems configuration and maintenance, troubleshoot problems, plan and direct upgrades, and test operations to ensure optimum systems functionality and availability.

Technical Contributions

- Pioneered the company's computerization from the ground floor; led the installation and integration of a state-of the-art and highly secure network involving 50+ workstations running on 6 LANs interconnected by V-LAN switching technology.
- Defined requirements; planned and accelerated the implementation of advanced technology solutions, deployed on a calculated timeframe, to meet the short and long-term needs of the organization.
- Orchestrated the introduction of sophisticated applications and multimedia technology to streamline workflow processes, expand presentation capabilities, and keep pace with the competition.
- Administered the life cycle of multiple projects from initial systems/network planning and technology acquisition through installation, training, and operation. Saved hundreds of thousands in consulting fees by managing IS and telecommunication issues in-house.

Business Contributions

- Created and produced high-impact multimedia presentations to communicate the value and benefits of individual investment projects to top-level company executives. Tailored presentations to appeal to highly sophisticated, multicultural audiences.
- Assembled and directed exceptionally well qualified project teams from diverse creative disciplines; collaborated with and guided photographers, videographers, copywriters, script writers, graphic designers, and artists to produce innovative presentations and special events.
- Performed market research and analyses to determine risks and feasibility of multiple investment projects valued at up to $150 million. Developed and recommended tactical plans to transform vision into achievement.

Broadcast, Print, and Radio Advertising & Production   *1971 - 1985*

DIRECTOR OF ADVERTISING, Schwarzer Advertising Associates, New York, NY (1983 - 1985)
ADVERTISING ACCOUNT EXECUTIVE, Schoppe, New York, NY (1984) / Rainbow Advertising, Brooklyn, NY
   (1981 - 1983) / Marcus Advertising, Phoenix, AZ (1980 - 1981) / WCHN, WTYR, AND WSCZ, Boston, MA (1979
   - 1980) / WFDX-TV, WFDX-FM, WKLU, WERS, WQRT, Lehigh Valley, PA (1971 - 1978)
WRITER/PRODUCER, RADIO PROGRAMMING, WPTR, Detroit, MI (1971)
   Early career involved a series of progressive creative and account management positions spanning all advertising mediums: multimedia, television, radio, and print. Worked directly with clients to assess complex and often obscure needs; conceptualized and developed advertising campaigns to communicate the desired message in an influential manner.

Achievement Highlights

- Designed, wrote, produced, and launched advertising campaigns that consistently positioned clients with a competitive distinction. Developed a reputation for ability to accurately intuit and interpret clients' desires and produce deliverables that achieved results.
- Hand-selected and led creative teams consisting of graphic designers, artists, musicians, talent, cartoonists, animators, videographers, photographers, and other freelancers and third-party creative services to develop and produce multimillion dollar advertising campaigns.
- Won accolades for the creation, production, and launch of a 4-color fractional-page advertisement that generated the greatest response in the history of the publication. Honored with a featured personal profile recognizing achievements.
- Developed and applied a unique style and advertising philosophy that accounted for the nuances of human psychology and utilized innovative, brainy, and sometimes startling techniques to capture attention and influence the target market.

EDUCATION & TRAINING
A.A.S, Broadcast Production, Russ Junior College, Boston, MA, 1971
Continuing education in Marketing Research and Broadcast Production, 1981 - 1983
The School of Visual Arts, New York, NY

TECHNICAL QUALIFICATIONS
Innate technical abilities and interest in emerging technologies and digital communications. Trained and fully versed in all aspects of network design, implementation, installation, and maintenance. Advanced skill in the installation, configuration, customization, and troubleshooting of software suites and applications, hardware, and peripherals within the Windows environment (3.x, 95, 98, NT 3.5, NT 3.51, NT 4). Proficient with most Web development, multimedia, word processing, spreadsheet, graphic/presentation, and database tools and applications.

Software Development

James Sharpe
9 Central Avenue
White Sulphur Springs, MT 59645
(406) 555-1212
James@careerbrain.com

Summary

IS professional recognized for broad-based skills encompassing Web, hardware and software solutions. Move effortlessly through and adapt readily to ever changing technologies. Areas of expertise encompass: project management, team leadership, staff supervision, coding, design, testing, user training/support, troubleshooting, customer relations.

Technical Skills

Software: MS Office Suite, Quattro Pro, DacEasy, Act!, Premier, Avid Cinema, Authorware, Director, PhotoShop, CorelDraw, VoicePad, Naturally Speaking, Impromptu, PowerPlay, Visio

Hardware: SCSI, RAID Systems, IDE, NIC's, video/audio network hubs, switches, and routers

Web/Internet: Netscape Commerce Server, MS IIS, HTML, CGI, ISAPI

Databases & Technologies: Dbase, Paradox, MS Access, MS SQL Server, Progress, DDE, OLE, OLE2, ActiveX, Automations Servers (in and out of process), Active Forms, DCOM, Memory Mapped Files, Compound Files, MS Transaction Server (version 1.0), NT Services, Named Pipes, Thunking, Multithreaded applications and libraries (Win32), WinSock, mail services, HTTP, FTP, NNTP, TCP, UDP, SMTP, POP3

Operating Systems/Services: MS DOS, MS Windows 3.11, 95, 98, NT Server/Workstation, UNIX, MS Exchange, MS SQL Server, WINS, RAS, DHCP, IIS

Programming Languages: Delphi, Pascal, Progress, C/C++, VB, Fortran, PowerBuilder, Perl, Assembly

Career Highlights

- Recruited to manage several major projects at Technical Services (TS):
    - Reconfigured entire IS department. Developed specifications for new servers for file sharing, Web, and database. Redesigned network 100 Base T; installed T1; and enables WINS, DHCP, Exchange Server, MS SQL Server and IIS.
    - Revamped networks, servers, and internet connections to resolve the weekly, sometimes daily, crashing of network.
    - Project manager for medical/Internet project that was designed to provide continuing education courses online.
    - Supervised two professionals in IS and Web development.
    - Wrote several interfaces for authorware, I.E. 4.0 and Exchange, and created Intranet as dynamic pages from MSQL database.

- Founded Holbrook Software, with sole responsibility for account development, project planning, staffing, and customer relations. Developed software solutions for several public agencies and private firms:
    - Created an employee scheduling software, Illinois married filing status software with yearly upgrades and conversion program
    - Developed a criminal history database, investigation and complaint software packages for City of Missoula, Montana Police Department.
    - Developed a UCR (uniform criminal reporting) software package for state of Ohio. Program enables small cities, villages, and townships to participate in computerized national UCR.
    - Created software to accommodate membership database, account histories, invoices, membership functions, bank deposits, reports, and rosters for the Joliet Brokers Association.

- Designed Vesex Computer Systems Web site, applying knowledge of HTML/CGI, security, and interactive pages, among other functions
  - Developed user-defined help feature for online help
  - Provided HTML CGI and Winhelp training
  - Created interfaces to third-party products
  - Gained extensive expertise with large relational databases

Professional Experience

Holbrook Software Software Developer/Proprietor	*1997 - Present*
Electronic Systems Director of IS, Programming and Web Development	*1994 - 1996*
MIC Software Developer	*1992 - 1993*
Vesex Computer Systems Interface Developer/Web Programmer/Webmaster; Online Help Programmer	*1990 - 1991*
B. Hevers & Co. Regional Computer Coordinator	*1985 - 1990*
CompuStat Customer Service Representative	*1984 - 1985*

Professional Development
Coursework in Advanced Programming, Pascal, and Fortran

Stock Trader's Assistant

James Sharpe
9 Central Avenue
Boston, MA 02127

(602) 555-1212
James@careerbrain.com

Career Focus

Exploring career opportunities as a Trader's Assistant where my related experience and extreme interest in stock market and trade activities will be of value to an organization and its clients. My ultimate goal is to advance to a Senior Trader position.

Financial Profile

Accomplished, decisive, market-driven professional offering 7 years of experience as a Financial Consultant and Day Trader. Extremely knowledgeable in NYSE and NASDAQ markets and continually monitor other stock market activities to make well-informed and profitable decisions. Successfully sold stocks, mutual funds, treasury bonds, municipal bonds, and retirement plans for 5 years. Orchestrated 10 IPOs valued at $5 million to $10 million. Thrive in dynamic, fast paced business environments. Capable of making quick decisions in stressful situations. Cognizant of industry regulations. Proficient in Windows 98, Office 97, Level 2, ILX, and Bloomberg terminals. Earned a Series 7 and 63 License.

Related Experience

Independent Stock Market Day Trader   *1998 to Present*

- Conduct personal trading activities during market hours utilizing Level 2 software through diverse electronic communication networks. Continually research and analyze NYSE and NASDAQ markets and activities to make prudent and profit-driven stock market investments.

Financial Consultant: Boston Capital Group   *1997 to 1998*

- Primarily executed NASDAQ and NYSE short-term trades for clients.
- Chosen to direct back office activities when Boston Capital consolidated with another broker dealer. Handled all client issues, which included resolving problems and re-establishing relationships with clients during this tumultuous period. Managed 5 Registered Consultants.
- Acquired a wealth of knowledge in trading by cementing relationships with traders.
  Accomplishments
  - Increased client base 50%, which resulted in a $2.5 million portfolio.
  - By establishing excellent relationships with clients during my previous employment, able to convince several of my major clients to transfer their portfolio to Boston Capital.

Financial Consultant: Boston Securities   *1992 to 1997*

- Joined financial service group to market stocks, mutual funds, treasury bonds, retirement plans, and municipal bonds to clients. Acquired a wealth of knowledge in stock market activities.
  Accomplishments
  - Captured over 300 retail accounts primarily through cold calling efforts and referrals.
  - Recognized as the only employee to receive the Chairman's Award in 1994 for exceptional performance.
  - Played a major role in raising capital ($5 million to $10 million) to launch 10 IPOs. Sold stock to various underwriting groups; instrumental in meeting critical deadlines.

Current Employment

Dakotas Restaurant: Headwaiter (part time)   *1998 to Present*

- Trained 12 new waiters.
- Named Employee of the Month for August, 1999 due to outstanding sales performance.

Education

Associates degree in Business Administration, East Coast Community College
Associates degree in Electrical Engineering, East Coast Community College

Store Manager

James Sharpe
9 Central Avenue
Oldsmar, FL 33557
(813) 555-1212
James@careerbrain.com

WORK EXPERIENCE

Manager, A National Kitchen Utensil Retailer. 1997-present
Manage daily operations of a $2-million annual business. Staff of 12 people. Responsible for increasing sales and profitability and decreasing expenses.

Increased gross margin by 25% and net contribution by 105% on a 3% sales increase.

Senior Assistant Buyer, Stern's, Oldsmar, FL. 1993-1997
Controlled open to buy purchase journal, profitability reports, weekly three month estimate of sales, stocks, and markdown dollars. Planned and negotiated sales promotions, advertising, and special purchases.

Coordinated training and teamwork with managers and merchants in the 22 stores.

Increased department sales 18% more than the Division's increase.

Assistant Buyer. Assisted selection and distribution of merchandise. Managed all buying office functions while learning to plan sales, control stocks, and markdown dollars. Created weekly, monthly, and seasonal financial plans.

Developed all systems to support the growth of the branch from a $1-million volume to a $4-million annual volume.

Buyer/Manager, Gulf Gifts, FL. 1990-1993

Bought merchandise for two different gift stores. Directed daily store operations and sales. Directed merchandise presentation, inventory control, and customer service. Scheduled and supervised a 7-person staff.

Increased sales volume 22% more than corporate projection.

Manager, Willis & Geiger, New York, NY. 1987-1990

Direct daily store operations. Analyzed trends in fashion, merchandise, and consumer needs. Planned effective marketing strategy, displays, advertising, and an employee sales program.

Increased annual net sales volume by 33%.

EDUCATION

Fashion Institute of Technology, New York, NY. B.A. Merchandising, 1986

Student System Project Specialist

Jane Swift
9 Central Avenue
Portland, OR 97204
(503) 555-1212
Jane@careerbrain.com

OBJECTIVE
Student System Project Specialist

PROFILE
Resourceful, creative, extremely pleasant person who is consistently evaluated outstanding for quality of work, use of time, technical knowledge, cooperation, and ability to work with others.

EXPERTISE
Complex computer applications • relational databases • business writing and editing • instructing/training-troubleshooting, problem solving, conflict resolution • modern office procedures

STRENGTHS
- High level of knowledge and use with the following software programs and tools: Course Master, SQL, Room Scheduling, Human Resources, Unix, W programs, Windows, and MS Office.
- Diplomatic, tactful, work effectively with employees at all levels.
- Organizational ability and systematic approach to problem-solving.
- Manage time well and work well under pressure situations and deadlines.
- Excellent ability to learn and assimilate new information, technical and functional.

EXPERIENCE
Virtual Solutions, Portland, OR
Computer Systems Analyst I   2000 - present
   Provide administrative and technical support to Banner Human Resources system implementation and users. Required extensive organization, attention to detail, analyses, and writing skills as well as expertise with complex computerized systems, documenting data and procedures, and training others.
      Highlights
      - Successful implementation of Banner Human Resources software.

Technology Trainers, Portland, OR
Program Assistant   1997 - 1999
Program Coordinator   1999 - 2000
   Explained information for submission and subsequent updates to course offerings, credits, and institutional policies and procedures. Self-trained in functions of job. Projects required high degree of planning, organization, and attention to detail.
      Highlights
      - Developed system configuration for room scheduling program.
      - Developed method to automate finals schedule process that was previously labor and time intensive.
      - Presented demonstrations of program and its usefulness.
      - Maintained high level of professionalism while mediating and resolving scheduling conflicts.

Microtech, Inc., Boston, MA

Systems Analyst   1993 - 1997

Worked independently and collaboratively in performing all operations of data processing including purchasing, installation, maintenance, training, feasibility studies for new computer systems, and provided system support to users.

Highlights

- Computerized accounting, human resource, and budget systems.

Data Processing Assistant Manager   1991 - 1993

Ensured uninterrupted operations of all computer equipment, programs, and related functions; monitored systems, trained staff, and provided support.

Highlights

- Main contact for trouble calls and repair requests, conducted problem analyses for repair technicians, modified software configuration.

EDUCATION AND PROFESSIONAL TRAINING

Specialized training, conferences, and workshops in Access, Banner Human Resources, HIS Project Manager, EECO computer operations.

College of William & Mary, Accounting

Emerson College, Computer Applications

Supermarket Management

James Sharpe
9 Central Avenue
New York, NY 10017
(212) 555-1212
James@careerbrain.com

Career Profile

- Extensive experience in the specialty and natural foods industries serving as consultant, manager, store designer, buyer, and lecturer.
- Expert in wholesale and retail sale of conventional and organic produce with total annual volume as high as $5 million. Achieve produce profit margins of up to 42 percent.
- Working background in Eastern, Western, and Midwestern United States markets; understand regional variances in food products, growing seasons, local economies, and consumer buying patterns.
- Active proponent of sustainable farming methods and profitable organic market development. Keen interest in historical and political perspectives on food and food production. Believe that eating is a political act.
- Recognized by the *New York Times* for establishing the best organic produce in the city.

Representative Customers and Clients

- Falducci's
- Union Market
- Gourmet Specialties
- Savannah River Club
- Market Square Cafe
- RKO Farms
- Carmel Market

Achievements and Qualifications

- Expert in forecasting, planning, trend spotting, and creating new opportunities. Specialist in cost and inventory control. Have increased product movement and reduced spoilage at every retail or wholesale client/employer.
- Increase typical produce department percentage of store sales from 15% to 25–35%. Run a profit margin usually 6 to 8 points over regional average. Total annual volume in produce has been $250,000 to $5 million.
- Experienced buyer with wide knowledge of farmers and wholesalers in key growing areas of the United States. Understand regional and cultural negotiating and buying patterns. Expert in foraging for the freshest and most unusual produce.
- Adept in the innovative and profitable presentation of produce and all types of specialty foods. Create effective and prize-winning displays using unusual props; mix texture and color, identify and react to food and visual trends.
- Directed design, construction, and opening management of $2 million annual sales, 4,000 square foot, full-line specialty foods store. Determined floor layout, product placement, lighting, fixturing, signage, and back-room production arrangements/equipment. Scouted for antiques and unusual fixtures to enhance store concept.
- Facility for selling to the specialty and organics customer and to the customer with a highly developed palate and a sense of aesthetic character—food stylists, personal and professional chefs, world travelers, society figures, and international clients. Develop and maintain an excellent rapport with customers accustomed to the best in quality and service.
- Interact with customers on a personal and instructional level that creates a redirected purchasing pattern based on a seasonal sensibility for produce and an understanding of ingredients. Direct total purchase for a loyal following of customers who shop with an "open list" and ask "What's good today?"

Experience as Manager, Buyer, and Consultant

Downtown Foods: Produce Manager and Buyer, 1998 - Present
Gourmet Specialties: Store Designer, Construction Project Manager, Store Opening Manager, 1997
Naraganset Farmers Market: Produce Consultant, 1996
Organic by Nature: Produce Manager, 1995
Magic Lettuce: Produce Consultant, 1994
Union Market: Produce Consultant, Manager/Buyer, 1993
Falducci's: Produce Manager, 1992

Systems and Networks Manager

James Sharpe
9 Central Avenue
Syracuse, NY 12345
(315) 555-1212
James@careerbrain.com

Profile
- 15 years of management and hands-on background working in IT infrastructure.
- Experience with world-class banks and financial institutions in New York, London, Paris.
- Hold MBA in Banking and Finance.
- Chosen for the 2000 International Who's Who in Information Technology.

Areas of Expertise

network design • systems management • LAN administration • strategic planning • team formation and leadership • budget preparation • project planning and management • presentation • business writing • resource management • product and design research • vendor interface and negotiation • systems conversion • computer operations • systems implementation • branch start-ups and automation • disaster recovery • system migrations • data center overhauls and moves • applications support

Executive Development
A Fortune 100 Company, Syracuse, NY

Vice President and Manager of Network Operations   1998 to present
Control $1 million budget and oversee five technicians in the design, implementation, and support of company's WAN and LAN infrastructure. Handle heavy resource management and coordination with internal departments, vendors, and network integration companies to define scopes of work, technical designs, product selection, required resources, schedules, and price negotiation. Budget resources and prepare reports. Hire, schedule, and review technicians.

Projects

AT&T frame relay and Cisco router implementation, TCP/IP address conversion, Compuserve RAS implementation, Cisco switched Ethernet 100mb/1 gb Catalyst implementation, HP Open View and Cisco Works implementation, MS DHCP and proxy server implementation. Managed project teams at remote sites to implement NT servers, routers, PC hardware upgrades, and Windows 95/NT images. Co-managed 1,100-user move.

A Major Investment Bank, London   1995 to 1998
Network Manager
Managed WAN daily support, hardware installation/configurations, and network changes. Monitored/configured private frame relay voice and data network. Monitored ACC routers and NT servers. Performed Windows NT 3.51 server and workstation installations. Configured ACC routers, Adtran CSU's, and Newbridge 3612 and 3606 multiplexors for remote site installations.

A Large Multinational Bank, Paris   1992 to 1995
Network Operations Supervisor
Managed all network and computer operations for the international hub site, reporting directly to the Technology Manager and supervising a team of technicians and computer operators. Supervised three direct reports, supported traders, reviewed/upgraded operations, handled troubleshooting, researched products and interfaced/negotiated with vendors.

James Sharpe (315) 555-1212

- Completed full office start-up in Luxembourg in three months. Implemented LAN, voice, data, and video capabilities. Hired and trained computer operator to support local users. Implemented support procedures and documentation.
- Saved company over $50,000 annually: Migrated video conferencing from leased lines to ISDN, cleaned up multiplexor maintenance contracts, discovered overpayment on WAN lines. Set up a new process to review all invoices and pre-approved all purchases and communications costs before forwarding to Technology Manager.

Technology Expertise

Hardware: Cisco 7206/4700/25XX, Cisco PIX firewall, Cabletron MMAC+/Smart Switch 6000's/MMAC8, Newbridge 46020/36XX, IDNX 20/12, CYLINK link encryptors, Paradyne CSU's, ACC routers, Northern Telecom Option 11, PictureTel 4000/M8000, VAX 4000/6310/8000, HSC50, RA60/80/82/90 disk drives, MTI disks in DSSI architecture, HP 9000 K100, Sun Ultra 10, HP Laserjet 3/4/5 and QMS laser printers, Dell/Digital/AST/IBM PC hardware, Intel/3Com NIC cards, Cabling knowledge includes category 3/5, IBM Type 1, fiber optic multimode, v.35, x.21, RS232.

Software: SWIFT Alliance v3.0, IBIS, ST400, Montran (CHIPS), Reuters, Telerate, ADP Executive Quotes, IFSL Green Bar Viewer, Euroclear, Tracs, Soar, MS Project 95, VISIO, MS Word/Excel/PowerPoint, Lotus Notes v4.6, MS Mail, Ami-Pro, Lotus 1-2-3, DOS, Chameleon v4.6, Sybase v11, COBOL, Pascal, BASIC.

Protocols/Operating Systems: Cisco IOS version 11.x, TCP/IP, IPX, frame relay, EIGRP, OSPF, RIP, PPP, ISDN, SNMP, DHCP, WINS/DNS, Netbeui, NetBIOS, DECnet, LAT, VAX/VMS v5.5-2, Pathworks v4.1/5.0, Windows NT Server 3.51 and 4.0, Netware 3.12, HP-UX v10.2, Solaris v2.6.1, OS/400 v2.3.

Education and Professional Development

M.B.A. in Banking and Finance, Syracuse University, Syracuse, New York

B.S. in Interdisciplinary Studies, Rensselaer Polytechnical Institute, Rensselaer, New York

Computer Operations Diploma (500 hour program), Institute for Data Systems, Mahopac, New York.

Additional technology courses: Network Design and Performance, Advanced Cisco Router Configuration, Microsoft Project 95. SYBASE SQL Server Administration, SYBASE Fast Track to SQL Server, Fundamentals of the HP UNIX System, Pathworks V5 Migration Planning, RDB Database Administration, Pathworks Tuning and Troubleshooting, PC Architecture and Troubleshooting.

Teacher (Entry-Level)

James Sharpe
9 Central Avenue
Mill Valley, CA 94941
(415) 555-1212
James@careerbrain.com

Page 1 of 2

OBJECTIVE   I seek a challenging position as an elementary school teacher where my drive and ambition will be rewarded.

EDUCATION   C.W. POST - Long Island University, Brookville, New York
Bachelor of Science in Elementary Education, expected date of graduation May 2001
Overall G.P.A.: 3.63   Last Semester's G.P.A.: 3.90
Dean's List 1998, 1999

Coursework included:

- Methods of Teaching Elementary Science, Math, and Social Studies
- Multicultural Education
- Educational Psychology
- Theory and Practice of Diagnosing Reading
- Basic Drawing

Extracurricular Activities: Founding brother of Delta Phi Epsilon - assisted with organizing and participating in sponsored events. As active member, helped with community service fund-raising campaigns. Member of Phi Eta Sigma (National Freshman Honor Fraternity).

STUDENT TEACHING

1/98 - Present   HILLSIDE GRADE SCHOOL
New Hyde Park/Garden City Park School District
Assist with assorted classroom duties (3rd and 6th graders). Draft lesson plans; organize planbook for review and approval; mark tests and record grades; average class size approximately thirty students; teach two to three lessons per day. Additionally responsible for dance program activities, including working with 6th graders twice a week for seven weeks.

9/96 - 12/96   WESTSIDE SCHOOL
Cold Spring Harbor School District
Participated in the daily activities, observation (six credits), of a first grade class once a week.

James Sharpe
(415) 555-1212
Page 2 of 2

EMPLOYMENT EXPERIENCE

8/93 - 1/98   FAZIO DANCE CENTER
Howard Beach, New York
Dance Instructor. Taught youngsters ages 3 1/2 to 9 years old the art of tap dancing, jazz, and ballet. Average class size approximately twenty students. Assisted with all aspects of yearly recitals.

6/97 - 8/97   SUMMER FUN DAY CAMP
Ozone Park, New York
Supervised the daily camp activities of large groups of youngsters. Responsible for weekly trips to museums, Hall of Science, Westbury Music Fair, and beaches. Also organized indoor play.

EXAMINATIONS   Passed NTE part I, II (March 1997) and III (December 1997).

OUTSIDE INTERESTS

As a member of the C.J. Dance Company my activities include studying tap, jazz, and ballet. Participate in charity work and fund-raising events.

REFERENCES   Furnished upon request.

Teacher's Aide

Jane Swift
9 Central Avenue
Chicago, IL 60606
(312) 555-1212
Jane@careerbrain.com

Profile

Experienced in classroom environments, teaching and working with children.
Self-motivated and detail oriented with a proven ability to build and foster strong relationships.
Possess excellent administrative and communications skills.

Summary of Qualifications

Classroom Experience

- Certified Teachers Aide with thorough knowledge and understanding of school structure and operations.
- Successfully utilized written and oral communication skills when working with teachers, students, and parents.
- Planned, developed, and implemented lesson plans ensuring comprehension of required materials.
- Assisted teachers with class assignments, working with students in both individual and group settings.
- Coordinated extracurricular meetings and activities.

Administration

- Provided administrative assistance including word processing, meeting coordination, copying, and filing.
- Managed concurrent responsibilities through effective time management.
- Identified and coordinated resources necessary to complete assignments.
- Managed the funds and budgets for multiple volunteer organizations.
- Accurately prepared a wide array of documentation.
- Experienced using multiple computer software packages including Microsoft Word, Excel, and PowerPoint.

Relevant Volunteer Experience

Classroom Volunteer, King Elementary School, Chicago, IL	1996 - Present
Publishing Center Coordinator, King Elementary School,	1998 - Present
Co-leader and Treasurer, Daisy Troop, Chicago, IL	1998 - Present
Children's Education Teacher, St. Ann's Church, Chicago, IL	1996 - 1998
Treasurer, Parent Teacher Organization, Chicago, IL	1996 - 1997

Work History

Accounts Receivable Clerk, Utilities Company, Pindrop, OH	1995 - 1996
Administrative Assistant, Electric Company, Bentwood, IL	1986 - 1989
Administrative Assistant, Electric Illuminating Company, Pindrop, OH	1985 - 1986

Education

Associates Degree, Community College of Chicago, Chicago, IL

Telecommunications Analyst

James Sharpe
9 Central Avenue
Jericho, NY 11753
(516) 555-1212
James@careerbrain.com

OBJECTIVE:

Challenging opportunity as Telecommunications Analyst

SUMMARY:

Eleven years' progressive experience providing network analysis, system planning, and product evaluation and selection. Comprehensive and cost-effective installation, troubleshooting, and maintenance of voice and data communications systems.

COMMUNICATIONS KNOWLEDGE:

Bell System, PBX's, Modems, MUX's and Fiber Optics. Specifically, Northern Telecom SLI, NEC NEAX 2400, Dimension 200, Rolm CBS, Mitel SX200, Strombergh Carlson DBX 1200/5000, GTE PIC, PCM Fiber Optic System, Equinox Data Switch and T1, Functional understanding of Packet Switches, WAGNET and ETHERNET.

EXPERIENCE:

A MAJOR BROKERAGE/FINANCIAL CORPORATION: TELECOMMUNICATIONS ANALYST

Project manager for the planning and implementation of a nationwide voice and data communications network. Included development of a multi-side RFP to replace fourteen phone systems. Issued RFP's to vendors, conducted evaluations according to formats and configurations. Network design and traffic engineering using ETN networks. 1991 - Present.

VIACOM, MANHATTAN: TELECOMMUNICATIONS VOICE/DATA ANALYST

Responsibilities included planning and implementing telecommunications for headquarters and field offices. Included long-range requirements, new products and software releases, and recommending upgrades as required. Reviewed and evaluated proposals, selected systems, assisted in system software design, and supervised implementation. 1989 - 1991.

CHASE MANHATTAN: TELECOMMUNICATIONS ANALYST

Responsibilities included: Coordinating installation for international data communications networks in Europe and Africa. Reviewed company's product usage, and provided recommendations for effective use of data switches or data through PBX. Assisted in the selection and implementation of data switch (RS-232) for a CM subsidiary. 1987 - 1989.

EDUCATION: B.S. Telecommunications. (New York University), 1990.

REFERENCES: Available upon request.

Telecommunications Management Professional

Jane Swift
9 Central Avenue
Kansas City, MO 64105

(816) 555-1212
James@careerbrain.com
Page 1 of 2

MANAGEMENT PROFESSIONAL
Telecommunications Industry
Project Management / Project Implementation

TOP PRODUCING PROFESSIONAL with more than 15 years experience building both regional and national technical service/support groups. Demonstrated expertise in customer support, sales, marketing, and key account management. Combine strong planning, organization and consensus building qualifications with effective writing, presentation and negotiation skills. Exceptional planning, analytical, and organizational skills.

Expert qualifications in identifying and capturing market opportunities to accelerate expansion, increase revenues, and improve profit contributions. Excellent team building and interpersonal skills. Expert qualifications include:

- Quality & Productivity Improvement
- Training & Development
- Cost Reduction
- Customer Service & Retention
- Project Lifecycle

- New Business Development
- Milestone Tracking
- Corporate Winbacks
- Cross Functional Team Leadership
- Staffing & Recruitment

MANAGEMENT PROFILE

- Organized, take-charge professional with exceptional follow-through abilities and detail orientation; able to oversee projects from concept to successful conclusion. Able to efficiently and effectively prioritize a broad range of responsibilities to consistently meet deadlines.
- Demonstrated success in surpassing productivity and performance objectives.
- Proven ability to resolve problems swiftly and independently.
- Possess strong interpersonal skills; able to work effectively with individuals on all levels.
- Recognized for maximizing ongoing employment opportunities for others within the organization.
- Demonstrated ability to provide vision and then translate that vision into productive action.
- Possess in-depth knowledge of T-1 provisioning.

SELECTED ACHIEVEMENTS

- Recognized for "continuously providing leadership in achieving business goals by managing herself and coaching others in delivering superior customer and client experience while minimizing cost."
- Commended for "bringing focus and stability to the successful completion of many large projects, business initiatives, and customer issues."
- "... continuously demonstrates a delightful ability to lead and enable individuals and team effectiveness, meeting business goals. . . . is supportive, effectively providing information and alignment with union partners, clients, process management, peers, and executives."
- Earned reputation for "achieving her objective to balance workloads and enable team effectiveness; eliminating costly, unnecessary training differentials, and yielding additional cost savings."
- Specially selected to participate in the elite Leadership Development Program designed for high performing managers.
- Peak performer, consistently place in top 10 percentile in comparison to peer group.

PROFESSIONAL EXPERIENCE

1985 - Present, Sprint Corporation, Kansas City, MO
Fast-track promotions through a series of increasingly responsible positions transitioning from financial/accounting and administrative to results-oriented project management. Performance-based promotions reflect strong network background; both long distance and local.

GENERAL MANAGER: Business Customer Care   *December 1999 - Present*
Supervise team of 380, including technical and clerical staff and 120 managers. Directly support top ten corporate customers, each billing in excess of $1 million per month. Built alignment with union partners to form new Inbound, M8 WPOF team addressing issues raised by front-line staff. Serve as local leader for Single Nodal Provisioning "Deliver It" Initiative; work with Process/Development team.

- Spearheaded ISDN implementation, keeping call center a viable entity.
- Championed provisioning for the Advantis Migration Project. Was asked to take the lead in this high profile project as a "direct result of strong leadership and management skills."
- Recognized for "empowering team to be innovative in resolving project issues with a sense of ownership and urgency, often exceeding expectation for facility designs, test, and turn up activities.
- Achieved status of company "Role Model." As member of National Center Support Model Team, recommended national prototype approach, which was deployed.
- Initiated efficiency improvement measures drastically slashing number of technician overtime hours to achieve significant cost savings.

MANAGER: Business Customer Care   *October 1996 - November 1999*
Directed the voice provisioning of outbound and inbound services for global and middle market stratas. Managed staff or 100+ employees. Employed and extensively trained staff in high-caliber customer service techniques.

- Consistently exceeded Customer Value Added, People Value Added, and Economic Value Added target goals.
- Implemented service delivery processing for the IBM Winback, providing over $100 million in monthly revenue.
- Recognized as one of 30 to receive Sprint's "Leading Legend" team award, out of a 1400 member universe.

SUPERVISOR: Business Customer Care   *August 1992 - September 1996*
Served as project manager of software defined networks for dedicated global Sprint customers. Achieved some of Sprint's highest profile winbacks utilizing strong customer interface skills.

SUPERVISOR: Network Services Division   *February 1989 - August 1992*
Functioned as Facility Planner. Implemented Sprint Message Network for the Eastern Region.

- Recipient of the 1989 Vice President Quality Award.

Previous administrative and accounting positions leading to consistent promotions   *1984 - 1989*

EDUCATION

Skidmore College, Saratoga Springs, NY
Bachelor of Business Administration   May 1983

REFERENCES

References will be furnished on request.

Telecommunications/Information Systems Management

James Sharpe
9 Central Avenue
San Francisco, CA 94127
(415) 555-1212
James@careerbrain.com

**Voice & Data Communications, Information Technology,
Project/Budget Management, Strategic Planning**

Expert in the design, development, and delivery of cost-effective, high-performance technology and communication solutions to meet challenging business demands. Extensive qualifications in all facets of projects from initial feasibility analysis and conceptual design through implementation, training, and enhancement. Excellent organizational, budget management, leadership, team building, negotiation, and project management qualifications.

Professional Experience

Food Systems International, San Francisco, CA   *1995 - Present*
Achieved fast-track promotion through positions of increasing responsibility for multibillion dollar international company with 30,000 employees worldwide.

Telecommunications Manager   *1998 - Present*
Responsible for management of $15 million department budget. Fully accountable for overall strategy for telecommunications technology acquisition and integration, vendor selection and negotiation, usage forecasting, workload planning, project budgeting, and administration. Plan and direct implementation of emerging telecommunications solutions at all domestic locations consisting of 125 facilities. Provide direction regarding telecommunications technology to affiliates throughout U.S. Lead cross-functional project teams; supervise technical and administrative staff with 20 direct reports. Fully accountable for department's strategic vision and leadership. Representative achievements include:

- Directed $40 million annual MCI network conversion at 200 locations within six months, saving company $15 million over three years.
- Designed and managed implementation of network utilizing Lucent and Octel at more than 100 locations in 12 months, realizing annual cost savings of $1 million.
- Served as technical project director for $12 million consolidation of East Coast headquarters with West Coast location.
- Facilitated move of corporate headquarters involving 3,000 employees over a four-day weekend.
- Implemented video conferencing technology at more than 60 sites.
- Built a four-digit dialing network for Food Systems locations within a four-month period.

Assistant Manager of Telecommunications   *1996 - 1998*

Management Trainee   *1995*

Education
BS in Political Science, Northwestern University, Chicago, IL
Professional Development/Continuing Education: Various American Management Association workshops and courses; BCR technical/technical management courses.

Telemarketing Professional

James Sharpe
9 Central Avenue
Waterbury, VT 05676
(802) 555-1212
James@careerbrain.com

Profile

Telemarketing Specialist/Sales Manager/Team Leader with proven ability to lead sales teams in fast-paced, high-volume environments. Able to coordinate multiple projects and meet deadlines under pressure. Outstanding record in training, motivating, and retaining employees. Knowledgeable in telemarketing business methods and applicable laws.

Telemarketing Experience

Telephone Sales Representative, United States Telemarketing, Waterbury, Vermont, 1999 - Present

Management Trainer, AT&T Net, Burlington, Vermont, 1998 - 1999
Directed performance, training, and recruiting for 13- to 15-person bay marketing long distance and wireless services by telephone to prospective customers across the country.
- Implemented creative sales contests and incentive programs that increased revenues, boosted morale, and minimized employee turnover.
- Trained top-performing sales teams on effective telephone sales and closing techniques.
- Supervised team performance through call splitting and statistical reporting. Maintained target levels for quality management.
- Exceeded corporate goals for team sales per hour and sales hours fulfillment. Consistently ranked in top three of 32 bays.

Team Leader, Domestic Features, Burlington, Vermont, 1997 - 1998
Managed 9-person telemarketing team marketing family-friendly videos for privately owned international film production company with $60 million in annual revenues.
- Led successful teams recognized for commitment to company cause of promoting nonviolent films with no sexual content or innuendo, and influencing the film industry to offer more films of this nature.

Sales Experience

Independent Sales Professional/Certified Flooring Inspector, Burlington, Vermont, 1996 - 1997

Store Manager, Stickly Carpets, Burlington, Vermont, 1994 - 1996
Managed sales and operations for retail flooring business. Directed sales teams, scheduling, goal setting, and motivational seminars. Purchased merchandise from mills, negotiated contracts, and administered promotions and product merchandising.
- Achieved annual retail sales averaging $0.5 million with a gross profit margin of 35%.
- Hired, trained, and managed goal-oriented sales teams with below average turnover.
- Conducted in-service training seminars for sales representatives teaching detailed product information and sales techniques.

Training

B.A. in Human Services, University of Vermont, Burlington, Vermont, 1994
Ongoing Professional Development: sales training and motivational seminars with Anthony Robbins, Tommy Hopkins, Zig Ziglar, Stephen Covey

Tour Director

James Sharpe
9 Central Avenue
Glendale, CA 91209
(818) 555-1212
James@careerbrain.com

Profile

- Highly successful Tour Director with 5+ years' experience providing the finest quality travel experiences for thousands of guests. Achieved 98% guest satisfaction rate throughout career.
- Recognized for outstanding organizational skills, creative programming, public speaking and presentation expertise, and the ability to consistently exceed guest expectation.
- Talent for conveying "vision" of a place, inspiring excitement and enthusiasm. Able to analyze and fulfill guests' dreams and expectations for their trip.
- Willing to do whatever it takes to ensure guests' comfort and enjoyment, making guests feel like family.

Experience

Tour Director, Zydeco Tours, Los Angeles, California   1994 - Present

- Top tour director for the #1 tour company in the world. Zydeco Tours specializes in upscale tours and cruises to destinations around the world, hosting 100,000+ guests annually.
- Personally direct 10 months of tours to Italy, Hawaii, Colorado Rockies, Texas, New Mexico, Canyonlands, Idaho, Yellowstone/Grand Tetons/Mount Rushmore. Oversee all aspects of 7 - 20 day tours for 40 guests including:

• Travel connections and transfers • Hotel and meal arrangement/confirmation •
• Anticipating and resolving problems • Individual tour coordination • Introducing new, innovative programs •
• Documentation and record keeping • Ensuring complete guest satisfaction •

Accomplishments:

- Personally hosted more than 100 return guests. Many more guests booked additional tours with Zydeco.
- Trained and mentored 75 new tour directors receiving praise for "the insights and standards that he can teach and impart to others."
- Selected by management to participate in program development, modifications, and enhancements. Successfully led many first run tours.
- Awarded excellent ratings from Product Manager for working to improve the product and level of customer service and for responsiveness to company's needs.

Education and Skills

Degree program: American History, University of California at Los Angeles
Extensive and ongoing research in the history, demographics, industry, geography, geology, customs, and culture of tour destination.
Skills: Internet research, e-mail, travel reservation/confirmation systems, conversational Italian.

Traffic Control (Shipping and Receiving)

JANE SWIFT

9 Central Avenue • Greenwich, CT 06830 • (203) 555-1212 • Jane@careerbrain.com

SUMMARY OF QUALIFICATIONS

- Extensive, large volume *Traffic Control, Shipping & Receiving* knowledge; strong leadership abilities.
- Solid record of promotions based on performance. Insightful commitment to positive communication.
- Willing to take on new challenges within demanding deadlines utilizing progressive, results-oriented performance style.
- Strong time management and interpersonal skills. Extremely organized.
- Self-motivated, adaptable, loyal team player. Impeccable work ethic.
- Competent blueprint reading capabilities. Computer literate—proficient with spreadsheets.

EXPERIENCE

ABC EXTRUSION, Division of General Corporation • Greenwich, CT   1992 to 2000
Manufacturer of machinery for the rubber & plastic industry. Company name changed several times due to new ownership. Retained as a valuable employee through each transfer.

- **Traffic Control Manager**—Facilitated all shipments of large machinery and spare parts. Coordinated all paperwork and documentation including Bill of Lading, Certificate of Origin and Customs documents. Entered applicable data into computer system.
- **Receiving Manager**—Handled all receiving and stockroom department responsibilities. Identified, tagged and located parts in stock area. Retrieved components and piece parts for assembly floor personnel. Skilled using Federal Express Powership & Pitney Bowes shipping equipment.
- **Receiving**—Supported all receiving department functions. Identified, verified and received parts optimizing the computerized database.
- **Stockroom**—Stocked parts; recorded and cataloged items in database. Assisted in retrieving parts for assembly floor work orders.
- **Shipping**—Prepared and arranged U.P.S. shipments and packing of parts. Operated U.P.S. equipment documenting size, weight and type of cargo. Typed Bills of Lading and Customs forms. Recorded all shipping data.
- **Data Entry**—Logged all new parts and stockroom locations into database.
- **Expediter**—Identified, traced and accelerated parts in process to the next manufacturing operation. Directed finished parts to appropriate assembly areas. Tracked and updated shortage lists.
- **Licensed**—to operate overhead crane, forklift and overhead lifts.

HOMETOWN MARKET • Greenwich, CT   1975 to 1992
Produce Market

- **Owner/Manager**—Directed and oversaw daily store operations. Supervised up to ten employees. Facilitated operational performance of store, implemented all phases of management functions inclusive of inventory, presentations, display, advertising, customer and employee relations, all accounting/bookkeeping, payroll and receivables. Generated and maintained reports, spreadsheets and mailing lists of over 10,000 people.

CONTINUING EDUCATION

- Blueprint Reading Certification, ABC
- Forklift Operation, ABC
- Crane Operation, ABC
- Accounting I, II, Connecticut State University

References Available Upon Request

VP of Operations

Jane Swift   Page 1 of 2
9 Central Avenue
Houston, TX 77002
(713) 555-1212
Jane@careerbrain.com

SUMMARY OF QUALIFICATIONS

Vice President of Operations, Manufacturing. 20+ years experience in the creative leadership of multisite manufacturing operations to improve productivity, quality, and efficiency. Facilitated significant cost savings through expertise in:

- Operations Systems
- Strategic Planning
- Cost Management
- Facilities Design
- Offshore Production

- Manufacturing Process
- Quality Control
- Supplier Partnership
- Human Resources/Labor Relations
- Compliance

PROFESSIONAL EXPERIENCE

Acme Automotive Products, Houston, Texas   *1989 - 1999*

A national leader in the manufacturing of automotive water pumps with annual sales of $380 million and 1,500 employees.

Vice President of Operations

- Managed the company's two plants in Texas and Mexico. Directly supervised two plant managers, a materials manager, advanced manufacturing systems manager, distribution manager, manager for special projects, and training and a Quality Control Division.
- Initiated and secured ISO9002 certification in two plants on the first application.
- Reorganized preventative maintenance schedules that decreased scrap rates by 50% and virtually eliminated rework rates.
- Orchestrated teamwork and communication between marketing and production to ensure customers received precise delivery dates and improved quality.
- Guided efforts with a major supplier to turnaround its sub-quality standards. Avoided a change to the competition's vendors that could have been costly. Result: vendor achieved ISO9000 certification and is now rated top in field.

A1 Heating Corporation   *1979 - 1989*

A residential and industrial water heater manufacturing company.

Vice President of Mexican Operations, Bordertown, Texas   1985 - 1989
Plant Manager/Director of Operations, Portland, Oregon   1981 - 1985
Manager of Manufacturing, Milwaukee, WI   1979 - 1981

- Instituted a quality control system in Mexican operation that resulted in highest product quality in industry. Responded to suspicions from customers and suppliers about quality of Mexican-produced goods by arranging for decision-makers to see plant in operation.
- Reduced accident rate 200% and turnover rate (from 12% to 3% per month in four years) in Mexican operations by implementing unilateral training programs (e.g., skills, teamwork, supervisory).
- Negotiated commitments from vendors to ensure JIT system.
- Established a 50,000 sq. foot distribution center to improve service to mid-continent customers.
- Prevented theft of valuable copper shipments by working with Mexican police.
- Selected by senior management to solve problems in Canadian plant, which resulted in opening on schedule. Efforts led to promotion to Vice President of Mexican Operations.

- Improved Portland plant operations efficiencies as a result of executing a comprehensive study. In four years increased output significantly and profits by 200% by optimizing space, decreasing product damage during production, and consolidating shipments.
- Oversaw Milwaukee plant closing and transfer to modern facilities. Responsibilities included identification of most economical way to equip new plant, comprehensive study on disposal of buildings, and employee transition management. Production levels remained stable and efforts led to promotion to Director of Operations.

Hillcrest Water Products, Inc., Dayton, Ohio   *1974 - 1979*
     Manufacturing Engineer

EDUCATION
MBA, Apex School of Management, University of Dayton, Dayton, Ohio
Bachelor of Science (Mechanical Engineering), University of Wisconsin, Madison, Wisconsin

ONGOING PROFESSIONAL DEVELOPMENT
- Strategic Planning Seminar, Columbia University Executive Program
- Leadership at the Peak, Center for Creative Leadership
- World Class Manufacturing & Process Capability Studies, K. W. Farn & Associates
- Human Resources Seminar, American Manufacturing Association
- The Employee Team Concept, The Center for Productivity
- MRP II, Oliver Wight
- Understanding Border Culture, Maquiladora Associates

Visual Merchandising Specialist

Jane Swift
9 Central Avenue
Manhasset, NY 11575
(516) 555-1212
Jane@careerbrain.com

With fifteen years' experience in Visual Merchandising Management, I have successfully:

- Coordinated all Visual Merchandising in Macy's third-most-profitable store.
- Supervised visual aspects of a successful $3 million store renovation with responsibility for new fixturing and merchandising.
- Conducted seminar in Visual Merchandising for all new department managers in Macy's eastern region.
- Utilized innovative image control techniques that contributed to a new high-fashion store's becoming the volume leader for its entire chain in one year.

RECENT ACCOMPLISHMENTS

Visual Merchandising Manager of a Macy's store with a $40 million sales volume, I coordinated fixturing, merchandising, and seasonal changes for all twelve departments, along with responsibility for overall store image.

- Analyzed stock levels to determine new fixture needs, prepared requirement reports, and coordinated on-time deliveries of all fixtures.
- Reporting directly to the Vice President for Corporate Visual Merchandising, I supervised five Visual Merchandising Managers brought in from other stores to assist in the project.
- Interfaced with both union and non-union construction personnel while directing movement of departments under construction.
- Guiding all Department Managers through renovation and construction, I familiarized them with new fixturing and applicable merchandising techniques.

EARLIER ACCOMPLISHMENTS

As District Display Director for Laura Ashley Inc., a 100-store specialty women's ready-to-wear chain, I developed fashion awareness, coordinated displays, and trained staff, including new District Display Directors throughout the country. Reporting directly to the Corporate Display Director, I was:

- Given responsibility for image control at the company's new flagship store on 57th St, where fashion image was crucial. My innovative merchandising and display techniques contributed to this store's becoming the number-one-volume store for the entire company by its first anniversary.
- Recognized for my planning, organizing, and coordinating abilities, I was involved in several new store openings throughout the U.S. and Canada.

As Display Coordinator/Visual Merchandising Manager with ESPRIT, Inc., I progressed to having a five-store responsibility. Developing my functional skills, I was promoted to Visual Display troubleshooter for a multi-state region.

JANE SWIFT (516) 555-1212 page 2 of 2

EMPLOYMENT

MACY'S, 1987 - Present
LAURA ASHLEY, 1983 - 1987
ESPRIT DE CORPS, 1979 - 1983

EDUCATION

A graduate of Harper College, Palatine, Illinois, with a specialty in Fashion Design, I have also completed intensive course work in Architectural Technology which has significantly contributed to my expertise in store renovation and floor plan know-how. Course work in photography has rounded out my background.

PERSONAL

Interests include apparel design and construction, sketching, and free-hand drawing.

Web Site Designer

Jane Swift
9 Central Avenue
Seattle, WA 98102
(206) 555-1212
Jane@careerbrain.com

Areas of Effectiveness

Professional Web Site Design	Site Planning & Renovation
Marketing & Maintenance	Business Solutions
Quality Custom Programming	Graphic Design

Experience

Web Site Designer, Co-Owner. Rainier Software 1999 - Present
Senior Researcher. University of Washington 1997 - 1999

Career Highlights

- Designed and implemented Web site for Mount Rainier Methodist Church (*www.mumc.com*)
- Created Web site for Ultimate Typographical Services based on client design and content specifications
- Stress user-friendly design, emphasizing ease of navigation, quick download times, and appealing graphics
- Maintain clients' Web site registration with Internet search engines; include HTML meta tags to ensure high ranking
- Advise clients on effective marketing techniques to increase Web site traffic

Technical Expertise

HTML	Javascript	Macromedia Fireworks
Dreamweaver	FTP protocols	search engine submittals
Adobe Photoshop	Microsoft Access, Word, and Excel.	

Education

University of Washington, BS (Biology) 1995, MS (Biology) 1997

Appendix

Resumes for Special Situations
Professional Resume Writing Services
Resume Banks
Resources

Resumes for Special Situations

These are resumes that performed above and beyond the call of duty for job seekers whose background didn't "fit the mold." They're invaluable guideposts in presenting your own experiences in the most flattering light.

James is leaving the military for a Finance Executive position.

James Sharpe
9 Central Avenue
Indianapolis, IN 46206

(317) 555-1212
James@careerbrain.com

Profile

Confident, dependable, versatile management professional with extensive and diverse experience in the areas of budget management, personnel management, and customer service. Global perspective based upon assignments and travel abroad. Articulate problem solver with superior analytical and communication skills. Organized, meticulous, and methodical; particularly adept in problem identification, research, analysis, and resolution.

Qualifications

- An established record of progressively responsible positions of trust at the highest levels of government.
- A proven history of success in the administrative management of military units
- An innate ability to develop loyal and cohesive staffs dedicated to the task at hand.

Competencies

- communications skills
- top secret security clearance
- training and development
- human resources

- long- and short-range planning
- leadership and supervision
- computer systems
- customer relations

- budget analysis/management
- senior staff coordination
- project management
- organizational skills

Experience

United States Navy, Worldwide Assignments   1990 - Present

Program Director, Naval Artillery School, San Diego, California   1998 - 2000
Oversaw operation of largest training complex in the U.S. Navy, with an operating budget over $2.5 million and $100 million in real property listing.
- Supervised 150 military and civilian personnel with 6 direct reports.
- Developed comprehensive 5-year development plan, resulting in $500K funding for improvements.
- Formulated, planned, and implemented $1 million in capital improvements. Actively participated in contract negotiations with vendors and coordinated projects.
- Overcame $400K budget shortfall through budget analysis and cost control.
- Developed organizational vision, goals, and key business drivers.

Program Manager, Eighth Fleet, Southeast Asia   1996 - 1998
Program and budget manager for large organization with annual budget over $800 million.
- Supervised 20 personnel with 3 direct reports.
- Funded $2.5 million in out-of-cycle, high priority projects.
- Overcame 10% funding decrement through analysis of congressional appropriation bills, identifying shortfall and authoring letters of justification.
- Developed and presented plan to reorganized budget analysts, streamlining executing by 40 - 50% and resulting in annual savings of more than $200K.

Senior Budget Analyst, Oostende, Belgium   1994 - 1996
Budget and Funds Manager for the acquisition, operation, and maintenance of communications and information systems.
- Prepared, presented, defended, and managed an $11 million budget.
- Generated $1.4 million savings in 1996 budget through analysis and tracking expenditures.

Project Officer/Instructor, Bellevue, Washington   1990 - 1993
Developed students for leadership and management responsibilities.
- Served as instructor, counselor, and mentor for 12 students during a 20-week course. Led 8 groups in four years.
- Redesigned core curriculum and introduced building block type of instruction.

Education

Bachelor of Business Administration, University of Washington, Seattle, Washington
Graduate--Senior Level Management/Leadership School, U.S. Naval Command College

Jane is changing careers.

Jane Swift
9 Central Avenue
Calabasas, California 91301
(818) 555-1212
Jane@careerbrain.com

OBJECTIVE

A responsible and challenging entry-level position that will utilize my education and background, expand my knowledge, and offer opportunities for personal and professional growth.

SUMMARY OF KNOWLEDGE AND EXPERIENCE

- CUSTOMER SERVICE
- INTERFACE WELL WITH THE PUBLIC
- EXCELLENT COMMUNICATION SKILLS
- SET, MEET DEADLINES/GOALS
- CASHIERING
- MARKETING
- INVENTORY CONTROL
- KNOWLEDGE OF WORDPERFECT

- HIGHLY ORGANIZED
- KNOWLEDGE OF SPANISH
- DETAIL/EFFICIENCY ORIENTED
- RECORD KEEPING
- TROUBLESHOOTING
- TUTORING
- COORDINATION
- PUBLIC RELATIONS

EDUCATIONAL HISTORY

California State University, Northridge
Los Angeles Valley College, Van Nuys

B.A. Psychology - 3.8 GPA - 1995
A.A. General Education

ACCOMPLISHMENTS AND ACHIEVEMENTS

- Awarded Recognition Certificate for achieving 100% on Shoppers Report Evaluation for food service performance, salesmanship, and hospitality at Marie Callender.
- PSYCHI - National Honor Society for Psychology
- Golden Key Honor Society - National Honor Society

EMPLOYMENT HISTORY

4/99 - Present   **WAITRESS**
Marie Callender, Sherman Oaks, California
2/97 - 3/99   **CASHIER / WAITRESS**
Denny's Restaurant, Northridge, California
9/94 - 12/96   **MARKET RESEARCHER**
Suburban Associates, Sherman Oaks, California
9/93 - 6/95   **ASSISTANT TO TEACHER / ART DIRECTOR**
Temple Beth Hillel

VOLUNTEER/COMMUNITY SERVICE

San Fernando Valley Child Guidance Clinic - Tutoring

REFERENCES FURNISHED UPON REQUEST

James is changing careers to Human Resources.

James Sharpe
9 Central Avenue
New York, NY 10012
(212) 555-1212
James@careerbrain.com

Objective
Key member of a human resources consulting team utilizing communication, organizational, and collaborative skills in a challenging environment.

Related Skills and Career Achievements
Project Management
- Led a project team for the successful launch of the Absolut bottle series.
- Managed the Absolut licensing program and facilitated the negotiation of a license agreement that generated significant incremental exposure and sales.

Presentation
- Taught English to 5th graders and gave American Culture lectures to high school students in Thailand for two months.
- Provided orientations to AFS teachers from China and Thailand upon their arrival in the United States.
- Presented regular Absolut marketing updates to staff.
- Contributed to the production of the winning Honda pitch at Saatchi & Saatchi Advertising.

Writing & Editing
- Launched a career services business to help clients define marketable skills and create results-oriented resumes.
- Developed three issues of a 10-page brand newsletter that promoted successful marketing concepts and international brand identity.
- Wrote legal correspondence to ensure adherence to brand license agreements.

Computer Applications
- Extensive knowledge of Windows and Macintosh applications for word processing, desktop publishing, spreadsheets, presentation, database management and Internet navigation.
- Developed contact databases for *House and Garden*'s advertising department.

Career Chronology

Career Marketing Consultant, Self-Employed, New York, NY	1999-2000
Contract Worker/Marketing, Lee Hecht Harrison, New York, NY	1998
Absolut Brand Coordinator, Allied Domecq Intl., Los Angeles, CA	1992-1997
Freelancer, *House and Garden* magazine, New York, NY	1991
Administrative Assistant, Saatchi & Saatchi, New York, NY	1990
Program Assistant, AFS Intercultural Programs, New York, NY	Summers 1988-1990

Education
Bachelor of Arts, 1990
Hunter College, New York, NY

James is an Educator in transition.

James Sharpe
9 Central Avenue
Lancaster, PA 17601

(717) 555-1212
James@careerbrain.com

SUMMARY

Skilled educator with 20+ years experience creating curricula and delivering instruction, evaluating students, developing and implementing strategic plans, and managing projects. Seeking opportunity to transition existing instructional, organizational, and human relations skills into a training or human resource position in a corporate environment.

QUALIFICATIONS

Instruction

- State Permanent Teaching Certification (N - 6)
- Prepare lesson plans in Social Studies, Science, Math, and Language Arts.
- Instruct 25 elementary students, addressing individual needs and learning styles.
- Evaluate students' performance and implement plans for improvement, as appropriate.
- Train students, parents, and staff in the use of computer systems.
- Fulfill on-site "Help Desk" role for students and staff using computers.

Planning

- Serve on numerous District Planning and Building Planning Committees that address ongoing concerns of staff and the community, identifying problems and solutions.
- Chair Positive School Climate Committee that promotes a comfortable learning environment and workplace for students and staff, respectively.
- Participated in developing five-year technology plan for Newark district.
- Wrote technology plan for Suburb School District and monitored implementation.
- Implemented computers in the classroom for Rural School District.
- Chaired committee that pioneered school yearbook at a time when the district had none.

Additional Skills

- Wrote grant proposal that resulted in $7,000 in funding from state government for purchase of capital equipment (computers) at Rural Central School.
- Proficient in Windows 95, Microsoft Office / Mac, ClarisWorks, Word Processing, Spreadsheets, and the Internet.
- Coached Soccer at Suburb Central School; Ski Club Advisor (Rural).

PROFESSIONAL EXPERIENCE

1989 - Present   Elementary Teacher, Rural Central School District, New Holland, PA
1976 - 1989   Elementary Teacher, Suburb Central School District, Lewisburg, PA

EDUCATION

1981   Master of Science, Education
Pennsylvania State University, State College, PA
     GPA: 3.77 / 4.00
1976   Bachelor of Science, Education
Pennsylvania State University, State College, PA
     Dean's List

PROFESSIONAL ENRICHMENT

Creative Learning Styles	Portfolio Assessment
Cooperative Learning	Gender Equity
Annual Computer Conference	Grant Writing
Essential Elements of Instruction	

James is an Electrician changing to a career in sales & promotion.

James Sharpe
9 Central Avenue
Ferndale, MI 48220
(313) 555-1212
James@careerbrain.com

CAREER OBJECTIVE

To support the growth and profitability of an organization that provides challenge, encourages advancement, and rewards achievement with the opportunity to utilize my substantial experience, skills, and proven abilities in a position involving Sales and Promotion within the Consumer Goods industry.

STRENGTHS

- Skilled in motivating and interacting with the public.
- Disciplined and well organized in work habits, with ability to function smoothly in pressure situations.
- Ability to identify problems and implement effective solutions.
- Possess a "pro" company attitude dedicated to the growth and profitability of the company.

EMPLOYMENT HISTORY

McMURRAY ELECTRIC, 22036 Woodward, Ferndale, MI 48220
Journeyman Electrician - April 1997 to Present
Responsible for the installation and servicing of commercial, residential, and industrial accounts. In my current position as Foreman Leader, I supervise the activities of four to five electricians/helpers and have been responsible for as many as thirteen employees.

- Ability to read and effectively implement blueprints, along with extensive layout skills.
- Because of vast knowledge of jobs performed for the company and ability to deal effectively with people, was selected by management to train new employees.

POWERS DISTRIBUTING COMPANY, INC., 2000 Pontiac Dr., Pontiac, MI 48053
On-Premise Promotions - August 1999 to Present
Responsible for representing Miller Brewing Company at promotional functions in on-premise accounts situated in Oakland and Macomb Counties.

- I possessed the energy, enthusiasm, and poise necessary for implementing successful brewery promotions, was selected for newly created position.
- Have acquired extensive knowledge of motivating/sales techniques, which has contributed substantially to increased sales at brewery promotions.
- Active in the development and coordination of brewery promotions.

EDUCATION

Associated Builders and Contractors, Inc. - Graduated June 1998
Course of Study: Electrical
Oakland Community College - Courses relating to Electronics Field (Attended 1989 and 1990)
Ferndale High School - Graduated June 1988

REFERENCES FURNISHED UPON REQUEST

Jane is changing careers after a period of self-employment.

Jane Swift
9 Central Avenue
Burlingame, CA 94010
(415) 555-1212

Jane@careerbrain.com

Objective	Sales representative or showroom position in the fashion industry

Summary of Qualifications

- Five years' experience in design and manufacture of Women's Wear
- Extensive production management and operations experience
- Fifteen years' sales experience in inside sales, showrooms, and tradeshows
- Expertise in conducting tradeshows, designing booths, and managing customers
- Capable and flexible self-starter who is able to travel for trade shows

Work Experience

1994 to 2000 **Owner/Designer**
Gene Sims Designs
Design and manufacture of Womens' Wear accessories, earrings, hair clips, purses, and pins. Extensive experience in buying, trade shows (Canada and Washington state), payroll, collections, billing. Hired 22 sales reps throughout the U.S. and Puerto Rico. Employed 12 people to make accessories.

1990 to 1994 **Outside Sales and Trainer**
West Coast Financial Services
Extensive selling experience cold-calling, canvassing, and prospecting to corporations for medical insurance plans. Organized and set up an entire department and trained department staff.

1984 to 1990 **Personnel and Collections Manager**
Physio-Control
Interviewed potential employees for several department heads. Managed credit and collections. Trained managers on how to interview and hire the right person.

1978 to 1984 **Office Manager/Executive Recruiter**
Betty White Employment Agency
Interviewed prospective employees for professional and clerical positions with corporations.

James has changed careers many times.

James Sharpe
9 Central Avenue
Aurora, CO 80014
(303) 555-1212
James@careerbrain.com

OBJECTIVE   A challenging position providing an opportunity to apply broad Management experience.

EDUCATION   University of Colorado
MBA program—presently enrolled
B.S. Public Administration, Colorado College

QUALIFICATIONS Progressively responsible management background in a large medical facility, with successful experience in the following areas:

Staff Supervision—presently responsible for 30 skilled, semi-skilled, unskilled, and managerial employees. Hire, train, direct, and evaluate the staff. Responsible for their output and the quality of their work. Maintain morale, motivation, and positive employee relations. Solve problems, take corrective action, apply company policy.

Operations Management—direct staff and activities in several support departments, including maintenance, grounds and buildings, laundry, housekeeping. Manage a budget of nearly a half million dollars. Schedule all departments for the most effective use of manpower, equipment, and facilities.

Inventory Control/Purchasing—maintain an inventory control system for non-medical supplies and food.

Other—frequent involvement in customer and public relations, promoting the facility; work with other staff to prepare for licensing, compliance reviews; involved in Real Estate Management—buying, renovating, and maintaining rental properties; licensed in real estate sales.

As public administration Intern at both the state and federal levels, involved in labor relations activities, legislative actions, communications.

EMPLOYMENT   Aurora Rest Home, Aurora, CO
1999 to present   Supervisor—promoted from Assistant

1995 to 1999   Coors Brewery, Golden, CO
Construction Worker

1993 to 1995   Intern—federal and state

Jane is a handicapped worker who wants to change careers.

Jane Swift
9 Central Avenue
Monroe, WI 53566
(608) 555-1212
Jane@careerbrain.com

OBJECTIVE   Seeking a challenging position in Customer Service.

SUMMARY

- Possess a combined Customer Service and Financial background. Responsible for administering several aspects of pension plans. Significant customer service responsibilities as Office Manager and Credit Coordinator.

QUALIFICATION

- Present position requires accuracy and efficiency in creation of files, calculation of benefits and options, analysis of IRS qualification, preparation of tax forms, and other similar activities.
- Effective verbal and written negotiations with agents, attorneys, plan participants, accountants, and others. Good communications skills are necessary for confidential interdepartmental communications.
- Experience includes Credit and Office Management. My responsibilities in credit include taking applications, securing credit approvals, ordering products, and arranging for delivery. I also calculated salespeople's commissions. As Office Manager, I handled customer service duties, accepted and booked payments, maintained inventories, and performed other functions associated with keeping the office running smoothly.

EXPERIENCE
1999 to present   BC/BC
Pension Technical Specialist

Sears
Credit Coordinator—for major appliance

3M Products
Office Manager

Big Brothers/Big Sisters; United Cerebral Palsy Assoc.
(6 years, part-time)
Office Manager/Clerical

James is a Technology Expert changing to Web Development.

James Sharpe
9 Central Avenue
Pittsburgh, PA 15222

(412) 555-1212
James@careerbrain.com

GOAL

To contribute to a Web development team where my strong technical and business skills and personal passion for computer technology will be of value.

PROFESSIONAL PROFILE

- 10+ years' experience working in cross-functional teams as a technical expert. Oversaw multiyear, multimillion dollar development programs. Produced proposals resulting in new work for organization totaling nearly $500,000.
- Achieved numerous official commendations during tenure for exceptional performance and special acts of service. Consistently received highly favorable customer feedback and successfully developed business relationships with the technical community.
- Enhanced personal productivity and contributions to team through initiative to learn MS Project, MS Office, MS FrontPage, basic HTML, Internet-related applications, and information technology trends.

Demonstrated competencies in:

Technical Analysis	System Design & Information Architecture
Strategic Planning & Problem Solving	Project & Budget Management
Research, Writing, & Presentations	Customer Focus

CAREER HIGHLIGHTS

- Challenged to create a Web site for the Joint Service Small Arms Program Office to increase awareness of their programs for Armed Services customers and to conduct management committee business. Within 3 months, learned basics of Web site design and programming, planned information architecture, and launched the site to positive reviews from customers and other external government agencies.
- Developed a business plan for the Power Sources Base Assessment program (a survey of batteries as power sources for ammunition systems) that was approved by the customer without changes after a competitive selection process. Team awarded $144,000 for the first year's work with potential for another $250,000 in the second year.
- Authored a 250-page technical report on the state of the art in laser technology that was the culmination of a 1-year independent research project. The study was approved and published in 1998 and is used in strategic planning by the Joint Services Committee. Selected to present conclusions to technical community at NDIA Infantry Symposium.
- Introduced a logical strategic planning tool that was used to overhaul several programs in order to meet new timelines for success required by the Pentagon and adopted office wide.
- Devised an innovative method for monitoring a system contractor's cost performance in 5 areas on a $15 million contract. Technical Director mandated that this method be management's standard for analysis of contractor performance in order to spot potentially dangerous trends early.
- Managed development of program's portion of a Department of Defense Master Plan required by the Pentagon. After Congressional Committee review, the program continued to receive financial and political backing.
- Spearheaded review process leading to the successful type classification and on-schedule deployment of mortar weapon systems. Required intense coordination with numerous support organizations and government agencies to produce documents and presentations for material release boards.

CAREER HISTORY

U.S. Army Engineering Facility, Pittsburgh, PA
Mechanical Engineer: First Division - 1999 - Present
Program Management Engineer: Second Division - 1996 - 1999
Systems Engineer: Support Center - 1992 - 1995

EDUCATION

MBA, 1989: University of Pittsburgh, Pittsburgh, PA - Dean's List Honors
BS, 1987: State University of New York at Brockport, Brockport, NY

James is a blue-collar worker and wants a white-collar job.

James Sharpe
9 Central Avenue
Claremont, NC 28610
(704) 555-1212
James@careerbrain.com

OBJECTIVE   An opportunity to apply technical skills and communications ability in a Sales or Customer Service position.

SKILLS SUMMARY Thoroughly familiar with the process of quoting and producing industrial products for a wide range of customer applications. Work with customers' specifications, ideas, or blueprints to produce parts on a special or stock basis. Call on accounts to assist with product development, to provide service in the event of discrepancies or quality questions. Duties require the ability to communicate effectively on technical problems, and to establish rapport.

In a retail setting, have held major responsibility for staff supervision and customer service, managing several functions with high customer and employee contact.

As a supervisor, held responsibility for training, scheduling, directing, and evaluating the work of skilled machinists. Keep areas of responsibility supplied with tooling, materials, and equipment to ensure the most effective use of manpower and machinery.

Acted as buyer of industrial products: drills, reamers, slotting saws, collects, high-speed carbide steels, ceramics, lubricants, and NC screw machine programs, among others.

Operated and troubleshot sophisticated machine shop equipment, including Swiss screw machines, grinders, lathes, milling machines, drill presses. Able to program CNC equipment. Conversant with the full range of machine shop practices, as well as quality and production control procedures.

EXPERIENCE
1998 to present **Jig Tools, Claremont, NC**
Supervisor, Quality Control Inspector
Production Machinist

1994 to 1998   **Finest Foods, Raleigh, NC**
Front End Manager, supervising an evening shift.
Involved in cashiering, packing, credit voucher cashing.

1989 to 1994   **Atlas Moving Co., Raleigh, NC**
Truck Driver, Mechanic

PERSONAL   References available upon request.

Jane has had multiple jobs and needs to combine her experience.

Jane Swift
9 Central Avenue
Kenner, LA 70062
(504) 555-1212
Jane@careerbrain.com

OBJECTIVE

A challenging Sales or Sales Management position, providing an opportunity to apply broad experience and a record of success in marketing a variety of products and services.

QUALIFICATIONS

Sales—Thoroughly familiar with techniques for generating new business in industrial, commercial, and consumer markets. Employed cold call, referral, and other prospecting techniques. Skilled at assessing client needs and making effective sales presentations, often involving technical product details.

Have regularly exceeded sales quotas.

Sales Management—Responsibilities included selecting, training, motivating, and supervising professionals in sales, service, and other operations.

Performed market research and promotions, forecasting, the development of distribution systems, and other marketing administration functions.

Developed marketing plans, arranged financing, helped establish distribution networks.

EMPLOYMENT

ADT Systems—Worcester, MA
Commercial Sales Representative   1995 to present

Patriot Marketing—Worcester, MA
Owner/Consultant   1993 to 1995

Maxxum Industries, Inc.   1980-1990
Self-Employed Restaurateur
Cherry Buick
Goodnick Miller
International Harvester

TRAINING

Studied Business Administration, Management, and Marketing at Louisiana Institute of Technology, the University of Texas, and Kenner Junior College. Have received technical product and sales training in numerous courses and seminars throughout my career.

PERSONAL

U.S. Navy—honorably discharged
References available upon request

Jane is changing careers to become a Salesperson.

Jane Swift
9 Central Avenue
Utica, MI 48087
(313) 555-1212
Jane@careerbrain.com

OBJECTIVE   An opportunity to apply Medical Technological background in a challenging Sales or Marketing position.

QUALIFICATIONS

- Over six years' experience in Medical Technology in hospital laboratory and outpatient settings. Have worked successfully with physicians in a number of disciplines, including pathology, geriatrics, oncology, other areas; interact daily with laboratory staff (supervisory and technical), patients, and other people throughout the hospital.
- Thoroughly familiar with complex, sophisticated laboratory equipment, such as Coulter S plus IV, Coulter 550, MLA 700, Fibrometer. Provide technical training to other operators and to medical technology students. Accountable for the accurate calibration of equipment, basic troubleshooting, and maintenance.
- Maintenance of inventory, purchase of supplies, and quality control procedures in general.
- These duties require a person who is thoroughly knowledgeable about laboratory and highly technical equipment and associated procedures, is familiar with materials, and is precise in performance of duties.

EMPLOYMENT

1992 to present   Utica Family Hospital—Utica, Michigan
Special Hematology Laboratory Technologist, promoted from Laboratory Technologist

EDUCATION   B.S. Medical Technology, 1992
Detroit State College (Detroit, Michigan)

Registry eligible in Hematology

Additional training by laboratory equipment manufacturers

REFERENCES   Excellent professional references are available upon request.

Jane is a recently divorced homemaker reentering the work force.

Jane Swift
9 Central Avenue
Wichita, KS 67218
(316) 555-1212
Jane@careerbrain.com

OBJECTIVE

An entry position in Personnel or Human Resources Management, providing an opportunity to apply formal education in the field, and business experience.

EDUCATION

Anna Maria College—Paxton, Massachusetts
B.A. Psychology
Graduated *magna cum laude*

SUMMARY
OF SKILLS

Studies have included courses in Industrial Psychology, Personnel Management, Marketing, Management, Accounting, other Psychology and Liberal Arts courses.

Experience in *Interviewing/Communications*, gained from extensive dealings with customers, clients, students, and peers in the organization. Capable of effective written and oral communication where the ability to gather precisely and act on it is critical.

Background in *Counseling*, with both adults and students in academic and professional settings. Assisted with *Career Counseling* and other forms of personal assistance.

Experience includes work as a *Telemarketing Representative* and as an Administrative Assistant. Have held leadership positions in volunteer organizations, including *Chairperson, Fundraiser, Advisory Board Member,* and *Counselor*. Duties have required the ability to organize, set up, and implement systems for getting tasks completed, as well as the ability to be persuasive and obtain cooperation.

EXPERIENCE

Wichita Employment Services
Telemarketing Representative. Working from research, leads, and cold calls, identifying target markets and make over 500 sales calls per month. Provide quotes, and refer results of research for further action. Set up relevant sales administration systems.

1998 to 2000

Kansas State University
Worked part and full time while attending college.
Assignments included:
Secretary in the Graduate Office, in the Development Office, and to the Director of the Nursing Program.

ACTIVITIES

Chairperson, Boy Scout Troop Committee; Member, Advisory Board; Fundraiser, Counselor, Navy Officers' Wives Association; Fundraiser, Library Committee.

PERSONAL

Health: excellent
Willing to travel/relocate

Professional Resume Writing Services

In the early stages of your job hunt, you might want to look into getting extra help from a professional resume writer. A professional in the field might be able to help you develop a more polished layout or present a particularly complex background more effectively.

The big question is, "Who should I use?" As in any other profession, there are practitioners at both ends of the performance spectrum. I am a strong believer in using the services of resume writers who belong to the field's professional associations. They tend to be more committed, have more field experience, and have an all-around higher standard of performance, partly because their membership demonstrates their commitment to the field and partly from the ongoing educational programs that these associations offer to their members.

Resume writers who are members of the appropriate professional associations are more likely to be able to help you fine-tune your resume into an effective marketing tool. Depending on the help you need, their services can range from $50 to $1000. (Don't gasp—the higher up the professional ladder you are aiming, the more important a polished and professional-looking resume becomes!)

Remember that a resume isn't just a piece of paper that gets your foot in the door. It also sits on every interviewer's desk as a road map to your professional background, giving them some guidance for the direction your interviews will take. It also works on your behalf long after you have left the interview, and it is probably the last document an employer will consider before making the final decision between candidates.

I am including a list of professional resume writers and professional colleagues, who generously helped me locate some excellent job hunting letters. If you need help in this area, these are all people for whom I can vouch. They all have impeccable credentials. To help you understand those credentials I'll give you a quick overview of the dominant professional associations in the field.

There are three dominant associations in the field: the Professional Association of Resume Writers (PARW, *www.parw.com*), the National Resume Writers Association (NRWA, *www.nrwa.com*) and Career Masters Institute (CMI).

Both PARW and NRWA have hundreds of members and provide ongoing opportunities for members to gain mentoring experience and additional training. Both offer resume-writing certification, and both operate e-mail list servers for members with access to e-mail. The professional training programs range from how to handle specific resume challenges to issues related to running a resume service. The associations build camaraderie between members and offer them access to the expertise of hundreds of other professional resume writers. Both organizations offer an annual convention with workshops on industry issues. PARW offers training seminars several times a year throughout the country. NRWA offers its members a Web-based training program.

Members of the Career Masters Institute tend to be serious tenured professionals. Almost all (about 95 percent) are Certified Professional Resume Writers (CPRW), a distinction that sets them apart and clearly validates their capabilities. Many (approximately 30-40) have also earned their Job & Career Transition Coach (JCTC) certification. Several (about 10-15—and as a member, I'm one of them) are nationally published authors on resume writing, job search, coaching, and related career topics. Also important—most CMI members offer more than just resume writing services.

Although a powerful resume is the foundation for virtually every successful job search, CMI members also offer a host of career marketing services that can help their clients accelerate their campaigns. These services include Internet resume postings, e-mail campaigns to recruiters, direct-mail campaigns to growth companies, executive job lead reports, career coaching, counseling, and more.

Here are some of the members of these three estimable associations who have contributed resumes and valuable insights to the book (with a special thanks to Wendy Enelow and Gwen Harrison):

Abilities Enhanced
PO Box 9667
Kansas City, MO 64134
Phone: (816) 767-1196
E-mail: M7125@aol.com
Web: www.abilitiesenhanced.com

Elizabeth J. Axnix, CPRW, IJCTC
Quality Word Processing
329 East Court Street
Iowa City, IA 52240-4914
Phone: (800) 359-7822 or (319) 354-7822
Fax: (319) 354-2220
E-mail: axnix@earthlink.net

Kathy Black
Career Recipes
P.O. Box 3686
Evergreen, CO 80437
Phone: (303) 679-1519
Fax: (303) 670-4414
E-mail: kathyjane@earthlink.net
Web: www.careerrecipes.com

Tracy A. Bumpus, CPRW, JCTC
Executive Director
RezAMAZE.com
Austin, TX
Phone: (512) 291-1404 or
(888) 277-4270
Fax: 208-247-2542
Web: www.rezamaze.com

Diane Burns, CPRW, IJCTC, CCM
President
Career Marketing Techniques
5219 Thunder Hill Road
Columbia, MD 21045
Phone: (410) 884-0213
E-mail: DianeCPRW@aol.com
Web: www.polishedresumes.com

Career Advantage
5536 Longview Circle
El Paso, TX 79924
Phone: (915) 821-1036
Fax: (915) 822-8146
E-mail: jmoore@dzn.com
CMI, CPPRW

Career Counsel
11 Hillside Place
Chappaqua, NY 10514
Phone: (914) 238-1065
E-mail: LinZlev@aol.com

Career Development Resources
1312 Walter Road
Yorktown Heights, NY 10598
Phone: (914) 962-1548
Fax: (914) 962-0325
E-mail: cardev@aol.com
Contact: Mark Berkowitz
CMI, CPRW,NCCC, International
Certified Job & Career Transition Coach

A CareerPro Inc.
201 North Federal Highway, Suite 108
Deerfield Beach, Florida 33441
Phone: (954) 428-4935
Fax: (954) 428-0965
E-mail: careerpro@mindspring.com
Web: www.faxrecruiters.com/amme.html

Career Solutions, LLC
Trenton, MI 48183
Phone: (734) 676-9170 or
(877) 777-7242
Fax: (734) 676-9487 or (877) 777-7307

Comprehensive Resume Services
5300 Spring Mountain Road,
Suite 212-D
Las Vegas, NV 89102
Phone: (702) 222-9411

Deborah Wile Dib, NCRW, CPRW, JCTC
President
Advantage Resumes of New York
Phone/fax: (631) 475-8513
Web: www.advantageresumes.com
Member, NRWA, PARW, AJST,
CPADN, CMI

Kirsten Dixson, JCTC, CPRW
New Leaf Career Solutions
Bronxville, NY
www.newleafcareer.com
info@newleafcareer.com
Toll-Free 866-NEW-LEAF (639-5323)

Jacqui Barrett Dodson, CPRW
Career Trend
7501 College Boulevard, Suite 175
Overland Park, KS 66210
Phone: (913) 451-1313
Fax: (913) 451-3242
E-mail: dodson@careertrend.net

Wendy S. Enelow, CPRW, JCTC, CCM
President
Career Masters Institute
119 Old Stable Road
Lynchburg, VA 24503
Phone: (804) 386-3100
E-mail: wendyenelow@cminstitute.com
Web: www.cminstitute.com
Past President, The Advantage
Executive Resume & Career Marketing
Service

Dayna Feist, CPRW, JCTC
Gatehouse Business Services
265 Charlotte Street
Asheville, NC 28801
Phone: (828) 254-7893
Fax: (828) 254-7894
E-mail: Gatehous@aol.com
Member, Certification Board, PARW65
Member, Career Masters Institute

A First Impression
www.resumewriter.com
Successful job search and career
management for professionals, highly
effective resumes, coaching, consulting,
Internet job exploration and more.
Professionally speaking...we have a
way with words.

Joyce Fortier, CCM
Create Your Own Career
23871 W. Lebost
Novi, MI 48375
Phone: (248) 478-5662
Fax: (248) 426-9974
careerist@aol.com
www.careerist.com

Fox Resume & Career Resources
24242 S. Navajo Drive
Channahon, IL 60410
Phone: (815) 467-6153
E-mail: pfoxhr@aol.com
Contact: Patty Fox

Louise Garver, CMP, CPRW, JCTC
Principal
Career Directions
Connecticut office:
115 Elm Street, Suite 104
Enfield, CT 06082
Phone: (888) 222-3731 or
(860) 623-9476
Fax: (860) 623-9473
Massachusetts office:
125 North Elm Street, Suite 301
Westfield, MA 01085
Phone: (413) 568-2356
E-mail: CAREERDIRS@aol.com
Web: www.resumeimpact.com

Gatehouse Business Services
265 Charlotte Street
Ashville, NC 28801
Phone: (828) 254-7893
Fax: (828) 254-7894
E-mail: Gatehous@aol.com

Wayne M. Gonyea, MS, CCM
President
Gonyea Career Marketing, Inc.
1810 Arturus Lane
New Port Richey, FL 34655
Phone: (727) 375-0489
E-mail: online@resumexpress.com
Web: www.resumexpress.com
Founding Member, Career Masters
Institute

Gwen Harrison
Advanced Resumes
438 Shearwater Drive
Fortson, GA 31808
Phone: (877) 353-0025
Fax: (888) 811-3241
Gwen@advancedresumes.com

Beverly Harvey, CPRW, JCTC
Phone: (888) 775-0916 or
(904) 749-3111
E-mail: beverly@harveycareers.com
Web: www.harveycareers.com
Certified Job & Career Transition Coach
Certified Professional Resume Writer
Charter Member Career Masters
Institute
Member National Association of
Resume Writers
Member Professional Association of
Resume Writers
Contributor to PARW's Training Manual

Maria Hebda, CPRW
Career Solutions, LLC
E-mail: careers@writingresumes.com
Web: www.writingresumes.com

Nancy Karvonen, CPRW, IJCTC
Executive Director
A Better Word & Resume
Galt, CA
Phone: (209) 744-8203
Fax: (209) 745-7114
Voice Mail/Pager: (888) 598-1995
E-mail: careers@aresumecoach.com
Web: www.aresumecoach.com
Certified Professional Resume Writer
(CPRW)
Internationally Certified Job and Career
Transition Coach (JCTC)
Member, Career Masters Institute
Member, PARW Certification Committee

Shanna Kemp
Kemp Career Services
2105 Via Del Norte
Carrollton, Texas 75006
Phone: (972) 416-9089 or
(877) 367-5367
Fax: (972) 478-2890
E-mail: respro@aresumepro.com

Cindy Kraft, CPRW, JCTC
Executive Essentials
P.O. Box 336
Valrico, FL 33595
Phone: (813) 655-0658
Fax: (813) 685-4287
Web: www.exec-essentials.com
Member: PARW and Career Masters
Institute

Louise Kursmark, CPRW, JCTC
Best Impression Career Services, Inc.
Cincinnati, Ohio
Phone: (513) 792-0030
Web: www.yourbestimpression.com

Lisa C. LeVerrier
President
Competitive Advantage Resumes
& Career Coaching
5523 N. Military Trail Suite #1212
Boca Raton, FL 33496
433 Plaza Real, Suite 275
Boca Raton, FL 33432
Phone: (561) 982-9573 or
(800) 750-5690
Fax: (561) 982-7312
E-mail: gethired@earthlink.net OR
lisalev@earthlink.net
Web: www.jobcoaching.com

Christine Magnus
Business Services Plus
Phone: (718) 519-0477
Fax: (718) 405-9894
E-mail: BizServ@aol.com
Member, PARW, Career Masters Institute

Chandra C. May
ccmay@webtv.net
740-772-6240
ACCESS RESUME, Chillicothe OH

Meg Montford
Abilities Enhanced
"managing careers in transition"
www.abilitiesenhanced.com

JoAnn Nix, CPRW
Beaumont Resume Service
Phone: (800) 265-6901
Fax: (409) 924-0019 or (419) 781-2971
E-mail: info@agreatresume.com
Web: www.agreatresume.com

Debra O'Reilly, CPRW, JCTC
Resumewriter.com
16 Terryville Avenue
Bristol, CT 06010
Phone: 860-583-7500
Fax: 860-585-9611
E-mail: debra@resumewriter.com
Web: www.resumewriter.com
Charter Member, Career Masters Institute
Member, Professional Association of
Resume Writers
Member, National Resume Writers
Association

Don Orlando, MBA, CPRW, JCTC
The McLean Group
640 South McDonough Street
Montgomery, Alabama 36104
Phone: (334) 264-2020
Fax: (334) 264-9227
E-mail: yourcareercoach@aol.com
Certified Professional Resume Writer
Certified Job and Career Transition Coach
Master Team Member: Career Masters
Institute

Professional Resume Services
1214 East Fenway Avenue
Salt Lake City, Utah 84102
Phone: (801) 883-2011
Fax: (801) 582-8862
E-mail: resumes@tacisp.com
Web: www.MyCareerResource.com
PARW, CMI, CPRW

A Resume Coach
www.aresumecoach.com
Phone: (209) 744-8203
Voice Mail/Pager: (888) 598-1995
Fax: (209) 745-7114
e-fax (801) 650-8140
Certified Professional Resume Writer
(CPRW)
Internationally Certified Job and Career
Transition Coach (JCTC)
Member, Career Masters Institute

Nadine Rubin
Adam-Bryce, Inc.
77 Maple Avenue
New City, NY 10956
Phone: (914) 634-1772 or
(845) 634-1772
Fax: (914) 634-1772 or (845) 634-1772
Web: www.adambryce.com

Kelley Smith, CPRW
Advantage Resume Services
P.O. Box 391
Sugar Land, Texas 77487
Phone: (281) 494-3330 or
(877) 478-4999
Fax: (281) 494-0173
E-mail: info@advantage-resume.com or
kands@concentric.net
Web: www.advantage-resume.com
Career Masters, PARW, NRWA

Rebecca Stokes, CPRW
President
The Advantage, Inc.
401 Mill Lane
Lynchburg, VA 24503
Phone: (800) 922-5353
Fax: (804) 384-4700
E-mail: advresume@aol.com
Web: www.advantageresume.com

Gina Taylor, CPRW
Gina Taylor & Associates, Inc.
1111 W. 77th Terrace
Kansas City, Missouri 64114
Phone: (816) 523-9100
E-mail: ginaresume @aol.com

Jean West, CPRW, JCTC
Career Services,
207 10th Avenue
Indian Rocks Beach, FL 33785
Phone: (727) 596-2534
Fax: (727) 593-7386
Web: www.impactresumes.com

Janice Worthington-Loranca CPRW, JCTC
Fortune 500 Communications
EVP National Resume Wriers
Association
"Top 10 Industry Leaders" Professional
Association of Resume Writers
Resident Resume Expert,
careerInvestors.com
F500resume@aol.com

Here are some other online resume services that have sterling reputations in the professional community:

1st Impressions Resumes and Careers
www.1st-imp.com

A+ Online Resumes
www.ol-resume.com

Affordable Resume
www.aaow.com/john_schwartz

Bakos Group
www.bakos.com

Career & Resume Management
www.crm21.com

Career Marketing-Resume service
www.careermarketing.com

Career Transitions
www.bfservs.com:80/bfserv.html

Careerpro
www.career_pro.com

eResumes
www.resumelink.com

Keyword Resume & Fax Service
www.ourworld.compuserve.com/home
pages/deckerservices

North American Business Concepts
www.digimark.net/noam/

One-way Resume
www2.connectnet.com/users/blorincz

Protype
www.members.aol.com/criscito

Resume Publishing Company
www.csn.net

Resumes on the Web
www.resweb.com

Resumexpress
www.resumexpress.com

Superior Resumes
www.mindtrust.com

Resume Banks

Resume banks are the reverse of job banks. Instead of employers listing available jobs to be scanned by job hunters, resume banks are made up of resumes supplied by job applicants, intended to be scanned by prospective employers. In most resume banks, you either upload your resume in file or HTML form into the site, or fill out an online form, which will generate a resume-like document for employers to scan.

It used to be fashionable for job search experts to advise job hunters to take out newspaper ads announcing their abilities. I never endorsed this approach because I'd never met an employer who saw it as a viable avenue for finding quality employees. Even though resume banks are, in effect, an electronic version of these ads, they seem to be working. I think the reason is twofold. First of all, these banks are set up so that a computer, not a person, is doing the initial searching for candidates, and second, people who are active online are, *ipso facto*, computer literate, and therefore more desirable as employees.

An employer requesting a search from a resume database will describe the available job with a number of descriptive words and/or phrases, known as keywords. The computer then searches for those words and phrases in all the resumes in the database. An employer can typically search for up to twenty keywords or phrases. It isn't necessary that you match all twelve keywords—just one match is usually all it takes.

If you are going to post your resume online, you will most likely use one of the resume generators supplied by the job bank in question. If not follow these guidelines.

- Use 14 point (size) Courier type, or a similar plain font.
- Avoid italics, script, underlining, and boldface, along with two-column or other nontraditional formatting.
- Use upper/lower case to differentiate headings.
- Use plenty of white space.
- Do not include large paragraphs of text.
- You can use bulleted lists, but use a dash as your bullet "point."

If you are an experienced professional with qualifications for more than one job, you may want to post additional resumes under appropriate job titles, including the appropriate keywords and phrases for that job. Some people are concerned about confidentiality. If you upload your resume into a resume bank, theoretically your employer may find your resume online. Practically speaking, most active resume banks have ways to protect your confidentiality. You can try to improve your odds by replacing the name of your current employer with a generic name. For example, you could change "The First International Bank of Last Resort" to "A Major Bahamian Bank"; headhunters do this for their clients all the time.

Resume banks are new for employers and employees alike. Resume banks now often have hundreds of thousands of resumes, and some of them already exceed a million. Resume banks are rapidly becoming an integral part of recruitment for all corporations and headhunters. My advice is to get used to maintaining your resume online on a permanent basis—it's better to find out about available jobs (no matter how) and have the opportunity to turn them down, rather than never having heard about them at all.

Most resume banks are free (at present). The few who do charge typically offer special additional services, and the fees for these are usually quite reasonable. Note that most job banks have resume banks and vice versa.

A+ Online Resumes
ol-resume.com/
e-mail: webmaster@ol-resume.com

This is a professional resume service that will convert your resume to HTML (Hyper Text Markup Language) and post it on the WWW, where HR professionals and business owners can have access to it around the clock. Employers can find your resume either by job category or location. Resumes are registered with the most popular Web search engines, such as Yahoo, Webcrawler, etc. You are given your own home page with a URL. Postings cost $40 for three months, $60 for six months, $80 for nine months, and $100 for a full year. A+ aggressively promotes the site throughout the Internet on highly targeted hyperlinks to ensure that it maintains a high profile.

You can view the guest book, which contains a list of employers who use the site. These companies are listed by state. California had 127 companies listed, Alabama had nine, and Hawaii had one. This site advises that you don't have to restrict a resume to one or two pages. While space considerations are different online, the reader's attention hasn't increased any, exceed the two-page-limit adhered to by most professionals at your own peril.

Academe This Week
www.chronicle.merit.edu/.ads/.links.html

This site is a service of the prestigious *Chronicle of Higher Education*, a weekly publication for college and university faculty members and administrators. The magazine is a fascinating read, but we need to concentrate on the service itself here. On this site you can browse through a list of available positions within these categories: humanities, social sciences, science and technology, and professional academics. Each of these categories offers more selections. In science and technology, for example, there were fourteen subcategories starting with agricultural science.

There were twenty-eight positions worldwide for teachers and professors of computer technology, most of which required a Ph.D. Most of the jobs listed here last year are no longer available.

America's Employers Resume Bank
www.americasemployers.com/resume.html

This subsidiary site of the America's Employers Career Center caters primarily to executives who have been prescreened by America's Employers career counselors. The resume database has grown by leaps and bounds since last year. When I searched this site, I found seventeen resumes in accounting and finance, eleven in health care, and twenty-six in information systems. This year I found several hundred resumes in accounting alone. Member companies are able to access contact information on the candidates directly. If a company who is not a member of America's Employers is interested in contacting you, the service will notify you.

America's Job Bank
www.ajb.dni.us

This is the big one, 1.4 million jobs, in all specialties, at all levels, and most importantly in your town. You can search for jobs by title or function, state, or zip code. How is such a large and detailed job bank possible? It's run by the Department of Labor.

You have three choices once you get into the Job Bank: menu search, keyword search, or code search (for those savvy individuals who know the D.O.T.—Dictionary of Occupational Titles—code for their profession). Menu search gives you a scroll list of 22 standard job categories. The 3,326 computer jobs on file for New York came up onto the screen in less than 30 seconds. I was impressed, having done so much waiting for so much less at other, more self-important sites. Each listing shows job title, location, salary, education required, experience required, and whether the job is full-time or part-time. I was even able to learn which industries the jobs were in. Jobs are listed alphabetically so it is easy to sort through them. New listings are asterisked to save regular users' time. The really neat thing about this site is that once the jobs are on screen, you can re-sort the order they are listed in by state, city, job title, salary, or new jobs. America's Job Bank is one site that lives up to its claims. It's friendly, flexible, fast—and it delivers.

America's Job Bank also has a resume builder, which will automatically load your profile in its resume database called America's Talent Bank. This database is also enormous and therefore frequently searched by employers and headhunters.

Now this is a government run site, so don't expect it to be too slick. Nevertheless, you would be a fool not to visit and use the resources. There's nothing bigger out there.

Bilingual Jobs
www.bilingual-jobs.com

If you are bi-lingual in English and one other language, this site can offer you an edge. The job bank offers jobs from all kinds of industries: Information Technology, Finance, Publishing, Construction, Manufacturing, and more. Many of the positions offer the opportunity of international exposure for the bi-lingual. In a global economy and with America's economic dominance in all fields, a job through this site could be the means to an important career boost. Obviously, you will post your resume in the resume bank too.

Brassring.com
www.brassring.com

A site with a strong IT slant, 50,000 jobs and 1200 plus advertisers. Brassring.com was one of the first to offer an active database that automatically matches candidates and employers and notifies both (via e-mail) of any and all matches—sending the matching resumes to the employer, and the job description to the job seeker. Job seekers can "protect" their resume—so that their current employer doesn't accidentally pick up their resume as a match—and can specify which Usenet newsgroups they want to be listed on. The database automatically discards job listings/resumes you have already reviewed, so that you don't constantly have to go over the same material when you check in. If you're not happy with the results, you can adjust your profile with more or less information at any point. And you have the option of independently searching the database just like on the listings systems. It costs $20 to post your resume for six months. You can also do a keyword job search, which gives you an idea of what they have to offer . . . 27 systems analysts and one merchandise manager nationwide.

Aside from the above, this site also offers goodies such as tips on resume writing and corporate profiles, and information on scholarships from educational institutions. The system is really quick, the information is well organized and comprehensible, and Brassring.com seems very service-oriented. I like these guys—they're well worth the visit.

Careerbabe
www.careerbabe.com

A great site. Fran Quittel (the Careerbabe) cares and really knows her stuff. You won't find the standard job and resume banks here but you will get good and timely advice from someone who knows her stuff.

"The babe" is a columnist for a number of newspapers and magazines. She answers questions and has regular chats, well as often as she can get worthwhile guests. The site also has a good library of articles with informative commentary on resumes, job hunting, and careers.

Careerbrain.com
www.careerbrain.com

Now this is something different, and right off the bat I have to tell you why: It's my site, and what is known in the business as a "heavy content" site. At Careerbrain you can take my free online job hunting course, which complements everything you are reading in this section and shows you how to use the Internet effectively in a job hunt. Also has free career choice tests, free resume evaluations, and free job hunting TV and radio shows starring yours truly. You'll also find resume blasters, reference checking tools, and other goodies. There's no site like it. You also get to ask me questions directly.

Careerbuilder
www.careerbuilder.com

A significant job bank with a similarly important resume bank, and e-mail alerts on suitable job openings make Careerbuilder worth a visit. Allied with ADP, Careerbuilder has marketing muscle and a presence in Canada, Europe, and Asia—which could be useful if you're seeking to gain a little international exposure.

A nice time-saving feature on the job bank page is that they tell you if there are advertised jobs in the bank for the geographic target of your search. The site also has some good job hunting tips and advice on other career management issues.

You should understand that all the job bank sites are driven by recruitment advertising dollars. As such their focus is on the paying customer—the corporate advertiser. This is why you will usually find the job hunting and career management advice bordering on the moronic. However, Careerbuilder seems to be making a genuine effort to give something real back to you, the job hunter.

An example of this is a brand new product that can save you an awful lot of surfing time. Careerbuilder has developed a job scout that does more than e-mail alert you to suitable job openings in their job bank. This new tool searches all the job banks on the net and tells you who has openings in your area of expertise. This is a first and I predict will cause tremendous upheavals in the online recruitment advertising field.

CareerCity
www.careercity.com

This site has been set up by Adams Media Corporation, one of the most successful publishers of career and job search-related books (and—truth be told—the publisher of *Knock 'em Dead*!). It includes an impressive array of features for job seekers, including:

- A meta job search tool that allows you to instantly search 4 million job openings at all the leading career sites
- Links to the *Knock 'em Dead* website, which features excerpts from this bestselling book and other *Knock 'em Dead* books in the series
- Descriptions and hot links to 27,000 U.S. companies

- Comprehensive salary surveys in all fields
- Job searches by state, country, job category, description, title, or company name
- Free electronic resume posting directly to potential employers

CareerCity also contains special sections for entry-level positions, computer/high-tech, health care, education, and government jobs; salaries and job searching; career planning; and unique diversity and women's centers.

CAREERMagazine
www.careermag.com/
e-mail: editor@careermag.com

You will never have time to peruse all of these sites thoroughly and ultimately first impressions do count. If a site appeals to your aesthetic senses, you're more likely to stick to it. This site is fun because it is formatted just like a magazine, so you periodicalholics will feel comfortable here.

CAREERMagazine has all the essentials of a thorough Career Site, a keyword-based job database, employer profiles, a resume bank, a career forum, job fairs, a recruiter directory, relocation resources. It also features articles on employment, employment book excerpts and reviews, a bookstore where you can order books, On Campus update, the 30 fastest growing occupations, and areas covering such subjects as diversity and self-employment.

This does not appear to have the most comprehensive job database; there were only 10 systems analyst positions on file for New York, 26 merchandise managers in America, and no swim coaches. Perhaps I need to be more precise in my search, but I got too distracted by all the other features on this site. Try it, you'll like it!

Like all career websites (and there are now thousands of them), CAREERMagazine is becoming more commercially oriented. They are adding banner advertising, more links, and information on advertisers. Most interesting is their addition of information on the legal aspects of employment.

Career Mosaic
www.careermosaic.com

The job bank is searchable by job title, geography (within a 50 mile radius of your specific location), or keyword. The company option allows you to keep a weather eye on a desired employer for when a suitable opening appears. As of my last visit they did not have an e-mail alert for suitable job openings, so you won't automatically get a "heads up" on a desired employer.

Career Mosaic also has links to countless professional associations, information about job fairs (increasingly common on job sites), and links to international jobs.

This great site is marred only by the abysmal career center run by *Fortune* magazine. *Fortune* somehow convinced Career Mosaic that because they had a professionally successful readership they were the font of all career knowledge. Looking at the career center it is obvious that they are not. You will find some good *Fortune* inspired lists (The *Fortune 500,* etc.) but no real job hunting or career advice of any significance.

This is definitely one of the larger employment sites around, and another that claims to be the first, biggest, and bestest. Career Mosaic offers a multitude of great services, including:

- A career resource center, containing advice for job seekers and links to other services
- Free resume posting!

- The College Connection—for students or first-time job searchers
- Online job fairs
- Employer profiles
- A special area for health care jobs
- USENET jobs offered featuring 60,000 postings daily, rebuilt daily, cleared weekly
- J.O.B.S. database featuring "thousands of up-to-date job opportunities"

This site is all business, and has expanded rapidly. Their international gateway features Career Mosaic for Japan, Canada, the UK, Australia, Asia, France, Hong Kong, Korea, New Zealand, and Indonesia.

CareerPath
www.careerpath.com
e-mail: webmaster@careerpath.com

Newspapers saw Internet recruitment advertising as a major threat to their recruitment advertising dollars. Careerpath is their response. Claims no job is older than two weeks.

Careerpath is an ever-growing alliance of newspapers that put their recruitment advertising together on Careerpath to create a mammoth job bank. Starting with just seven newspapers, you can now check the Help-Wanted advertising of 80 plus newspapers; and this number will continue to grow. There are hundreds of thousands of job listings on the site, and you can search for jobs by newspaper, industry, or a keyword.

The site also has a resume bank for employers and headhunters to search. It is worth taking a few minutes to use their resume creator, which will then automatically load your resume in the resume bank. The ads are updated daily by 6 A.M. Eastern Standard Time. They also post each day's number of ads—when I searched they boasted 303,000 plus ads for the week!

You can search this site without registering to get a feel for what's available, but I guarantee that you will ultimately register. For one thing, the price is right; registration is free. Registering involves filling in your name and e-mail address, and choosing a password and a screen name. (Your choice of online moniker must be really unique—I resorted to "Battlerager" when all else failed. Dinner for two to the first reader who gets the reference! Contact me at martinyate@careerbrain.com.) The security for this site is very tight, but the administrators claim they're just keeping track of how people use the site. They are quite adamant that they are not trying to sell you something!

Once you begin your search, the site is responsive, and easy to use. You simply select a job title and geography. You can also enter additional keywords that the database will use to narrow your search.

Career Shop
www.careershop.com
e-mail: webmaster@tenkey.com

A substantial career site with the usual job bank (national but strongest in the Southeast); the job bank also has an e-mail alert: a resume bank, job fair listings, relocation, a salary calculator, and links round out the standard fare. They do however have a few features that help them stand out.

They have a training area within the site that enlightens you about online, self-paced (CDROM), and on the ground-in-your-town training seminars. However, most of these are computer related and feature the fare of Microsoft and Novell. Navigation through this area is clean and simple, as is the rest of the site.

They recently introduced careertv.com which, glamorous as it sounds, is basically the opportunity to see a couple of minor TV actors pitch the jobs of technology companies. This is one of the early applications of video streaming on the Internet and you'll need to download one of the players to make it work on your computer. However, the process is fairly painless—even for a Luddite like me. If streaming is beyond you and your computer, careershop TV is now available on a number of local stations (they barter airtime on a station for advertising). Look at the broadcast schedule on the site and maybe they'll have a relationship with the station in your area.

My favorite part of this whole site is their Career Dr. Most of the Internet career Drs and career Coaches are either bogus or simply don't answer the questions posted to them. Dr Randall Hansen is different; he does answer the questions and his input is relevant. Especially nice is that he'll give you an answer and then refer you to other resources and provide the links right there on the page. Good guy, sensible advice, kudos to careershop.com for a site worth visiting. This site has recently been bought by Personnel Group of America. There are no visible changes on the site at time of publication, but by the time you read this there may be additions to this site.

Career Tips
www.careertips.com

An interesting take on the global workplace. If you want to pursue work or education outside of the U.S. this is a good place to start. The site addresses career prospects, education and training facilities, employment opportunities and immigration rules in developed countries all around the world. This is an intelligently conceived site and well worth a visit if you are considering working overseas or completing part of your education in another country.

CareerWeb
www.careerweb.com
e-mail: info@cweb.com

A continually growing site with the requisite job and resume bank. Once you have filled out a job profile, careerweb.com alerts you to suitable job openings via e-mail. This neat service is becoming increasingly common on the majority of career sites with job banks.

Careerweb also has a resume bank that is well worth the time to load a resume. However from the job hunters viewpoint, there is a problem with this resume bank—and every other resume bank! Your resume gets wiped out after 90 days. Fresh resumes are thought to be a selling point to employers and recruiters, but if you aren't settled in a new job in 90 days you'll have to make a point to come back and re-register. You will have to do this with almost every resume bank out there, so this is not meant solely as a criticism of Careerweb.

- Articles and essays (The Career Doctor)
- Associations
- Books, publications, and news articles
- Career advice
- Career fairs
- Consulting and counseling services
- Directories
- Future societies
- Healthcare and human resource, professional information, opportunities, and organizations
- Internships and career advice
- Networking
- Professional training and career development
- Salary calculator
- Career assessment
- Resume bank
- Job Bank
- Job hunting tips

Check Your References
www.myreferences.com

Ever wonder what your references really say about you? Getting interviews but not job offers? Maybe Myreferences.com could be the solution for your situation. For as little as $59 the people at Myreferences will do a professional reference check on your behalf and report to you on exactly what past employers say about you, including tone of voice and how difficult they were to reach. An exemplary service that's been in business since the early eighties. I've been recommending it in *Knock 'em Dead* since the late eighties.

Community Career Center
www.nonprofitjobs.org

A job and resume bank site focused on community centered non-profit jobs.

Contract Employment Connection
www.ntes.com

A job bank addressing the needs of employers looking for contractors rather than full-time employees. Its strength is Information Technology people, although there are contract jobs from other professions.

Contract Executives
www.imcor.com

Now owned by Norrel, a temporary help company, Imcor specializes in contract positions for executives; you won't find anything here for under $75K a year. All of the jobs in the job bank are contract positions; many of them come with a greater or lesser degree of opportunity for converting the contract position to permanent employment. If you are an executive in the 75K-plus range the resume bank is worthwhile too.

Cool Works
www.coolworks.com

Jobs away from the madding crowd. A cool job bank with thousands of jobs in ski resorts, theme parks, national parks, sports, and the travel industry.

Diversity
www.eop.com

This site is the home of The Career Center for Workplace Diversity. A publisher who specializes in special interest diversity magazines for equal opportunity, engineering, and the disabled own it. The site has a job bank, which leverages the recruitment advertising from the magazines, so if you belong to an identifiable minority these advertisers would love to hear from you.

There are articles from the magazines re-purposed for the site, plus updates on career fairs around the country. If you are part of a minority or are challenged in some way, you know it can be tough finding good jobs and career advice, so spread the word.

DiversityLink
www.diversitylink.com

Another good diversity job bank with some very visible corporate advertisers. DiversityLink also has a resume bank you can be sure is accessed by the same major corporations and by recruiters whose clients are striving to achieve and maintain diversity in their workforce. If you belong to an identifiable minority you can gain an edge by posting your resume and responding to matching job openings.

The Education Jobsite
www.edjobsite.com

A job bank for teachers, and boy are teachers in demand right now! Jobs from all over the nation for K through 12th grade teachers. You can search by geography, certification, or specialty.

Employment Spot
www.employmentspot.com

The site features lots of links to job and resume banks, as you would expect, plus career related news, diversity oriented employers, government organizations, internships, relocation resources, and maps to your next interviews. Well thought out and worth a visit.

Exec.U.Net
www.execunet.com
e-mail: Canada@execunet.com

This is a good database and networking connection for professionals in the 100K plus category. The site is also different in that while the job bank is free to employer and recruiters, there is a fee to the job hunter. The site requires membership at $135 for three months. For the Internet phobic, job leads can also be delivered through regular mail. Execunet also sponsors networking meetings around the country.

Exec.U.Net continues to add useful information, including more data on market trends, and resources for job search and career management. A great specialist site, this is where you'll get the best chance to meet and be wooed by the headhunters.

This site has been acclaimed by *Business Week, Fortune, Money, Investor's Business Daily, ABC Nightly News,* and the *New York Times.* Perhaps even more important, it now gets a top rating from *Knock 'Em Dead.* Go and visit—it will elevate your career. Great site, run by good professional, and conscientious people.

Executive Jobs
www.jobreports.net

A special site that focuses on higher level jobs (50–300K) in the sales and marketing disciplines. The site claims that none of these jobs are widely advertised and that many of them have never been advertised at all. The site relies for its sources on an extensive network of higher level recruiters who specialize in S & M. This is a subscription site with monthly issues of a 50-page report that features 250–300 jobs per issue. Jobs are not repeated from issue to issue. If you register your resume, they will give you e-mail alerts when matching jobs are located from the newsletter. One monthly issue costs $29.95; the price drops the more issues you subscribe to.

Jobreports also offers a free resume evaluation service; Terra Durlain (a very knowledgeable woman in this field) and her people review your resume and give you feedback. There is also a for fee resume wiring and distribution service.

This is a conscientiously run service, and for the Internet phobic it can all be done through hardcopy and the telephone. Reach them at (716) 485-3454.

FedWorld
www.fedworld.gov
e-mail: webmaster@Fedworld.gov

The FedWorld Information Network is a service designed to give the general public access to government information. FedWorld provides access to 100-plus dialup bulletin boards that are not otherwise available on the Internet. Search the job bank, register your profile and needs, and an e-mail alert will update you about appropriate openings.

FedWorld's Federal Job Announcement search capability allows you to search a database of about two thousand U.S.

government job announcements that are updated daily from Tuesday through Saturday at 9:30 A.M. Eastern Standard Time. From the initial home page key in "Job Announcements," which brings you to a keyword search that allows you to enter one or two relevant job field words, you can choose to scan alphabetically, reverse alphabetically, or in the most relevant job order. You can narrow your search by location and start to search. I found that most of the jobs with the government were in Washington, D.C. (Gee, don't you just love learning something new every day!)

Flipdog.com
www.flipdog.com

This is part of the new trend. To date most job sites are mostly the graduation of Help Wanted advertising from the newspaper; not that this is a bad thing, they have greatly speeded up the job hunting process. Nevertheless, you are still restricted to the positions being advertised by a particular company on a particular site.

Flipdog is something new. It will link you to the sites of upwards of fifty thousand employers and their specific job openings. They are claiming over half a million job openings, which doesn't surprise me at all. The vast majority of the jobs are in the continental U.S., although I did find jobs as far away as Sweden, 140 IT jobs; and Thailand with 60 plus manufacturing jobs.

Register with their job hunter tool (a variation on the standard e-mail alert), and it will alert you to when any company in their database has jobs posted on that company's own website that fit your needs.

How is this different? Flipdog isn't asking you to rely on companies who advertise with them, it goes directly to company websites and

searches their Job Opportunity pages for you. This is a great tool for the job hunter.

You can also subscribe to their monthly Job Opportunity Index, which gives you an overview of employment in 50 major Metropolitan areas and the number of jobs available in different major categories. This won't help you find a specific job, but if you are considering relocation it can give you a snapshot of types of employment opportunities in a given area, and the concentration of the core industries in that area. From an ongoing employability factor, lots of employers in your field in a destination area means it will be easier to progress your career in that area than one where there is not a concentration of employers in your chosen profession.

They also have a fairly neat research tool for information on a specific company. Type in a company name and it will reply with a list of links that provide both public and insider information about that company. They also have many of the other features you would find on the standard job site. Flipdog is different, check it out.

Getting a Job
www.americanexpress.com/student/

A good-sized database of intern programs from corporate America and the non-profit world. Backed by Amex Financial Assistance services you can also learn a good deal about how far in debt you'll get for a good education!

Global careers
www.globalcareers.com

A job bank with international appeal. Jobs from around the world, mainly in finance, business, management, and transportation. There is also a resume bank, so if you want international exposure, or are bi-lingual this is a good place to post your resume.

Gonyea Online Career Center

You must be a subscriber to America Online to access these services. For $19.95 a month (at this writing) and the cost of the phone call, you have access to a very impressive array of job search tools. To get to this site, search AOL by keyword and type in either "career" or "career center." You'll see the Gonyea Online Career Center as one of the search results. Formerly the America Online Career Center, the Gonyea Online Career Center was the power behind that throne, and still offers a good selection of career-related services, including:

- Help Wanted–USA
- Worldwide Resume Bank
- Career Guidance Services
- Government Jobs Central
- Career Resource Mall
- Occupational Profiles
- Employment Agencies
- Online Job Hunting.

One service that will be of primary interest is Help Wanted—USA, where you can key in a preset job code and location for job categories and receive a list of matching job openings. I ran the same test on every set of job listings I encountered. I searched for three distinct jobs: a systems analyst and a retail merchandise manager, both located in New York, and a swim team coach located in California. I chose the first two jobs because they are both growing careers in growing industries, and added the swim coach as a wild card—because it would be a dream job!

In Help Wanted—USA I found 97 listings in the computer category for New York, about one-third of which were for systems analysts or something closely related. There were absolutely no listings for retail trade (which I found odd) and none under the sports/recreation category either. This isn't meant as a criticism, since these sites are growing and changing all the time, and no one can keep track of all of the jobs or careers. It is meant as a caution for you. Just because a site is big or well known doesn't mean it has what you need, or that what you need isn't out there somewhere. By the time you read this, there may be dozens of retail merchandise managers popping out of Help Wanted—USA.

This site claims to have ten thousand new job listings per week, updated weekly. It recommends that the best time to check for new listings is Wednesday morning.The Gonyea Online Career Center also boasts over 1 million users a month. This makes it one of the most visited career sites available today.

Good Works
www.essential.org/goodworks/

A job bank for those with a social conscience. Good Works advertisers are non-profit organizations looking for professionals wanting to make a difference with their work through social change and the public interest.

Great Summer Jobs
www.gsj.petersons.com

Another niche site. This one offering a job bank with an endless supply of counselor jobs at summer camps around the country. Good content fills you in on what camp directors look for in the counselors they hire, what the jobs are, and how much they pay.

This is a seasonal site to the degree that you simply won't find jobs posted in the summer, because they have all been filled. The job listings start building in October and begin to tail off in the spring.

If you are interested in a camp counselor job, you'll find it a valuable exercise in the forward planning skills you can use throughout your career; you'll develop an appreciation for planning ahead as an important component of lifetime career management.

Headhunter.net
www.headhunter.net

The other awesome headhunter site. A major job bank with multiple postings from thousands of headhunting firms in most disciplines. This is a great job bank that gets you in front of the elusive headhunter with hundreds of thousands of job openings, with an e-mail alert option. It also has an extensive resume bank you'll want to be in. This site has enormous respect in the professional community. If you are a mid-career professional (there's not a lot for entry level here) you must visit headhunter.net

Help Wanted USA
www.iccweb.com

Run by Jim Gonyea, an Internet careersite pioneer, you can also find this site on AOL as the Gonyea Career Center. A comprehensive job bank that feature jobs from cities throughout the nation, and an equally important resume bank. You'll also find a resume blaster, salary calculator, and other useful job hunting tools here. It is one of the most comprehensive sites around and reflects Jim's depth of knowledge.

Hoovers Online
www.hoovers.com

This is the online version of the Hoovers directories, a valuable research tool to job hunters. Use it to identify potential employers, or gather background information for an upcoming interview. This is a subscription site costing about $12 a month, although many parts of the site are free.

Hot Jobs
www.hotjobs.com

A good and getting better, job bank with e-mail alerts. Great companies advertise with hotjobs.com in most fields, from Internet companies to entertainment conglomerates. This growing job bank has lots of mid- to higher-level postings with plenty of information about the job, but not much about the employer, so you'll have to do that research yourself.

The site also has a pretty decent resume bank frequently scanned by employers and recruiters. A neat feature of the resume bank is that it can tell you how many times your resume has been accessed. This could give you useful feedback on the effectiveness of your resume; many hits but no calls for interview might suggest a review of your resume structure and content.

Industry Insite
www.industryinsite.com

A networking site for college graduates from an increasing number of colleges like Stanford, Harvard, Yale, Duke, Northeastern, Berkeley, University of Chicago, Cornell, Princeton, and MIT, to name a few. There is a job bank, but the real benefit is the opportunity to network with alumnae from your and other schools who have similar professional interest areas as you.

Industry Insite is a community-oriented site and a great way to leverage the contacts that can come from an expensive education. Expect this site to continue adding alumnae associations to its membership.

International Jobs
www.internationaljobs.org

Online version of a print newsletter. Job bank of openings outside the U.S., but you pay to see them, about $26 dollars for six weeks. You also get the hardcopy newsletter.

Internet Business Network
Interbiznet.com

Fresh news everyday that's relevant to online jobhunters. This site is geared mainly towards the professional recruitment community. However, you can glean lots of information about specific recruiters and trends in employment. They also have a career advice section that is way above average. The advice is really quite sensible, and often insightful. You get the idea that the writers know something about job hunting, which is a refreshing change from most sites. It wouldn't hurt to bookmark this site and go to it at the start or end of a job hunting day, there is usually some useful advice, at least I have found it so on my visits. Each day's fare features three to six short articles with links to other information sources.

Internet Sourcebook.com
www.internetsourcebook.com

Now this is a nice little site that I expect will grow in importance over the years, or at least until someone buys them! Last year this site offered profiles of over 500 Internet companies and provided direct links to the job openings on their Web pages. This year they feature 2000 sites. The site is owned by Gateway.

Jaegers' Interactive
www.jaegerinc.com

A job bank run by a recruitment-advertising agency, and is their foray into the online world. The jobs come from their corporate advertisers.

Jobs are across the board, most valuable if you are in the Ohio area.

JobDirect.com
www.jobdirect.com

Job and resume bank with a strong presence in the college educated entry level space. Jobdirect has aggressively pursued colleges and graduating students across the U.S. and the resume bank shows it. Consequently employers scan the resume bank and post jobs in the job bank. If you are at the entry-level point of your career, this is a must go-to site.

JOBTRAK
www.jobtrak.com
e-mail: www@jobtrak.com
phone: (800) 999-8725

Established in 1987 as a service for college students, graduates, and alumni, this has developed into one of the most critically acclaimed sites on the Web. Also chosen as one of the University of Michigan's top four "Best of the Best" in job search sites, JOBTRAK was distinguished in 1992 as Entrepreneur of the Year by the state of California, semifinalist in the 1997 National Information & Infrastructure Awards as well as earning 10 other online awards. This service is completely free to job seekers. There is only one prerequisite. You must be a college student or an alum, since the only way you can get a password is through your campus or *alma mater*.

You can see why employers would register with and frequent this site! It is also user-friendly for employers: They can phone in their ads rather than have to master the Net in order to get access to this wonderful pool of talent. You begin by choosing a college from a scroll list (I went into the UCLA database). This brings you to a menu from which you choose how you would like to conduct your search: by type of work, location, keyword, company name, or date of job listings.

In the past year Job Track has continued its regular launch of new features, including salary calculators, Career Fair calendars, more relocation information and an expanded resource center.

Job Web
www.jobweb.org
e-mail: webmaster@jobweb.org

The first Internet site developed by a human resources organization, this one is owned and maintained by the National Association of Colleges and Employers (NACE), a nonprofit organization comprised of over seventeen hundred colleges and universities and over fourteen hundred business organizations. It caters to the college-educated work force, including students, recent graduates, and experienced professionals.

Winner of the 1997 Gutenberg award for the Best HTML Career/Employment Publications, the features of Job Web are impressive, including:

- Jobs—a keyword search database, free for job seekers
- Employer profiles, hundreds of companies listed alphabetically
- A database of U.S. school districts (representing 16,588 schools)
- Job search and industry information
- Career planning resources
- Career services professionals
- Catalogs for job seekers
- Minorities/disabilities resources
- Relocation resources
- International resources
- The Catapult—a resource gem for grads

This site is especially worth visiting if you are in the human resources field or if you are a college graduate looking for your first job. This job site is likely to be a winner because of all the campus recruiters who belong to the sponsoring organization. Expect it to achieve greatness!

Kelly Services
www.kellyservices.com

The job bank features jobs from all over the Kelly Temporary Services network. The resume bank makes your resume available to the thousand plus Kelly offices and their recruiters. Lots of administrative positions and also an increasingly good source for technical and managerial temporary positions.

Local Opportunities
www.Abracat.com

Sick of the city and yearning for a meaningful career with small-town quality-of-life? Then visit this site, the job bank has Help-wanted advertising from over 700 small town newspapers throughout North America. Register and identify your skills and geographic interests and you'll get e-mail alerts of matching jobs. Nifty site.

Manpower
www.manpower.com

A global employment services company (temporary and permanent) with a presence in 435 countries. You can search by title, keyword, state, or nation. There is a significant resume bank too, which makes your resume available to all the Manpower branch offices.

Med Search America
www.medsearch.com

There is no better site for health care professionals to find the perfect job. Thousands of job opportunities from all over the country are accessible to job seekers for *free!* It is powered by Monster Board and features a similar format. When you see a Website that says "powered by" it means the site has reached a commercial agreement to use products and services of another vendor under their own banner. As time goes by you will see more and more of such announcements.

Minorities Job Bank
www.minoritiesjobbank.com

This eponymously named site is owned by Black Collegian magazine, and offers community to many minorities on job hunting and career management issues. There are communities or "villages" for African Americans, Hispanic Americans, Asian Americans, Native Americans, and women.

If you belong to one of these groups this is a great site to visit. Each village has relevant articles on different aspects of career management all focused toward your special challenges in the workplace. There are also message boards and chats.

There are workplace related news stories supplied by a wire service, and last but not least there is a job and resume bank. The job bank is loaded with job openings from companies that are demonstrably interested in having a properly diversified workforce. Now while these jobs may well appear on other sites (employers don't advertise their employment needs in just one place), making the connection through a minority site may well help get your application noticed, and that's half the battle isn't it? The same applies to the resume bank, use them both.

Monster Board
www.monster.com

The aptly named Monster Board was one of the very first job search web sites. In fact their founder Jeff Taylor tells me their site was the 436th domain name registered.

The Monster job bank approaches the size of the one at Careerpath. It has hundreds of

thousands of jobs for people at all levels and in all fields, it's a must visit job bank; and with over a million resumes, their resume bank may be the biggest there is. Combined, this tells you that employers and recruiters will all consider advertising in the job bank and searching the resume database.

The site has chats and resident "experts" to address your questions, although the response isn't always timely and sometimes lacks depth. This trend setting site also has a lot of other bells and whistles.

- Career Insight & Advice—including links to other career sites and career advice columns by renowned employee advocate Joyce Lain Kennedy
- A resume builder
- A resume database
- Relocation services including apartment search, moving services, housing, and international rentals. You can see photographs of the area, see a floor plan, and (with a little download capability) you can actually do a 3-D tour of your potential digs online!
- Personal job search agent—you fill in a profile with details of the job you seek and all matches are displayed each time you log on.

The jobs listed here seem to be primarily located on the East Coast and are mostly in technical fields. You can search the database by discipline (almost 300 very specific titles), location (over 200 towns/states), or keyword, and get a list of available positions.

Nationjob
www.nationjob.com

An excellent national site with strong job and resume banks and perhaps the premier site for jobs in the heartland. E-mail alerts on suitable jobs for registered users. Lots of additional content and a site owner who understands the world of work and cares about his customers make this site a consistent winner.

Newspage
www.newspage.com

No job or resume bank. What you do get is daily news coverage about corporate expansion and contraction activities. This is a subscription site with a nominal price of $5 a month; you can request news in a number of different areas. For example, you might request news stories about "corporate expansions in Illinois." You can specify any region in the world. A useful research tool.

Non Profit Jobs
www.philanthropy-journal.org

An online venture of the Philanthropy Journal, this site comprises a job bank featuring the magazine's advertisers, and content addressing the workings and financing of the non-profit world. If you are looking for non-profit jobs through the Internet this is a good site.

The site gives you access to in-depth Philanthropy Journal articles about the non profit world. This can be really useful, as you'll learn who has just raised what money. When you hear that this charity or that non-profit has just raised twenty million dollars that's a clear indication that they're looking for people. You can also sign up for a free weekly newsletter, which you can think of as Philanthropy Journal Lite. The Journal has far more meat than the web site.

Penton Publishing
www.penton.com

Another job bank site owned by a publisher of professional niche magazines: sales, hospitality, travel, electronics, manufacturing,

and management. The job bank reflects these specialties. It is not a big job bank, but because the magazines are also published overseas, there is an international component to some of the jobs.

Recruiters Online Network
www.ipa.com

This is one of the best places to get your resume in front of some 8,000 headhunters from around the world. You can now also view all those job openings the mysterious headhunters are working to fill. Once you have loaded your resume in the resume bank you'll get e-mail updates on suitable opportunities. At the same time, the member recruiters will be alerted to your presence when your skills match an open requisition. There are so many different specialist recruiters using this site, your profession and specialty are almost certainly represented.

Resume Express
www.resumexpress.com

Load your resume onto the Resume Express launcher and get it automatically distributed to over four thousand targeted employers and recruiters. The cost is $99, and when you consider the time saving and comprehensive coverage, it is well worth the bucks. Started in 1994 by pioneer Wayne Gonyea this site was the first of its kind. It is often said that you can't get 100K plus jobs on the Internet. I recommended a friend making way over the magic 100K mark to Resume Express, he got twenty calls, multiple interviews, and a great job well into six figures. It was also the only vehicle that got his resume any significant response. Wayne understands careers and knows professionals in the industry who supply responsible articles on job hunting and resumes for his site.

Resume Network
www.resumenetwork.com

This site features a resume database linked to the world of recruiters and headhunters. It's a subscription site that costs you $125 a year. For this they will convert your resume to an HTML format (suitable for electronic distribution) do a weekly e-mail to their recruiter members, submit your resume to 30 plus resume banks, and provide resume hosting for a year. Of course as almost every single resume bank trashes your resume after 90 days it would be nice if they would submit your resume four times in the year for your subscription fee, such a service would cost them virtually nothing. Without it you are paying for a year's worth of service but your resume is only going to be in those resume banks for a quarter of that time. Until they change this try negotiating with them, require that they blast your resume four times, for the reasons I've stated.

Resumes on the Web
www.resweb.com
e-mail: sdas@ifu.net

Resume postings are now free and this site now has a jobbank (powered by jobsonline) with over 200,000 listings.

There is no fee for searching the site, making it attractive to recruiters and employers alike. You simply click onto the job category and the names of candidates appear. Click again and a complete resume with contact information appears—very straightforward. This is not a huge resume bank as yet, but the resumes I looked at had impressive credentials, making this site a place that employers and recruiters could well come to respect.

Retail Jobs
www.retailjobnet.com

A good niche site for the retail profession, if you are in the management or executive ranks, but not strong in sales floor positions. There is also a resume bank which in the last couple of years has been both for free and for fee, so who knows what it will be when you get there, as there are rumors that it may flip again.

Shawn's Internet Resume Center
www.inpursuit.com/sirc/

For a one-time fee of $30 you can post your resume on this very heavily visited site, which caters to high-end management. Check out the guest book, and you'll be impressed by the employers and recruiters who are searching the site. Check out your competition by doing a resume search on others looking for work in your field—an idea of what kind of qualifications they have and how they're presenting themselves to employers could be time and money well spent.

Socrates Careers
www.socratescareers.com

No job or resume bank, as such. This is an association of career management professionals whose common bond is services to working professionals and executives. All the members are respected in their professional community, and all of them have extensive track records. The site will link you to individual members who provide a wide range of services: reference checking, career counselling, resume writing and distribution, headhunter lists, job lists by industry (sales, marketing, HR, finance, sports, legal, federal, executive, and international), testing and assessment tools, employment law and discrimination attorneys including the attorney who won the much publicized discrimination case against the Hooters restaurant chain. There's a lot of qualified help here for people in transition.

Telecommuting Jobs
www.tjobs.com

A niche site which will develop growing importance in the changing world of work. You will find jobs here that don't require you in the office everyday: Mostly you'll find sales, programming, graphics, and writing jobs. There is a resume bank, but one that you pay to be in, albeit a token ten bucks a year. Also you'll find useful content on telecommuting trends and the issues that face telecommuters and their employers.

Wall Street Journal
www. wsj.com

On the homepage click on careers. This is the Wall Street Journal's foray into online Help-Wanted advertising. The job bank features recruitment advertising from all the prestigious business-oriented advertisers who also use the newspaper's national and regional editions for Help-Wanted advertising.

What makes the site stand out though is some truly useful content. The site now includes a significant amount of job hunting and career management articles written not by journalists but by respected career and job hunting experts. These articles are now available online and comprise some of the most sensible advice available on the Internet.

Yahoo Resume Bank
www.yahoo.com

Good old Yahoo—one of the Web's most popular search engines and most visited sites—really comes up roses here. When you get into Yahoo, just type in "individual resumes" and you will be presented with 91 headings you can link to, covering all major industries. The categories at the time of writing was somewhat scattered; for instance, there are six listings for "Computers and Internet" randomly interspersed amongst science and art and business. Click onto any one of these and a plethora of resumes are at your fingertips. This is a gold mine for computer graphic artists, both to show off your capabilities and to check out the competition . . . there are a lot of very talented people out there looking for work; just scanning their resumes is like walking through a cyber museum!

This bank has a growing roster of thousands of professional resumes. When you check on a category (in some areas there are also subcategories within job categories) you are instantly presented with a list of names, each annotated with a quick quip designed to attract your attention. One of these "headlines" read, "will bring you a smile." Now, on a resume, this might make a hardened HR pro vomit and move on. (I would have been put off by the coyness in a flash.) Online, as you'll soon see, things are different. Here, that human touch didn't seem to offend so much; in fact, I checked out the resume!

Once you click on a name, you get a full resume with all the details: experience, education, activities, references, etc. For an employer, the Yahoo resume bank is accessible, easy to use, and fast; for you, it is free. Go on, post your resume!

Also see these valuable resume sites:

Resumail Network
www.rsumail.com

Resumania Online
www.umn.edu/ohr/ecep/resume

Resume link
www.resume-link.com

Resources

HEALTH CARE

Publications

Hospital Phone Book
U.S. Directory Service, Miami, FL
Provides information on over 7,940
government and private hospitals in the U.S.

*National Association of County Health Officials
Sustaining Membership Directory*
National Association of County Health
Officials, Washington, DC
Lists national health officials for almost every
county in the U.S. Published annually. $10.
Call 202-783-5550 for more information.

National Jobs in Dietetics
Jobs in Dietetics, Santa Monica, CA
Lists jobs nationwide in the field of dietetics.
Published monthly; an annual subscription is
$84. Call 310-453-5375 for more information.

U.S. Medical Directory
U.S. Directory Service, Miami, FL
Over one thousand pages of information on
doctors, hospitals, nursing facilities, medical
laboratories, and medical libraries.

Associations

HEALTH CARE ADMINISTRATION

American Association of Medical Assistants
20 North Wacker Drive, Suite 1575
Chicago, IL 60606-2903; tel: 312-899-1500

American College of Healthcare Executives
1 North Franklin, Suite 1700
Chicago, IL 60606-3491; tel: 312-424-2800

American Health Care Association
1201 L Street NW
Washington, DC 20005; tel: 202-842-4444

American Health Information Management
Association
919 North Michigan Avenue
Chicago, IL 60611; tel: 312-787-2672

American Medical Technologists
710 Higgins Road
Park Ridge, IL 60068; tel: 708-823-5169

Healthcare Financial Management Association
Two Westbrook Corporate Center, Suite 700
Westchester, IL 60154; tel: 708-531-9600

National Association of Emergency Medical
Technicians
102 West Leake Street
Clinton, MS 39056; tel: 601-924-7747

Nuclear Medicine Technology Certification
Board
2970 Clairmont Road, Suite 610
Atlanta, GA 30329-1634; tel: 404-315-1739

NURSING

American Association of Nurse Anesthetists
222 South Prospect Avenue
Park Ridge, IL 60068-4001; tel: 708-692-7050

American Association of Occupational Health
Nurses
50 Lenox Pointe
Atlanta, GA 30324; tel: 404-262-1162
or 800-241-8014

American Hospital Association
1 North Franklin
Chicago, IL 60606; tel: 312-422-3000

American Nurses Association
600 Maryland Avenue SW, Suite 100 W
Washington, DC 20024-2571;
tel: 202-651-7000

Medical Economics Publishing
5 Paragon Drive
Montvale, NJ 07645-1742; tel: 201-358-7200

National Association for Home Care
519 C Street NE
Washington, DC 20002; tel: 202-547-7424
(send SASE for general information)

National Association for Practical Nurse
Education and Service
1400 Spring Street, Suite 310
Silver Spring, MD 20910; tel: 301-588-2491

National Association of Pediatric Nurse
Associates and Practitioners
1101 Kings Highway N, Suite 206
Cherry Hill, NJ 08034-1921;
tel: 609-667-1773

National Federation of Licensed Practical
Nurses
1418 Aversboro Road
Garner, NC 27529-4547; tel: 919-779-0046

National League for Nursing Communications
Department
350 Hudson Street
New York, NY 10014; tel: 212-989-9393

National Rehabilitation Association
633 South Washington Street
Alexandria, VA 22314; tel: 703-836-0850

PHYSICAL HEALTH

Accreditation Council for Graduate Medical
Education
515 North State Street, Suite 2000
Chicago, IL 60610; tel: 312-464-4920

American Association for
Respiratory Care
11030 Ables Lane
Dallas, TX 75229-4593; tel: 214-243-2272

American Association of Colleges of Pediatric
Medicine
1350 Piccard Drive, Suite 322
Rockville, MD 20850; tel: 301-990-7400

American Board of Preventive Medicine
9950 West Lawrence Avenue, Suite 106
Schiller Park, IL 60176; tel: 847-671-1750

American Medical Association
515 North State Street
Chicago, IL 60610; tel: 312-464-5000

American Occupational Therapy Association
4720 Montgomery Lane, P.O. Box 31220
Bethesda, MD 20824-1220; tel: 301-652-2682

American Physical Therapy Association
1111 North Fairfax Street
Alexandria, VA 22314;
tel: 703-684-2782 or 800-999-2782

American Podiatric Medical Association
9312 Old Georgetown Road
Bethesda, MD 20814-1621;
tel: 301-571-9200

American Society of Radiology Technologists
15000 Central Avenue SE
Albuquerque, NM 87123-4605;
tel: 505-298-4500

Society of Diagnostic Medical Sonographers
12770 Coit Road, Suite 508
Dallas, TX 75251; tel: 214-239-7367

DENTISTRY

American Association of Dental Assistants
203 North LaSalle Street, Suite 132
Chicago, IL 60601-1225;
tel: 312-541-1550

American Association of Dental Schools
1625 Massachusetts Avenue NW
Washington, DC 20036; tel: 202-667-9433

American Association of Orthodontists
401 North Lindbergh Blvd.
St. Louis, MO 63141-7816;
tel: 314-993-1700

American Dental Association
211 East Chicago Avenue
Chicago, IL 60611; tel: 312-440-2500
(for Commission on Dental Accreditation, direct
correspondence to Suite 3400; for SELECT
Program, direct correspondence to Department
of Career Guidance, Suite 1804)

American Dental Hygienists Association
Division of Professional Development
444 North Michigan Avenue, Suite 3400
Chicago, IL 60611; tel: 312-440-8900

National Association of Dental Laboratories
555 East Braddock Road
Alexandria, VA 22305; tel: 703-683-5263

National Board for Certification in Dental
Technology
555 East Braddock Road
Alexandria, VA 22305; tel: 703-683-5263

MENTAL HEALTH

American Association for Counseling and
Development
5999 Stevenson Avenue
Alexandria, VA 22304; tel: 703-823-9800

American Association for Marriage and Family
Therapy
11331 5th Street NW, Suite 300
Washington, DC 20005; tel: 202-452-0109

American Association of Mental Retardation
444 North Capitol Street, NW, Suite 846
Washington, DC 20001-1512;
tel: 202-387-1968 or 800-424-3688

American Psychiatric Association
1400 K Street NW
Washington, DC 20005; tel: 202-682-6000

American Psychological Association
750 First Street NE
Washington, DC 20002; tel: 202-336-5500

National Board for Certified Counselors
3 Terrace Way, Suite D
Greensboro, NC 27403-3660;
tel: 910-547-0607

BIOTECHNOLOGY AND ENVIRONMENTAL TECHNOLOGY

Publications

Corporate Technology Directory
CorpTech, Woburn, MA
Lists over 35,000 businesses and 110,000
executives. Describes products and services in
such fields as automation, biotechnology,
chemicals, computers and software, defense,
energy, environment, manufacturing
equipment, advanced materials, medical,
pharmaceuticals, photonics, subassemblies
and components, testing and measurements,
telecommunications, and transportation and
holding companies. Published annually.

CorpTech Fast 5,000 Company Locator
CorpTech, Woburn, MA
Lists over five thousand of the fastest-growing
companies listed in the Corporate Technology
Directory, but includes addresses and phone
numbers, number of employees, sales, and
industries by state. Published annually.

Directory of Environmental Information
Government Institutes, Rockville, MD
Lists federal and state government resources,
trade organizations, and professional and
scientific newsletters, magazines, and
databases. Published every other year.

Environmental Telephone Directory
Governmental Institutes, Rockville, MD
Lists detailed information on governmental
agencies that deal with the environment. The
directory also identifies the environmental
aides of U.S. Senators and Representatives.
Published every other year.

Sales Guide to High-Tech Companies
CorpTech, Woburn, MA
Covers over three thousand company profiles
and twelve thousand executive contacts.
Includes specific details on each company's
products and services. Published quarterly; a
yearly subscription is $185. Call 617-932-3939
for more information.

Transportation Officials and Engineers Directory
American Road and Transportation Builders
Association, Washington, DC
Lists over four thousand state transportation
officials and engineers at local, state, and
federal levels. Published annually.

Associations

Air and Waste Management Association
1 Gateway Center, 3rd Floor
Pittsburgh, PA 15222; tel: 412-232-3444

American Chemical Society
1155 16th Street NW
Washington, DC 20036;
tel: 202-872-4600 or 800-227-5558

American Institute of Biological Sciences
1444 Eye Street NW, Suite 200
Washington, DC 20005; tel: 202-628-1500

American Institute of Chemists
501 Wythe Street
Alexandria, VA 22314-1917; tel: 703-836-2090

American Institute of Physics
1 Physics Ellipse
College Park, MD 20740-3843;
tel: 301-209-3100

American Society for Biochemistry and
Molecular Biology
9650 Rockville Pike
Bethesda, MD 20814-3996; tel: 301-530-7145

American Society for Microbiology
1325 Massachusetts Avenue NW
Washington, DC 20005; tel: 202-737-3600

American Society of Biological Chemists
9650 Rockville Pike
Bethesda, MD 20814-3996; tel: 301-530-7145

American Zoo and Aquarium Association (AZA)
Office of Membership Service
Oglebay Park, Route 88
Wheeling, WV 26003; tel: 304-242-2160

Association of American Geographers
1710 16th Street NW
Washington, DC 20009-3198; tel: 202-234-1450

Botanical Society of America
1735 Nell Avenue
Columbus, OH 43210; tel: 614-292-3519

Center for American Archeology
P.O. Box 366
Kampsville, IL 62053; tel: 618-653-4316

Department of Energy Headquarters
Operations Division
1000 Independence Avenue SW, Room 4E-090
Washington, DC 20585; tel: 202-586-4333
(hotline for job vacancies, updated every Friday)

Environmental Protection Agency Recruitment
Center
401 Main Street SW, Room 3634
Washington, DC 20460;
tel: 202-260-2090/3308

Federation of American Societies for
Experimental Biology
9650 Rockville Pike
Bethesda, MD 20814; tel: 301-530-7000

Genetics Society of America
9650 Rockville Pike
Bethesda, MD 20814-3998;
tel: 301-571-1825
Geological Society of America
3300 Penrose Place, P.O. Box 9140
Boulder, CO 80301; tel: 303-447-2020

National Accrediting Agency for Clinical
Laboratory Sciences
8410 West Bryn Mawr Avenue, Suite 670
Chicago, IL 60631; tel: 312-714-8880

National Solid Wastes Management Association
4301 Connecticut Avenue NW, Suite 300
Washington, DC 20008; tel: 202-244-4700

Natural Resource Conservation Service,
Personnel Division
P.O. Box 2980
Washington, DC 20013; tel: 202-720-4264

ENGINEERING

Associations

American Association of Engineering Societies
1111 19th Street NW, Suite 608
Washington, DC 20034; tel: 202-296-2237

American Chemical Society
1155 16th Street NW
Washington, DC 20036;
tel: 202-872-4600 or 800-227-5558

American Institute of Chemical Engineers
345 East 47th Street
New York, NY 10017;
tel: 212-705-7338 or 800-242-4363

American Society for Engineering Education
1818 N Street NW, Suite 600
Washington, DC 20036; tel: 202-331-3500

American Society of Civil Engineers
1801 Alexander Bell Drive
Reston, VA 20191-4400; tel: 800-548-ASCE

American Society of Mechanical Engineers
(ASME)
345 East 47th Street
New York, NY 10017; tel: 212-705-7722
Institute of Electrical and Electronics Engineers
345 East 47th Street
New York, NY 10017; tel: 212-705-7900

Institute of Industrial Engineers
25 Technology Park
Atlanta, GA 30092-0460; tel: 770-449-0460

Society of Manufacturing Engineers (SME)
1 SME Drive, P.O. Box 930
Dearborn, MI 48121; tel: 313-271-1500

INFORMATION TECHNOLOGY

Publications

Access
1900 West 47th Place, Suite 215
Shawnee Mission, KS 66205; tel: 800-362-
0681
(initial six-month nonmember listing, $15;
each additional three months, $15; initial six-
month listing for members of the Data
Processing Management Association, $10)

AIIM Job Bank Bulletin
Association for Information and Image
Management
1100 Wayne Avenue, Suite 1100
Silver Spring, MD 20910;
tel: 301-587-8202
(four-month subscription: nonmember, $100;
member, $25; issued semimonthly)

Associations

ASIS Jobline
American Society for Information Science
8720 Georgia Avenue, Suite 501
Silver Spring, MD 20910-3602;
tel: 301-495-0900
(free; monthly)

Association for Computing Machinery
1515 Broadway
New York, NY 10036; tel: 212-869-7440

Association for Systems Management
1433 West Bagley Road, P.O. Box 38370
Cleveland, OH 44138; tel: 216-243-6900

COMPUTERS

Publications

ComputerWorld
500 Old Connecticut Path
Framingham, MA 01701-9171; tel: 508-879-
0700 or 800-343-6474
(annual subscription: U.S., $39.95; Canada,
$110; issued weekly)

ComputerWorld, Campus Edition
500 Old Connecticut Path
Framingham, MA 01701-9171;
tel: 508-879-0700
(annual subscription, $5; free to students;
published each October)

High Technology Careers Magazine
4701 Patrick Henry Drive, Suite 1901
Santa Clara, CA 95054; tel: 408-970-8800
(six issues per year, $29)

Technical Employment News
P.O. Box 1285
Cedar Park, TX 78613;
tel: 512-250-9023 or 800-678-9724
(weekly subscription, $55; annual subscription,
$88, U.S. and Canada)

Associations

IEEE Computer Society
1730 Massachusetts Avenue NW
Washington, DC 20036; tel: 202-371-0101
(available to members only)

CU Career Connection
University of Colorado, Campus Box 133
Boulder, CO 80309-0133; tel: 303-492-4727
(two-month fee for passcode to the job hotline,
$30)

Data Processing Management Association
505 Busse Highway
Park Ridge, IL 60068; tel: 708-825-8124

Institute for Certification of Computing
Professionals
2200 East Devon Avenue, Suite 247
Des Plaines, IL 60018;
tel: 708-299-4227

Quality Assurance Institute
7575 Philips Boulevard, Suite 350
Orlando, Fl 32819; tel: 407-363-1111

Semiconductor Equipment and Materials
International
805 East Middlefield Road
Mountain View, CA 94043; tel: 415-964-5111

BUSINESS AND PROFESSIONAL

Publications

The Almanac of American Employers
Corporate Jobs Outlook
Boerne, TX
Lists five hundred of the country's most
successful, large companies; profiles salary
ranges, benefits, financial stability, and
advancement opportunities.

Corporate Jobs Outlook
Corporate Jobs Outlook, Inc., Dallas, TX
Each issue reviews fifteen to twenty major
(five thousand employees or more) firms.
The report rates the firms and provides
information on salaries and benefits, current
and projected development, where to apply
for jobs, potential layoffs, benefit plans, the
company's record for promoting women or
minorities to executive positions, and college
reimbursement packages. Also includes
personnel contact information for each firm.
Published bimonthly; a yearly subscription is
$159.99. Call 214-824-3030. Note: This
resource is also available online at
www.vinnelljobcorps.org.

Directory of Corporate Affiliations
Reed Reference Publishing Company, New
Providence, NJ
Lists key personnel in 4,700 parent companies
and forty thousand divisions, subsidiaries, and
affiliates. Includes addresses and phone
numbers of key executives and decision makers.
Published once a year, with quarterly updates.
For more information, call 800-323-6772.

Directory of Leading Private Companies
National Register Publishing Company,
Wilmette, IL
Profiles over seven thousand U.S. private
companies in the service, manufacturing,
distribution, retail, and construction fields.
Includes companies in such areas as health
care, high technology, entertainment, fast-food
franchises, leasing, publishing, and
communications. Published annually.

Encyclopedia of Associations
Gale Research, Inc., Detroit, MI
Published in three volumes. Volume 1 lists
national organizations in the U.S. and includes
over twenty-two thousand associations,
including hundreds for government
professions. Volume 2 provides geographic
and executive indexes. Volume 3 features full
entries on associations that are not listed in
Volume 1. Note: This resource is also available
online through Dialog Information Services at
www.dialog.com (or 800-334-2564). Call for
more information.

International Directory of Corporate Affiliations
National Register Publishing Company,
Wilmette, IL
Lists over fourteen hundred major foreign
companies and their thirty thousand U.S. and
foreign holdings. Published annually.

The JobBank Series
Adams Media Corporation, Holbrook, MA
A top-notch series of paperback local
employment guides. The recent editions profile
virtually every local company with over fifty
employees in a given metro area. Company
listings are arranged by industry for easy use;
also included is a section on the region's
economic outlook and contact information for
local professional associations, executive search
firms, and job placement agencies. The series
covers twenty-nine major metropolitan areas,
including Atlanta, Boston, the Carolinas, Chicago,
Dallas/Ft. Worth, Denver, Detroit, Florida,
Houston, Los Angeles, Minneapolis/St. Paul,
Missouri, New York, Ohio, Philadelphia, Phoenix,
San Francisco, Seattle, Tennessee, and
Washington, DC. Many listings feature contact
names, common positions hired for, educational
backgrounds sought, benefits, fax numbers,
internship information, staff size, and more.
Available at most bookstores. Updated yearly.

National Trade and Professional Associations
of the United States
Columbia Books, Washington, DC
Lists information on over sixty-five hundred
trade and professional associations. Published
annually.

Resume Bank
American Corporate Counsel Association
1225 Connecticut Avenue NW, Suite 302
Washington, DC 20036; tel: 202-296-4522
(six-month registration: nonmembers, $65;
members, $25; complete job-matching
application, and five copies of resume free)

FINANCIAL SERVICES

Associations

BANKING

American Bankers Association
1120 Connecticut Avenue NW
Washington, DC 20036; tel: 202-663-5000
American Institute of Banking
1213 Bakers Way
Manhattan, KS 66502; tel: 913-537-4750

Association of Master of Business
Administration Executives
AMBA Center
South Summit Place
Branford, CT 06405; tel: 203-315-5221

Banking Federation of the European Economic
Community (BFEC)
Federation Bancaire de la Communaute
Europeenne (FBCE)
c/o Umberto Burani
10, rue Montoyer, B-1040
Brussels, Belgium; tel: 32-2-5083711;
fax: 32-2-5112328

Banking Law Institute (BLI)
22 West 21st Street
New York, NY 10010;
tel: 212-645-7880 or 800-332-1105;
fax: 212-675-4883

BANKPAC
(formerly: Bankers Political Action Committee;
Banking Profession Political Action Committee)
c/o Meg Bonitt
American Bankers Association
1120 Connecticut Avenue NW
Washington, DC 20036;
tel: 202-663-5115/5076
or 202-663-7544 (fax)

Electronic Banking Economics Society (EBES)
P.O. Box 2331
New York, NY 10036; tel: 203-295-9788

Savings and Community Bankers of America
Educational Services
Center for Financial Studies
900 19th Street NW, Suite 400
Washington, DC 20006; tel: 202-857-3100

U.S. Council on International Banking (USCIB)
1 World Trade Center, Suite 1963
New York, NY 10048;
tel: 212-466-3352; fax: 212-432-0544

Women in Banking and Finance
55 Bourne Vale
Bromley, Kent BR2 7NW, England;
tel: 44-181-4623276

Women's World Banking—USA
8 West 40th Street
New York, NY 10018;
tel: 212-768-8513; fax: 212-768-8519

SECURITIES

Association of Securities and Exchange
Commission Alumni
West Tower, Suite 812
1100 New York Avenue NW
Washington, DC 20005; tel: 202-408-7600;
fax: 202-408-7614

International Securities Market Association—
England
7 Limeharbour
London E14 9NQ, England;
tel: 44-171-538-5656; fax: 44-171-538-4902

National Association of Securities Dealers
(NASD)
1735 K Street NW
Washington, DC 20006-1506;
tel: 202-728-8000; fax: 202-293-6260

National Association of Securities Professionals
(NASP)
700 13th Street NW, Suite 950
Washington, DC 20005;
tel: 202-434-4535; fax: 202-434-8916

North American Securities Administrators
Association (NASAA)
1 Massachusetts Avenue NW, Suite 310
Washington, DC 20001;
tel: 202-737-0900; fax: 202-783-3571

Securities and Futures Authority
Cottons Centre, Cottons Lane
London SE I 2QB, England;
tel: 44-171-378-9000;
tel: 44-171-403-7569

Securities Industry Association (SIA)
120 Broadway
New York, NY 10271; tel: 212-608-1500;
fax: 212-608-1604

Securities Transfer Association (STA)
55 Exchange Place
New York, NY 10260-0001; tel: 212-748-8000

Western Pennsylvania Securities
Industry Agency
1 Oxford Centre, 40th Floor
Pittsburgh, PA 15219; tel: 412-731-7185

ACCOUNTING

Academy of Accounting Historians (AAH)
University of Arkansas, Department of
Accounting
Fayetteville, AR 72701; tel: 501-575-6125;
fax: 501-575-7687

Accounting Aid Society of Detroit (AASD)
719 Griswold, Suite 2026
Detroit, MI 48226; tel: 313-961-1840;
fax: 313-961-6257
E-mail: itpass@igc.apc.org

Affiliation of Independent Accountants
9200 South Dadeland Boulevard, Suite 510
Miami, FL 33156; tel: 305-670-0580;
fax: 305-670-3818

American Accounting Association
5717 Bessie Drive
Sarasota, FL 34223; tel: 941-921-7747

American Institute of Certified Public
Accountants (AICPA)
1211 Avenue of the Americas
New York, NY 10036-8775;
tel: 212-596-6200 or 800-862-4272 or
212-596-6213 (fax)

American Society of Tax Professionals
P.O. Box 1024
Sioux Falls, SD 57101; tel: 605-335-1185

American Society of Women Accountants
1255 Lynnfield Road, Suite 257
Memphis, TN 38119;
tel: 901-680-0470

American Women's Society of Certified Public
Accountants
401 North Michigan Avenue, Suite 2200
Chicago, IL 60611; tel: 312-644-6610

Associated Accounting Firms International (AAFI)
(formerly: Association of Regional CPA Firms)
1000 Connecticut Avenue, Suite 1006
Washington, DC 20036; tel: 202-463-7900;
fax: 202-296-0741

Associated Regional Accounting Firms (ARAF)
3700 Crestwood Parkway, Suite 350
Duluth, GA 30136; tel: 770-279-4560;
fax: 770-279-4566 (fax)

Association for Accounting Administration (AAA)
136 South Keowee Street
Dayton, OH 45402; tel: 513-222-0030;
fax: 513-2212-5794

Association of Accounting Technicians (AAT)
154 Clerkenwell Road
London EC I R 5AD, England;
tel: 44-171-837-8600/814-6999;
fax: 44-171-837-6970
E-mail: aatuk@pipex.com

Association of Government Accountants
2200 Mount Vernon Avenue
Alexandria, VA 22301; tel: 703-684-6931

EDP Auditors Association
3701 Algonquin Road, Suite 1010
Rolling Meadows, IL 60008; tel: 708-253-1545

European Accounting Association (EAA)
European Institute for Advanced Studies in
Management
13 Rue d'Egmont, B-1050
Brussels, Belgium; tel: 32-2-511-9116;
fax: 32-2-512-1929
E-mail: vandyck@ciasm.be

Foundation for Accounting Education (FAE)
530 Fifth Avenue, 5th Floor
New York, NY 10036; tel: 212-719-8300 or
800-537-3635

Governmental Accounting Standards Board
(GASB)
401 Merrit 7, P.O. Box 5116
Norwalk, CT 06856-5116; tel: 203-847-0700;
fax: 203-849-9714

Information Systems Audit and Control
Association
3701 Algonquin Road, Suite 1010
Rolling Meadows, IL 60008;
tel: 708-253-1545

Institute of Certified Management Accountants
(ICMA)
10 Paragon Drive
Montvale, NJ 07645; tel: 201-573-9000 or
800-638-4427; fax: 201-573-8438

Institute of Internal Auditors
249 Maitland Avenue
Altamonte Springs, FL 32701-4201;
tel: 407-830-7600

Institute of Management Accountants
10 Paragon Drive
Montvale, NJ 07645; tel: 201-573-9000;
fax: 201-573-9000

InterAmerican Accounting Association (IAA)
(formerly: InterAmerican Accounting
Conference)
275 Fontainebleau Boulevard, Suite 245
Miami, Fl 33172; tel: 305-225-1991;
fax: 305-225-2011

National Association of State Boards of
Accountancy
545 Fifth Avenue
New York, NY 10168-0002;
tel: 212-490-3868

National Society for Public Accountants
1010 North Fairfax Street
Alexandria, VA 22314; tel: 703-549-6400

INSURANCE

Publications

Insurance Field Directories
Insurance Field Company
P.O. Box 948
Northbrook, IL 60065; tel: 708-498-4010
($55; published each September)

Insurance Phone Book and Directory
US Directory Service
121 Chanlon Road
New Providence, NJ 07074;
tel: 908-464-6800
($67.95, plus $4.75 shipping)

Associations

ACFE Job Bank
Association of Certified Fraud Examiners
716 West Avenue
Austin, TX 78701; tel: 512-478-9070 or 800-
245-3321
(membership fee $75; send two copies of
resume and cover letter indicating salary
requirements and where you are willing to
relocate)

Actual Training Program Directory Society of
Actuaries
475 North Martingale Road, Suite 800
Schaumburg, IL 60173-2226;
tel: 708-706-3500
(free; published each January)

American Academy of Actuaries
1100 17th Street NW, 7th Floor
Washington, DC 20036;
tel: 202-223-8196

American Agents & Brokers
330 North 4th Street
St. Louis, MO 63012; tel: 314-421-5445

Best's Insurance Reports, Property/Casualty
Edition
A.M. Best Company
Ambest Road
Oldwick, NJ 08858-9988; tel: 908-439-2200
(annual fee $70)

Independent Insurance Agents of America
127 South Peyton
Alexandria, VA 22314;
tel: 703-683-4422 or 800-962-7950

Insurance Information Institute
110 William Street
New York, NY 10038; tel: 212-669-9200

Insurance Institute of America
720 Providence Road
Malvern, PA 19355; tel: 610-644-2100

Life Insurance Marketing and Research
Association
P.O. Box 208
Hartford, CT 16141-0208; tel: 203-777-7000

National Association of Life Underwriters
1922 F Street NW
Washington, DC 20006; tel: 202-332-6000

National Association of Professional Insurance
Agents
400 North Washington Street
Alexandria, VA 22314; tel: 703-836-9340

Professional Insurance Agents
400 North Washington Street
Alexandria, VA 22314; tel: 703-836-9340

Society of Actuaries
475 North Martingale Road, Suite 800
Schaumburg, IL 60173-2226;
tel: 708-706-3500

FINANCIAL MANAGEMENT

Associations

American Education Finance Association
(AEFA)
5249 Cape Leyte Drive
Sarasota, FL 34242; tel: 941-349-7580;
fax: 941-349-7580
E-mail: gbabigianc@aol.com

American Finance Association (AFA)
Stern, 44 West 4th Street, Suite 9-190
New York, NY 10012; tel: 212-998-0370

Association of Commercial Finance Attorneys
(ACFA)
1 Corporate Center, 18th Floor MSN 712
Hartford, CT 06103; tel: 203-520-7094; fax:
203-240-5077

Commercial Finance Association (CFA)
225 West 34th Street
New York, NY 10122; tel: 212-594-3490 or
212-564-6053

Financial Analysts Federation
P.O. Box 3726
Charlottesville, VA 22903; tel: 804-977-8977

Financial Management Association International
College of Business Administration
University of South Florida
Tampa, FL 33620-5500

Financial Management Service
Department of the Treasury
401 14th Street SW
Washington, DC 20227;
tel: 202-874-6750

Financial Managers Society
8 South Michigan Avenue, Suite 500
Chicago, IL 60603; tel: 312-578-1300

Government Finance Officers Association of United States and Canada
ISO North Michigan Avenue, Suite 800
Chicago, IL 60601; tel: 312-977-9700; fax: 312-977-4806

Institute of Certified Financial Planners
3801 East Florida Avenue, Suite 708
Denver, CO 80210; tel: 303-751-7600; fax: 303-759-0749

Institute of Chartered Financial Analysts
P.O. Box 3668
Charlottesville, VA 22903; tel: 804-977-6600

Institute of International Finance (IIF)
2000 Pennsylvania Avenue NW, Suite 8500
Washington, DC 20006-1812; tel: 202-857-3600; fax: 202-775-1430

International Association for Financial Planning
2 Concourse Parkway, Suite 800
Atlanta, GA 30328; tel: 404-395-1605

National Association of County Treasurers and Finance Officers
c/o National Association of Counties
440 First Street NW, 8th Floor
Washington, DC 20001;
tel: 202-393-6226

National Society for Real Estate Finance (NSREF)
2300 M Street NW, Suite 800
Washington, DC 20037; tel: 202-973-2801

New York State Consumer Finance Association (NYSCFA)
90 South Swan Street
Albany, NY 12210; tel: 518-449-7514;
fax: 518-426-0566

New York State Government Finance Officers Association
119 Washington Avenue
Albany, NY 12210-2204;
tel: 518-465-1512; fax: 518-434-4640

North American Economics and Finance Association (NAEFA)
Department of Finance
Syracuse University
Syracuse, NY 13244-2130;
tel: 315-443-2963; fax: 315-443-5389

Securities Industry Association
120 Broadway
New York, NY 10271; tel: 212-608-1500

HUMAN RESOURCES

Publications

HR Magazine
606 North Washington Street
Alexandria, VA 22314; tel: 703-548-3440

Associations

American Society for Training and Development
1640 King Street, Box 1443
Alexandria, VA 22313; tel: 703-683-8100
Employment Management Association
4101 Lake Boone Trail, Suite 201
Raleigh, NC 27607; tel: 919-787-6010

Institute of Management Consultants
521 Fifth Avenue, 35th Floor
New York, NY 10175; tel: 212-697-8262

International Personnel Management Association
1617 Duke Street
Alexandria, VA 22314; tel: 703-549-7100

National Training Laboratory
1240 North Pitt Street
Alexandria, VA 22314; tel: 703-548-1500

Society for Human Resource Management
606 North Washington Street
Alexandria, VA 22314; tel: 703-548-3440

LAW

Publications

ALA Management Connections
Association of Legal Administrators
175 E. Hawthorn Parkway, Suite 325
Vernon Hills, IL 60061-1428;
tel: 708-816-1212
(free; updated weekly)

Federal Careers for Attorneys
Federal Reports, Inc., Washington, DC
A guide to legal careers with over three hundred U.S. government general counsel and other legal offices in the U.S. Explains where to apply, the types of legal work common to each field, and information on special recruitment programs.

Judicial Staff Directory
Staff Directories, Ltd., Mt. Vernon, VA
Lists over eleven thousand individuals employed in the 207 federal courts, as well as thirteen thousand cities and their courts. The book also has information on court administration, U.S. marshals, U.S. attorneys, and the U.S. Department of Justice. Includes eighteen hundred biographies.

NDAA Membership Directory
National District Attorneys Association, Alexandria, VA
Lists all district attorneys' offices across the U.S. $15 for nonmembers, $10 for members. Call 703-549-9222 for more information.

Paralegal's Guide to Government Jobs
Federal Reports, Inc., Washington, DC
Explains federal hiring procedures for both entry-level and experienced paralegals. The volume describes seventy law-related careers for which paralegals qualify and lists over one thousand federal agency personnel offices that hire the most paralegal talent. Also profiles special hiring programs.

Associations

American Association for Paralegal Education
P.O. Box 40244
Overland Park, KS 66204; tel: 913-381-4458

American Bar Association Information Services
750 North Lake Shore Drive
Chicago, IL 60611; tel: 312-988-5000 or 800-621-6159

Internships for College Students Interested in Law, Medicine, and Politics
Graduate Group
86 Norwood Road
West Hartford, CT 06117;
tel: 203-236-5570 or 203-232-3100
($27.50, published annually)

National Association for Law Placement
1666 Connecticut Avenue, Suite 328
Washington, DC 20009; tel: 202-667-1666

National Association of Legal Assistants
1516 South Boston Avenue, Suite 200
Tulsa, OK 74119; tel: 918-587-6828

National Federation of Paralegal Associations
P.O. Box 33108
Kansas City, MO 64114;
tel: 816-941-4000
National Paralegal Association
Box 406
Solebury, PA 18963; tel: 215-297-8333

NCRA Employment Referral Service
National Court Reporters Association
8224 Old Courthouse Road
Vienna, VA 22182; tel: 703-556-6272
(six-month registration: nonmembers, $20;
free to members)

Paralegal Placement Network Inc.
P.O. Box 406
Solebury, PA 18963; tel: 215-297-8333
(regular fee, $10; Nat. Paralegal Association
members, $15)

MEDIA/COMMUNICATION/ PUBLIC RELATIONS

Publications

P.R. Reporter
P.O. Box 6000
Exeter, NH 03833

Public Relations Consultants Directory
American Business Directories Inc.
5711 East 86th Circle
Omaha, NE 68127; tel: 402-331-7169

*SMPS Employment Referral Society for
Marketing Professional Services*
99 Canal Plaza, Suite 250
Alexandria, VA 22314;
tel: 703-549-6117 or 800-292-7677
(nonmembers, $100; members, $50; five
copies resume and SMPS application—on file
for three months)

Associations

American Society for Health Care Marketing
and Public Relations
American Hospital Association
1 North Franklin
Chicago, IL 60606; tel: 312-422-3737

American Society of Journalists and Authors
1501 Broadway, Suite 302
New York, NY 10036; tel: 212-997-0947

Council of Sales Promotion Agencies
750 Summer Street
Stamford, CT 06901; tel: 203-325-3911

Dow Jones Newspaper Fund
P.O. Box 300
Princeton, NJ 08543-0300; tel: 609-452-2820

Editorial Freelancers Association
71 West 23rd Street, Suite 1504
New York, NY 10010; tel: 212-929-5400

Institute for Public Relations Research and
Education (IPRRE)
University of Florida
P.O. Box 118400
Gainesville, FL 32611-8400;
tel: 904-392-0280

International Advertising Association
521 Fifth Avenue, Suite 1807
New York, NY 10175; tel: 212-557-1133

Investigative Reporters & Editors
University of Missouri
26A Walter Williams Hall
Columbia, MO 65211; tel: 314-882-2042

League of Advertising Agencies Directory
2 South End Avenue #4C
New York, NY 10280; tel: 212-945-4314

National School Public Relations Association
(NSPRA)
1501 Lee Highway, Suite 201
Arlington, VA 22209; tel: 703-528-5840

PR Newswire Job Bank
865 South Figueroa, Suite 2310
Los Angeles, CA 90017;
tel: 213-626-5500 or 800-321-8169
(send resume and cover letter)

Promotion Marketing Association of America, Inc.
Executive Headquarters
257 Park Avenue South, 11th Floor
New York, NY 10001; tel: 212-420-1100

Public Relations Society of America
33 Irving Place, 3rd Floor
New York, NY 10003; tel: 212-995-2230

Public Relations Student Society of America
(PRSSA)
33 Irving Place, 3rd Floor
New York, NY 10003; tel: 212-460-1474

Society for Technical Communication
901 North Stuart Street, Suite 904
Arlington, VA 22203; tel: 703-522-4114

Writers Guild of America
555 West 57th Street
New York, NY 10019; tel: 212-767-7800

SALES AND MARKETING

Associations

TRAVEL

Adventure Travel Society
6551 South Revere Parkway, Suite 160
Englewood, CO 80111;
tel: 303-649-9016; fax: 303-649-9017

Air Transport Association of America
1301 Pennsylvania Avenue NW, Suite 1100
Washington, DC 20004-7017; tel: 202-626-4000

Airline Employees Association, Intl.
Job Opportunity Program
5600 South Central Avenue
Chicago, IL 60638-3797

American Society of Travel Agents (ASTA)
1101 King Street, Suite 200
Alexandria, VA 22314;
tel: 703-739-2782; fax: 703-684-8319

American Travel Inns (ATI)
(formerly: American Travel Association)
36 South State Street, Suite 1200
Salt Lake City, UT 84111-1416;
tel: 801-521-0732; fax: 801-521-0732

Association of Flight Attendants
1625 Massachusetts Avenue NW
Washington, DC 20036; tel: 202-328-5400

Association of Retail Travel Agents (ARTA)
845 Sir Thomas Court, Suite 3
Harrisburg, PA 17109; tel: 717-545-9548 or
800-969-6069; fax: 717-545-9613

Cruise Lines International Association
500 Fifth Avenue, Suite 1407
New York, NY 10110; tel: 212-921-0066

Freighter Travel Club of America
3524 Harts Lake Road
Roy, WA 98580; tel: 360-458-4178

Future Aviation Professionals of America
4959 Massachusetts Boulevard
Atlanta, GA 30337; tel: 404-997-8097 or
800-JET-JOBS

Greater Independent Association of National
Travel Services (GIANTS)
2 Park Avenue, Suite 2205
New York, NY 10016; tel: 212-545-7460 or
800-442-6871; fax: 212-545-7428

Independent Travel Agencies of America
Association (ITAA)
5353 North Federal Highway, Suite 300
Fort Lauderdale, Fl 33308; tel: 305-772-4660
or 800-950-5440; fax: 305-772-5797

Institute of Certified Travel Agents (ICTA)
148 Linden Street, P.O. Box 812059
Wellesley, MA 02181-0012; tel: 617-237-0280
or 800-542-4282; fax: 617-237-3860

International Association for Air Travel Couriers
P.O. Box 1349
Lake Worth, FL 33460;
tel: 407-582-8320; fax: 407-582-1581

International Association of Travel Exhibitors
(IATE)
P.O. Box 2309
Gulf Shores, AL 36547;
tel: 205-948-6690; fax: 205-948-6690

International Association of Travel Journalists
(IATJ)
P.O. Box D
Hurleyville, NY 12747; tel: 914-434-1529

International Federation of Women's Travel
Organizations (IFWTO)
13901 North 73rd Street, #210B
Scottsdale, AZ 85260-3125; tel: 602-596-6640; fax: 602-596-6638

Travel Industry Association of America
1100 New York Avenue NW, Suite 450
Washington, DC 20005-3934;
tel: 202-408-8422

U.S. Travel Data Center
(affiliate of the Travel Industry Association of America)
2 Lafayette Center
1100 New York Avenue NW, Suite 450
Washington, DC 20005; tel: 202-408-1832

Yours in Travel Personnel Agency
12 West 37th Street
New York, NY 10018; tel: 212-697-7855

MARKETING/ADVERTISING

American Advertising Federation
Education Services Department
1101 Vermont Avenue NW, Suite 500
Washington, DC 20005; tel: 202-898-0089

American Marketing Association
250 South Wacker Drive, Suite 200
Chicago, IL 60606-5819; tel: 312-648-0536

The Convention Liaison Council
1575 Eye Street NW, Suite 1190
Washington, DC 20005; tel: 202-626-2764

Direct Marketing Association
1120 Avenue of the Americas
New York, NY 10036-6700; tel: 212-768-7277

Meeting Planners International
Informant Building, Suite 5018
1950 Stemmons Freeway
Dallas, TX 75207; tel: 214-712-7700

Retail Advertising and Marketing Association
500 North Michigan Avenue, Suite 600
Chicago, IL 60611; tel: 312-251-7262

Sales and Marketing Executives International
977 Statler Office Tower
Cleveland, OH 44115; tel: 216-771-6650

Sales and Marketing Management
355 Park Avenue South
New York, NY 10010; tel: 212-592-6300

FOOD SERVICES

Associations

Alaska Culinary Association
P.O. Box 140396
Anchorage, AK 99514; tel: 907-265-7116

American Culinary Federation
10 San Bartola Road, P.O. Box 3466
St. Augustine, FL 32085-3466;
tel: 904-824-4468

Berks Lehigh Chef's Association
2012 Redwood Avenue
Wyomissing, PA 19610; tel: 610-678-1217

National Food Broker Association
2100 Reston Parkway, Suite 400
Reston, VA 22091; tel: 703-758-7790

National Restaurant Association
1200 17th Street NW
Washington, DC 20036; el: 202-331-5900

SUPPORT SERVICES

Associations

American Society of Corporate Secretaries
521 Fifth Avenue
New York, NY 10175-0003; tel: 212-681-2000

California Federation of Legal Secretaries
2250 East 73rd Street, Suite 550
Tulsa, OK 74136; tel: 918-493-3540

National Association of Executive Secretaries
900 S. Washington Street, No. G-13
Falls Church, VA 22046; tel: 703-237-8616

PUBLIC SERVICES/SOCIAL SERVICES

Publications

*Directory of Legal Aid and Defender Offices in
the U.S. and Territories*
National Legal Aid and Defender Association,
Washington, DC
Lists legal aid and public defender offices across
the U.S. Published annually.

Associations

ACTION International
120 Beacon Street
Somerville, MA 02143;
tel: 617-492-4930

American Counseling Association
5999 Stevenson Avenue
Alexandria, VA 22304;
tel: 703-823-9800 or 800-347-6647

American Friends Service Committee
1501 Cherry Street
Philadelphia, PA 19102; tel: 215-241-7000

American School Counselor Association
801 North Fairfax Street, Suite 301
Alexandria, VA 22314; tel: 703-683-2722

American Vocational Association
1410 King Street
Alexandria, VA 22314;
tel: 703-683-3111 or 800-892-2274

Child Welfare League of America
440 First Street NW, Suite 310
Washington, DC 20001; tel: 201-638-2952

Council for Standards in Human Service
Education
Northern Essex Community College
Haverhill, MA 01830; tel: 508-374-5889

Council on Social Work Education
1600 Duke Street, Suite 300
Alexandria, VA 22314-3421;
tel: 703-683-8080
(send $10 for Directory of Accredited BSW and
MSW Programs)

Educators for Social Responsibility
23 Garden Street
Cambridge, MA 02138; tel: 617-492-1764

Human Service Council
3191 Maguire Boulevard, Suite 1150
Orlando, FL 32803; tel: 407-897-6465

National Association of Social Workers
750 First Street NE, Suite 700
Washington, DC 20002-4241;
tel: 202-408-8600

National Center for Charitable Statistics
1828 L Street NW, Suite 1200B
Washington, DC 20036; tel: 202-223-8100

National Civic League
1445 Market Street, Suite 300
Denver, CO 80202-1728; tel: 303-571-4343

National Exchange Club Foundation for the
Prevention of Child Abuse
3050 Central Avenue
Toledo, OH 43606; tel: 419-535-3232
or 800-760-3413

National Network for Social Work Managers
1316 New Hampshire Avenue NW, Suite 602
Washington, DC 20036; tel: 202-785-2814

National Organization for Human Service
Education
Fitchburg State College, Box 6257
160 Pearl Street
Fitchburg, MA 01420; tel: 508-345-2151

Save the Children Federation
54 Wilton Road
Westport, CT 06880; tel: 203-221-4000

Social Service Association
6 Station Plaza
Ridgewood, NJ 07450; tel: 201-444-2980

EDUCATION

Publications

Who's Who in Special Libraries and Information Centers
Gale Research Inc., Detroit, MI
Lists special libraries alphabetically and geographically. Published annually.

Associations

Academy for Educational Development (AED)
1875 Connecticut Avenue NW
Washington, DC 20009;
tel: 202-884-8000; fax: 202-884-8400
admind@aed-org (E-mail)

American Association of School Administrators
1801 N Moore Street
Arlington, VA 22209-9988;
tel: 703-528-0700

American Association of School Librarians
50 E. Huron Street
Chicago, IL 60611; tel: 312-944-6780

American Association of University
Administrators
1012 14th Street NW, Suite 500
Washington, DC 20005; tel: 202-737-5900

American Association of University Professors
1012 14th Street NW, Suite 500
Washington, DC 20005; tel: 202-737-5900

American Educational Studies Association
(AESA)
University of Cincinnati
Graduate Studies and Research
Cincinnati, OH 45221; tel: 513-556-2256

American Federation of Teachers
555 New Jersey Avenue NW
Washington, DC 20001; tel: 202-879-4400

American Library Association
50 East Huron Street
Chicago, IL 60611; tel: 312-944-6780

Association for Community Based Education
(ACBE)
1805 Florida Avenue NW
Washington, DC 20009;
tel: 202-462-6333 or 202-232-8044

Association for Educational Communications and
Technology (AECT)
1025 Vermont Avenue NW, Suite 820
Washington, DC 20005;
tel: 202-347-7834; fax: 202-347-7839

Center for Adult Learning and Educational
Credentials (CALEC)
1 Dupont Circle NW
Washington, DC 20036;
tel: 202-939-9475; fax: 202-775-8574

College and University Personnel Association
1233 20th Street NW, Suite 301
Washington, DC 20036-1250;
tel: 202-429-0311

Council on International Educational Exchange
(CIEE)
205 East 42nd Street
New York, NY 10017;
tel: 212-661-1414; fax: 212-972-3231

Earthwatch
(formerly: Educational Expeditions
International)
680 Mount Auburn Street, Box 403
Watertown, MA 02272;
tel: 617-926-8200 or 800-776-0188;
fax: 617-926-8532
E-mail: info@earthwatch.org

Educational Research Service (ERS)
2000 Clarendon Blvd.
Arlington, VA 22201;
tel: 703-243-2100; fax: 703-243-1985

Federal Librarians Round Table
American Library Association, Washington
Office
1301 Pennsylvania Avenue NW, No. 403
Washington, DC 20004;
tel: 202-608-8410

High/Scope Educational Research Foundation
600 North River Street
Ypsilanti, MI 48198-2898;
tel: 313-485-2000 or 800-40-PRESS;
fax: 313-485-0704

Independent Educational Services (IES)
(formerly: Cooperative Bureau for Teachers)
353 Nassau Street
Princeton, NJ 08540; tel: 609-921-6195 or
800-257-5102; fax: 609-921-0155

Institute for Educational Leadership (IEL)
1001 Connecticut Avenue NW, Suite 310
Washington, DC 20036;
tel: 202-822-8405; fax: 202-872-4050

Intercultural Development Research
Association (IDRA)
5835 Callaghan Road, Suite 350
San Antonio, TX 78228;
tel: 210-684-8180; fax: 210-684-5389

International Association for Educational Assessment (IAEA)
P.O. Box 6665
Princeton, NJ 08541; tel: 609-921-9000; fax: 609-520-1093

Madison Center for Educational Affairs (MCEA)
455 15th Street NW, Suite 712
Washington, DC 20005;
tel: 202-833-1801; fax: 202-467-0006

National Association of Educational Office Professionals (NAEOP)
P.O. Box 12619
Wichita, KS 67277; tel: 316-942-4822; fax: 316-942-7100

National Association of Secondary School Principals
1904 Association Drive
Reston, VA 22091; tel: 703-860-0200

National Association of Student Personnel Administrators
1875 Connecticut Avenue NW, Suite 418
Washington, DC 20009; tel: 202-265-7500

National Council for Accreditation of Teacher Education
2010 Massachusetts Avenue NW, Suite 500
Washington, DC 20036; tel: 202-466-7496

National Council of Educational Opportunity Associations (NCEOA)
1025 Vermont Avenue NW, Suite 1201
Washington, DC 20005; tel: 202-347-7430

National Council on the Evaluation of Foreign Educational Credentials
c/o AACRAO
1 Dupont Circle NW, Suite 330
Washington, DC 20036;
tel: 202-293-9161 or 202-872-8857
E-mail: aacrao@umdd

National Education Association
1201 16th Street NW
Washington, DC 20036; tel: 202-833-4000

National Rural Education Association (NREA)
Colorado State University
230 Education Building
Fort Collins, CO 80523-1588;
tel: 970-491-7022; fax: 970-491-1317

Special Libraries Association
1700 18th Street NW
Washington, DC 20009-2508;
tel: 202-234-4700; fax: 202-265-9317

University Council for Educational Administration (UCEA)
Pennsylvania State University
212 Rackley Bldg.
University Park, PA 16802-3200;
tel: 814-863-7916/7917 or
fax: 814-863-7918

GOVERNMENT

Publications

The Capitol Source
National Journal, Inc., Washington, DC
Includes names, addresses, and phone numbers for key figures in the District of Columbia; also features information about corporations, interest groups, think tanks, labor unions, real estate organizations, financial institutions, trade and professional groups, law firms, political consultants, advertising and public relations firms, private clubs, and the media. Published twice a year.

Congressional Yellow Book
Monitor Publishing Co., New York, NY
Gives detailed information on congressional staff positions, committees and subcommittees, and top staff in congressional support agencies. Published annually.

COSLA Directory
The Council of State Governments, Lexington, KY
Provides information on state library agencies, consultant and administrative staff, plus ALANER numbers, electronic mail letters, and fax numbers. Published annually.

Directory of Federal Libraries
Includes library's administrator and selected staff for three thousand special and general, presidential and national libraries, as well as library facilities in technical centers, hospitals, and penal institutions.

Federal Executive Directory
Carroll Publishing Co., Washington, DC
Profiles a broad range of agencies, both executive and legislative, including cabinet departments, federal administrative agencies, and congressional committee members and staff. The directory also outlines areas of responsibility for legal and administrative assistants. Published six times a year; an annual subscription is $178. Call 202-333-8620 for more information.

Federal Organization Service: Military
Carroll Publishing Co., Washington, DC
Lists direct-dial phone numbers for 11,500 key individuals in fifteen hundred military departments and offices. Updated every six weeks; an annual subscription is $625. Call 202-333-8620 for more information.

Washington Information Directory
Congressional Quarterly Inc., Washington, DC
Provides important information on the federal government as a whole, and on each federal department and agency. The volume also provides details on regional federal information sources, nongovernmental organizations in the Washington area, and congressional committees and subcommittees. Published annually.

Washington 2000
Columbia Books, New York, NY
Contains addresses, phone numbers, and profiles of key institutions in the city. Includes chapters on the federal government, the media, business, national associations, labor unions, law firms, medicine and health, foundations and philanthropic organizations, science and policy research groups, and educational, religious, and cultural institutions. Published annually.

Associations

American Federation of State, County, and Municipal Employees
1625 L Street NW
Washington, DC 20036; tel: 202-429-1000

American Planning Association
122 South Michigan Avenue, Suite 1600
Chicago, IL 60603; tel: 312-431-9100

Civil Service Employees Association
P.O. Box 7125
Capitol State
Albany, NY 12210;
tel: 518-434-0191 or 800-342-4146

Council of State Governments
P.O. Box 11910
3560 Iron Works Pike
Lexington, KY 40578; tel: 606-244-8000

International Association of Fire Fighters
1750 New York Avenue NW
Washington, DC 21006; tel: 202-737-8484

International City/County Management
Association
777 North Capitol Street NE, Suite 500
Washington, DC 20002; tel: 202-289-4262

National Association of Counties (NACO)
440 First Street NW, 8th Floor
Washington, DC 20001; tel: 202-393-6226

National Association of Government
Communicators
669 South Washington Street
Alexandria, VA 22314; tel: 703-519-3902

National Planning Association
1424 16th Street NW, Suite 700
Washington, DC 20036; tel: 202-265-7685

New York State Professional Firefighters
Association
111 Washington Avenue, Suite 207
Albany, NY 12210; tel: 518-436-8827

State Services Organization (SSO)
444 North Capitol Street NW
Washington, DC 20001; tel: 202-624-5470

DISABILITIES

ADA Regional Disabled and Business Assistance Centers

Connecticut, Maine, Massachusetts, Rhode Island, and Vermont:
New England Disability and Business Technical
Assistance Center
145 Newbury Street
Portland, ME 04101;
tel: 207-874-6535 (voice/TDD)

New Jersey, New York, Puerto Rico, and Virgin Islands:
Northeast Disability and Business Technical
Assistance Center
354 South Broad Street
Trenton, NJ 08608; tel: 609-392-4004 (voice),
609-392-7044 (TDD)

Delaware, District of Columbia, Maryland, Pennsylvania, Virginia, and West Virginia:
Mid-Atlantic Disability and Business Technical
Assistance Center
2111 Wilson Boulevard, Suite 400
Arlington, VA 22201;
tel: 703-525-3268 (voice/TDD)

Alabama, Florida, Georgia, Kentucky, Mississippi, North Carolina, South Carolina, and Tennessee:
Southeast Disability and Business Technical
Assistance Center
1776 Peachtree Street, Suite 310 North
Atlanta, GA 30309;
tel: 404-888-0022 (voice/TDD)

Illinois, Indiana, Michigan, Minnesota, Ohio, and Wisconsin:
Great Lakes Disability and Business Technical
Assistance Center
1640 West Roosevelt Road (M/C 627)
Chicago, IL 60608;
tel: 312-413-1407 (voice/TDD)

Arkansas, Louisiana, New Mexico, Oklahoma, and Texas:
Southwest Disability and Business Technical
Assistance Center
2323 South Shepherd Boulevard, Suite 1000
Houston, TX 77019; tel: 713-520-0232 (voice),
713-520-5136 (TDD)

Iowa, Kansas, Nebraska, and Missouri:
Great Plains Disability and Business Technical
Assistance Center
4816 Santana Drive
Columbia, MO 65203;
tel: 314-882-3600 (voice/TDD)

Colorado, Montana, North Dakota, South Dakota, Utah, and Wyoming:
Rocky Mountain Disability and Business
Technical Assistance Center
3630 Sinton Road, Suite 103
Colorado Springs, CO 80907-5072;
tel: 719-444-0252 (voice/TDD)

Arizona, California, Hawaii, and Nevada:
Pacific Coast Disability and Business Technical
Assistance Center
440 Grand Avenue, Suite 500
Oakland, CA 94610; tel: 510-465-7884 (voice),
510-465-3167 (TDD)

Job Accommodation Network
P.O. Box 6123
809 Allen Hall
Morgantown, WV 26505-6123;
tel: 800-526-7234 (voice/TDD)

The President's Committee on Employment of
People with Disabilities
1331 F Street NW
Washington, DC 20004;
tel: 202-376-6200 (voice),
202-376-6205 (TDD)

U.S. Department of Justice, Civil Rights Division
Office of the Americans with Disabilities Act
P.O. Box 66118
Washington, DC 20035-6118; tel: 800-514-
0301 (voice), 800-514-0383 (TDD)

Index

A

Abbreviations, avoiding, 16-17, 32
Accomplishments. *see* Achievements
Accreditation/licensing, identifying in resume, 26
Achievements. *see also* Skills
    highlighting in resume, 39-41, 44, 57-59
    scholastic, 29
Acronyms. *see also* Jargon
    avoiding, 66
Action, 1, 99
Action verbs, using in resume, 63-65
Address, as used on resume, 16-17
Age, don't mention in resume, 33
Alumni networks, 115
ASCII files, 86, 110
Attention, 83, 94
Availability, don't talk about in resume, 30

B

Broadcast letter. *see also* Cover letters
    discussed, 106-108
Business. *see also* Employer
    basics of, 57
Business and trade publications, using, 115

C

Capitalization, avoiding, 75
Career Crossroads (Crispin/Mehler), 91
Career objectives. *see also* Job objectives
    choosing to discuss, 35
    compared to job objective, 45
    identifying, 44-45
Career summary, in combination resume, 11, 34-35
careerbrain.com, 91
Certified Personnel Consultant (CPC), 114
Charitable service, listing in resume, 26-27, 44
Charts, don't use in resume, 32-33
Chronological history, in combination resume, 11
Civil service grade, stating in resume, 27
College placement offices, using, 115
Community service, listing in resume, 26-27
Company. *see* Employer
Company role. *see also* Job titles
    identifying in resume, 55
Computerized screening.
    see also Keywords

    in general, 85-86
        ASCII files, 86
        etiquette, 90-91
        HTML files, 87
        resume services, 89-90
    help for, *www.careerbrain.com*, 91
    Internet myths
        length, 89
        updating, 88, 110
    keywords for, 21-22, 61-63, 83-84
        ranking scores, 22
    resume distribution, 109-110
    resume preparation for
        in general, 79-82
        getting computer's attention, 83
        keyword use, 83-84
        technical considerations, 86
        things to avoid, 83
Confidentiality, 24-25, 88. *see also* Privacy
Copying, suggestions for, 77
Cover letters. *see also* Broadcast letter;
Executive briefing
    examples, 102-104
    in general, 93-94
    length, 99
    rules for, 94-102
    stationery choices for, 77
    writing, 102
CPC. *see* Certified Personnel Consultant

D

Dates
    employment dates, including in resume, 20-21
    indicating in functional resume, 9
Demands, don't make any, 33-34
Desire, 98
Dictionary of Occupational Titles, 44
Directory of Job Descriptions, 57
The Directory of Directories, 116
Duties. *see* Responsibilities

E

e-mail
    finding addresses, 111
    including address in resume, 18
    precautions with, 111-112
    recruiters don't use, 87-88
Editing. *see* Resume preparation
Education. *see also* Achievements; Skills
    presenting in resume
        in general, 9, 11

    recommendations for, 28-29, 42-43, 70
Electronic resume. *see* Computerized screening
Employee, confidentiality concerns for, 24-25, 88, 112
Employer. *see also* Business
    identifying in resume, 24-25, 39, 41-42, 88, 112
    using phone number of, 17-18
    Web site of, 85, 111
Employment
    don't talk about reasons for leaving, 31
    part-time, listing in resume, 29-30
    personal conceptions of, 37-38, 116
Employment agencies
    Certified Personnel Consultant, 114
    private, 114
    state, 113
Employment history
    hiding gaps in, 20-21
    typical, 37
Encyclopedia of Associations (Bowker), 115
Endorsements. *see also* References
    quotes and third-party, 25-26, 59
    using in resume, 25-26
Entry-level candidate
    importance of scholastic achievements, 29
    part-time employment history, 29-30
Executive briefing. *see also* Cover letters
    discussed, 105-106
Executive recruiters, using, 115
Executive search firm, cover letter to, 98

F

Fees, employment agency, 114
Follow up, 99
    recommendations for, 116
    useful phrases for, 100-101
Fonts
    for computerized resume, 82
    selecting, 74-75
        variations of, 75
Foreign languages, listing in resume, 28, 43
Fraternities/sororities, choosing to identify, 29

G

Graphs, don't use in resume, 32-33
The Guide to Internet Job Searching (Riley), 91

H

Health, don't talk about, 33
Honesty, 21, 41
HTML files, 87

I

Interest, 95
Internet. *see* Computerized screening
Interview
    getting without having resume,
        106-108
    preparing for by writing resume,
        2-3
Interviewer
    offering resume to, 116
    resume as basis of questions
asked by, 2-3

J

Jargon. *see also* Acronyms
    avoiding, 15, 32
Job. *see* Employment
Job application form, 3
Job banks, 85
Job description
    keywords for, 62
    positioning your skills for, 98-99
Job objectives. *see also* Career
    objectives
    compared to career objective, 45
    identifying in resume, 18-20,
        54-55, 69
Job search, six-prong approach, 109
Job titles. *see also* Company role
    Dictionary of Occupational Titles, 44
    generic, 23
    reference numbers and, 90
    using in resume, 22-24, 39, 41,
        55-56
Junk mail, 93

K

Keywords. *see also* Computerized
screening
    in computerized resume, 83-84
    finding in newspaper ads, 62, 84
    in resume, 21-22, 61-63, 69
    synonyms for, 62
    using, 84

L

Languages skills, listing in resume,
    28, 43
Layout, choices for, 54
Library, resources at, 116
Licensing, identifying in resume, 26

M

Marital status, choosing to reveal, 35
Military service, discussing in
resume, 35-36, 42
Motivation, 41

N

Name
    addressing cover letter to, 95
    on computerized resume, 82
    on resume, recommendations
        for, 16, 69
Name dropping, avoiding, 66
National origin, don't mention in
    resume, 33
The National Job Bank, 116
Networking, 85, 115
Newsgroups, 85
Newspaper ads
    keywords in, 62, 84
    mentioning in cover letter, 97-98
    using, 112-113

O

Objectives. *see* Career objectives;
    Job objectives
OCR. *see* Optical character
    recognition
Optical character recognition (OCR)
    software. *see also* Computerized
    screening
    computerized screening and, 82

P

Paper, selecting, 76-77, 94
Patents, listing in resume, 27, 43
Personal discovery, in resume
    preparation, 3, 37
Personal history, don't include in
    resume, 33
Personal interests, discussing in
    resume, 43

Personal paragraphs, choosing to
    include, 36
Phone calls, preparing for, 87
Phone number
    don't use employer's number,
        17-18
    as used on resume, 17-18
Photographs, don't use in resume,
    15, 33
Physical description, don't talk about,
    33
Preparation, resume writing as, 2
Printing
    choosing quality for, 74
    suggestions for, 77
Privacy. *see also* Confidentiality
    with e-mail, 18
    with electronic distribution, 111-112
Problem-solver, all job hires as, 1, 38
Professional affiliations, listing in
resume, 26-27, 43
Professional training, listing in
    resume, 29
Professionalism, 67
Profit, 57
Publications, listing in resume, 27, 43

R

Race, don't mention in resume, 33
References. *see also* Endorsements
    don't include in resume, 31
Referrals, indicating in cover letter, 97
Rejection, dealing with, 116
Relocation, discussing in resume, 35
Research, 95
Responsibilities, listing in resume,
    25, 39, 56-57
Resume
    appearance of, 74, 76
    components of
        accreditation/licensing, 26
        address, 16-17
        civil service grade, 27
        e-mail address, 18
        education, 28-29
        employer's name, 24-25
        employment dates, 20-21
        endorsements, 25-26
        in general, 15
        job objective, 18-20
        job titles, 22-24
        keywords, 21-22
        languages, 28

name, 16
part-time employment, 29-30
patents, 27
phone number, 17-18
professional affiliations, 26-27
professional training, 29
publications, 27
responsibilities, 25
summer employment, 29-30
copying, 77
faults of, 74
goals for, 5
length concerns, 67
maybe's
    career objectives, 35
    marital status, 35
    military service, 35-36
    personal flexibility, 35
    personal interests, 36
    personal paragraphs, 36
    relocation willingness, 35
    summary, 11, 34-35
no no's
    abbreviations, 32
    age, religion, sex, national origin, 33
    availability, 30
    charts/graphs, 32-33
    demands, 33-34
    health/physical description, 33
    jargon, 32
    personal history, 33
    photographs, 33
    reason for leaving, 31
    references, 31
    salary references, 32
    titles, 30
    weaknesses, 33
    written testimonials, 31-32
preparation. see Resume preparation
printed quality, 74
qualities of, 1-4
review by management, 73-74
risks of not having, 3
strategy for, 5
styles. see Resume styles
taking to interview, 116
Resume bank, 85, 86
discussed, 110
Resume preparation
for computerized screening
    in general, 79-82
    keywords for, 21-22, 61-63
editing and polishing
    in general, 60-61

keywords, 61-63
in general, 37-38
    appearance, 74, 76
    avoiding typewritten copy, 74
    checklist, 78
    common errors, 73-74
    fonts selection, 74-75
    paper choices, 76-77
    printed appearance, 74
    proofing, 75-76
as interview preparation, 2
multiple, 72, 73, 92
proofreading checklist, 68-71
sample questionnaire, 46-52
writing basics
    chronological resumes, 54-60
    in general, 53, 71-72
    layout choices, 54
    length concerns, 67
    preparation, 54
writing secrets
    details, 42-44
    in general, 38-39
    objectives, 44-45
    raw materials, 39-42
Resume services, 89-90
Resume styles
chronological, 6
    example, 7
    preparation basics, 54-60, 70-71
combination, 11
    example, 12-13
    preparation basics, 59-60
functional, 8-9
    example, 10
    preparation basics, 59-60
Resume writing. see Resume preparation
Riley, Margaret, 91, 92

S

Salary
    don't talk about in resume, 32
    for team players, 36
Sentence structure, variation in, 65-66
Sex, don't mention in resume, 33
Skills. see also Achievements; Education
    demonstrating in cover letter, 94
    highlighting in resume, 8-9, 11, 39
    taking stock of, 38
    technological literacy, 43
Sports, 36
Standard & Poor's, 116
Stationery, selecting, 76-77, 94

Summary, using in resume, 11, 34-35, 69
Summer employment
    listing in resume, 29-30
    searching for, 96-97

T

Talents, 83. see also Keywords
Technological literacy. see also Skills
    highlighting in resume, 43
Tense, of writing style, 66-67
Testimonials. see Written testimonials
The Thomas Register, 116
Titles. see also Job titles
    don't use in resume, 30
Truthfulness, 21
Typewriter, do not use, 74

V

Verbs. see Action verbs
Voice, of writing style, 66-67
Voice mail, 87
Volunteer work, listing in resume, 44

W

Weaknesses, don't discuss in resume, 33
Word-processing services, 77
Written testimonials. see also References
    don't use in resume, 31-32
www.careerbrain.com, 91

Cover Letters That Knock 'em Dead

Essential information on composing a cover letter that wins attention, interest, and job offers!

The final word on not just how to write a "correct" cover letter, but how to write a cover letter that offers a powerful competitive advantage in today's tough job market.

Helpful features include a layout of the initial steps, a review of cover letter essentials, and checklists for proofing.

Also includes:

- Responses to newspaper advertisements
- "Cold" cover letters to potential employers
- Requests for informational interviews
- Broadcast letters

- Networking letters
- Follow-up letters
- Resurrection letters
- Rejection of offer letters
- Acceptance letters
- Resignation letters
- Thank-you letters

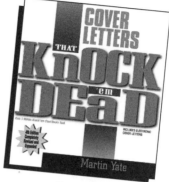

4th edition
Trade paperback, $10.95
ISBN: 1-58062-423-5
304 pages, 8" x 9¼"

Knock 'em Dead, 2002

The Ultimate Job-Seeker's Handbook

Trade paperback, $12.95
ISBN: 1-58062-537-1
352 pages, 8" x 9¼"

The newest edition of Marin Yate's *New York Times* Business Bestseller *Knock 'em Dead* features the most up-to-date advice available on recent developments in the job market. It also features invaluable advice on getting organized, landing interviews, and how to follow up on job opportunities, as well as what to do when layoffs and downsizing are on the horizon. The new edition includes a full section on electronic job search resources. And, of course, the book still feaures hundreds of great answers to tough interview questions!

The JobBank Series

There are 30 *JobBank* books, each providing extensive, up-to-date employment information on hundreds of the largest employers in each job market. The #1 best-selling series of employment directories, the *JobBank* series has been recommended as an excellent place to begin your job search by the *New York Times*, the *Los Angeles Times*, the *Boston Globe*, and the *Chicago Tribune*. *JobBank* books have been used by millions of people to find jobs. Titles available:

The Atlanta JobBank • The Austin/San Antonio JobBank • The Boston JobBank • The Carolina JobBank • The Chicago JobBank • The Connecticut JobBank • The Dallas-Fort Worth JobBank • The Denver JobBank • The Detroit JobBank • The Florida JobBank • The Houston JobBank • The Indiana JobBank • The Las Vegas JobBank • The Los Angeles JobBank • The Minneapolis-St. Paul JobBank • The Missouri JobBank • The New Jersey JobBank • The Metropolitan New York JobBank • The Ohio JobBank • The Greater Philadelphia JobBank • The Phoenix JobBank • The Pittsburgh JobBank • The Portland JobBank • The San Francisco Bay Area JobBank • The Seattle JobBank • The Tennessee JobBank • The Virginia JobBank • The Metropolitan Washington DC JobBank • The JobBank Guide to Computer & High-Tech Companies • The JobBank Guide to Health Care Companies

EACH JOBBANK BOOK IS 6" X 9¼", OVER 300 PAGES, PAPERBACK, $16.95.
For ISBNs and ISSNs, please visit http://www.careercity.com/booksoftware/jobbank.asp

The Adams Internet Job Search Almanac 2001-2002

Uncover thousands of jobs in minutes using your own computer! This comprehensive guide features hundreds of online resources available through commercial online services, the World Wide Web, newsgroups, and more. *The Adams Internet Job Search Almanac 2001-2002* also includes a selection of company joblines, advice on posting an electronic resume, and strategies for researching companies on the Internet. The book also features information on a variety of job-hunting software. 5½" x 8½", 320 pages, paperback, $10.95.
ISBN: 1-58062-426-X, ISSN: 1099-016X

Available wherever books are sold.

**For more information, or to order, call 800-872-5627
or visit www.adamsmedia.com**
Adams Media Corporation, 57 Littlefield Street, Avon, MA 02322

Visit our exciting job and career site at www.careercity.com

From the publishers of this book

CareerCity.com

Search *4 million* job openings at all the leading career sites with just one click!

Find all the great job openings without having to spend hours surfing from one career site to the next.

Now, with just one click you can simultaneously search all of the leading career sites . . . at CareerCity.com!

You can also have jobs come to you! Enter your job search criteria once and we automatically notify you of any new relevant job listings.

Plus! The most complete career center on the Web including . . .

- Descriptions and hot links to 27,000 U.S. companies
- Comprehensive salary surveys in all fields
- Expert advice on starting a job search, interviews, resumes and much more

You'll find more jobs at CareerCity.com!

Post your resume at CareerCity and have the job offers come to you!

It's fast, free, and easy to post your resume at CareerCity—and you'll get noticed by hundreds of leading employers in all fields.